The Limits of Medicine

What are the final limits of medicine? What should we not try to cure medically, even if we have the necessary financial resources and technology?

This book philosophically addresses these questions by examining two mirror-image debates in tandem. Members of certain groups, who are deemed by traditional standards to have a medical condition, such as deafness, obesity, or anorexia, have begun arguing that they have created their own cultures and ways of life. Curing their conditions, they claim, would be a form of genocide. At the same time, members of other groups are seeking medical cures for what would conventionally be deemed "cultural conditions." Mild neurotics who take antidepressants to elevate their mood, runners who use steroids, or men and women seeking cosmetic surgery are pursuing medical treatment for problems that arguably might better be solved culturally, by changing norms, pressures, or expectations in the broader culture.

Each of these two debates endeavors to locate medicine's final frontier and to articulate what it is that we should not treat medically even if we could. This volume analyzes what these two contemporary debates have to say to each other and thus offers a new way of determining medicine's final limits.

Andrew Stark is professor of strategic management and political science at the University of Toronto. He is the author of *Conflict of Interest in American Public Life* and editor, with Michael Davis, of *Conflict of Interest in the Professions*.

for my parents,
Lois and Marvin Stark

The Limits of Medicine

ANDREW STARK

University of Toronto

CAMBRIDGE
UNIVERSITY PRESS

CAMBRIDGE UNIVERSITY PRESS
Cambridge, New York, Melbourne, Madrid, Cape Town, Singapore, São Paulo

Cambridge University Press
40 West 20th Street, New York, NY 10011-4211, USA

www.cambridge.org
Information on this title: www.cambridge.org/9780521856317

First published 2006

Printed in the United States of America

A catalog record for this publication is available from the British Library.

Library of Congress Cataloging in Publication Data
Stark, Andrew, 1956–
The limits of medicine / Andrew Stark.
p.   cm.
Includes bibliographical references and index.
ISBN–10: 0-521-85631-0 (hardback)
ISBN–10: 0-521-67226-0 (pbk.)
ISBN–13: 978-0-521-85631-7 (hardback)
ISBN–13: 978-0-521-67226-9 (pbk.)
1. Medicine – Philosophy.   2. Therapeutics – Philosophy.   3. Medical innovations –
Social aspects.   4. Perfection.   I. Title.
R723.S755   2006
610'.1–dc22   2005015859

ISBN-13   978-0-521-85631-7 hardback
ISBN-10   0-521-85631-0 hardback

ISBN-13   978-0-521-67226-9 paperback
ISBN-10   0-521-67226-0 paperback

Contents

Acknowledgments

I am grateful to Don Herzog, Mark Lilla, Vivian Rakoff, Paul Thompson, and three anonymous Cambridge University Press reviewers for their valuable comments on various drafts of the book. I am indebted as well to the Social Sciences and Humanities Research Council of Canada, the Donner Canadian Foundation, and the "Defining the Medicare Basket Project" – funded jointly by the Canadian Health Services Research Foundation and the Ontario Ministry of Health and Long Term Care – for financially supporting my research and writing. Frances Boquiren, Shehryar Khan, Stephen Penner, and Aaron Peters provided exceptionally able research assistance. My appreciation also goes to Beatrice Rehl, philosophy editor at Cambridge University Press; Louse Calabro; and Helen Greenberg for all their editorial support and guidance. Over the past several years, my daughters, Rachel and Zoe, have given me their keen insights on the questions the book discusses. My wife, Deborah, knows the many senses in which this book wouldn't even have come into existence without her support. I thank her for that, as for so much else.

Introduction

Reversing Our Lenses

Imagine that money is no object. Would it be a good thing if medical science developed – and if universal public insurance then paid for – surefire cures for blindness or deafness? What about an advanced generation of Prozac that could eradicate neurotic anxiety and mild depression? Or an advanced form of genetic engineering that would furnish every competitive runner with the same peak physical resources? How about a "Michael Jackson pill" that, "if taken by black people," would "remove all vestiges of being black?"[1] Or new techniques of plastic surgery that would unerringly and permanently provide beautiful skin, lips, and noses? What about a fail-safe drug that cured obesity? Or anorexia? And what if none of these had any side effects?

Notwithstanding the protests of some analysts, who remind us that our financial resources are as limited as our technological hubris is boundless, questions such as these have assumed surpassing prominence in public debate.[2] Despite their futuristic aura, they address an intensely contemporary need to stake out the final limits to medicine, to locate the perimeters beyond which medicine would have no obligation to assist us – indeed, should not assist us – even if it could assist us.

Possibly, we treat these matters with urgency as much because of a sense of moral fallibility as technological hubris. It is often claimed that our scientific capacities continually outrun our moral ones, presenting us with new breakthroughs before we have had a chance to pave the moral way for them or ponder their ethical implications. True, the process of developing new generations of mood-altering or body-shaping or skin-rejuvenating or muscle-building drugs, especially if they are to be 100 percent effective and side effect free, will be long and error-ridden.

But, as those who engage in pitched contemporary debates about them note, so will be the process of thinking through their moral implications. We have every reason to begin asking now whether these are pursuits on which medicine should even embark or, if it does so embark, where it should stop. Put another way, it is precisely because the technologies for a super-Prozac or a side-effect-free steroid will take time to get right that their supporters, whether doctors, scientists, or potential patients, are so keen to broach them as possibilities right now. They want to begin dealing with the moral issues so as to get the scientific show on the road. Hence, we find ourselves today thinking about what medicine should do in a world without technological limits.

We also find ourselves thinking about what medicine should do in a world without financial limits. Of course, any given advocate for a super-Botox or a side-effect-free muscle-growth treatment will generally concede that in a world of limited medical budgets, they do not have the priority of, say, cardiac research or cancer care. Yet that same advocate can also insist, quite reasonably, that the cost of treating a condition should have nothing to do with the question of whether it is legitimately a medical one. "[D]ialysis machines and tomography units are enormously expensive," Arthur L. Caplan notes, and even now we haven't enough of them to help everyone in need. "But," Caplan says, "these facts do not in any way change the disease status of . . . schizophrenia [or] kidney failure . . . ."[3] Suppose that we are denied a particular medical treatment or that medical science opts not to pursue a cure for our particular condition. We are entitled to know whether, and we will reconcile ourselves differently to the decision according to whether, the reasons are financial, technological, or, instead, philosophical, having to do with medicine's final limits.[4]

The eight questions that I pose in the opening paragraph – having to do with blindness and deafness, mild depression and slow running, black racial features and plain facial features, obesity and anorexia – have become, even in today's world of limited resources and imperfect technology, principal lightning rods for debate over the final limits to medicine. They lend themselves, typically, to two approaches. According to bioethicists and others who adopt the first, it is the task of medicine to provide legitimate cures. Advanced performance boosters for competitive runners, however, or side-effect-free pharmaceuticals to lift people's moods, or new-wave Botox for permanently youthful skin, raise the question as to whether they might not be mere "enhancements" instead of cures for real medical conditions. They provoke impassioned argument as to whether they might not lie wholly beyond the province of medicine, even if we had the financial and technological wherewithal to provide them.

Those taking the second approach also affirm that the task of medicine is to furnish legitimate cures. The problem, however, is that treatments for conditions such as deafness, obesity, or anorexia may actually be a form of cultural genocide. People harboring conditions such as these, so the claim goes, have generated their own unique ways of life, historical traditions, means of understanding and interpreting the external world, or modes of expressing and communicating their inner beings: in short, their own irreplaceable and much-loved cultures. The notion of a cure for deafness, obesity, or anorexia, this line of argument concludes, is as offensive as would be a "cure" for being French or Hispanic.

These two endeavors – the attempts to make the cure/enhancement and the cure/cultural genocide "cuts" – are not inconsistent with each other, even though they are generally undertaken by different people, directed at different conditions, and advanced without much mutual recognition. But they have something important in common. Together, they comprise the contemporary attempt to draw the final limits to medicine, to say what it is that we shouldn't treat medically even if we could: even if we had the resources and the technology. The two cuts are attractive in some ways. Each captures moral intuitions we have; and many of us, including myself, would want to draw final limits to medicine. Unfortunately, these two cuts, as they are typically advanced, fail to do that. In this book, I offer an alternative way of setting medicine's final limits. But first: what's wrong with the way the lines currently get drawn?

Cure versus Enhancement

Bioethicists making a cut between cure and enhancement typically argue as follows: Cure, the proper function of medicine, restores or takes us to a social norm – think of plastic surgery to correct deviated septums – while enhancement, say plastic surgery to make ordinary noses more beautiful, takes us beyond the social norm.[5] Alternatively, by shifting from the social to the individual level, the cure/enhancement cut gets made in this way: If an individual whose pneumonia, say, has been cured by an antibiotic wins a race, then we should have no problem crediting the individual himself with that achievement. If, however, someone wins a race having taken steroids, then we can no longer be certain whether that individual himself is responsible for the accomplishment.[6] As a working paper for the President's Council on Bioethics puts it, cure makes an individual "whole, while enhancement alters the whole."⁷ Whether it flouts a social norm or some line demarcating the true individual, enhancement – unlike cure, which honors both – is to be resisted. Even assuming unlimited resources, we would have no obligation to pursue the development and fund the delivery of enhancement in the way we might for cure.

While these cuts between cure and enhancement hold intuitive appeal, they have not been successfully argued. The notion that medicine should be about bringing us to a social norm founders on the observation that the social norm is always moving: moving, in particular, in the direction of enhancement. Currently, half of all Americans over sixty-five have arthritis or a related form of chronic joint inflammation. It would, then, be considered socially normal, normal in our society, for an elderly person to suffer from arthritis. But if it's medicine's job merely to restore people to a state of social normality when they depart from it, wouldn't the medical community be exceeding its bounds if it embarked on the research, and delivered the services, necessary to alter whatever the existing state of social normality happened to be? It would seem so. Yet few would define as beyond the legitimate purview of medicine the work of those rheumatologists who, refusing to take the social norm as given, are busy developing new therapies to palliate, delay, prevent, or cure arthritis and rheumatism in the elderly.

Some philosophers might reply that developing such an arthritis cure would be justified even on a "social norm" criterion, properly understood. What's socially normal, Norman Daniels argues in his influential book *Just Health Care*, is whatever is necessary for human beings to pursue a great many "life plans" in a given society – lawyer, mountaineer, doctor, designer – as distinct from what's necessary for the pursuit of only a few idiosyncratic life plans, such as the ability to play piano like Glenn Gould or hit a ball like Joe DiMaggio. Since healthy and pain-free joints are necessary for the pursuit of a societywide array of life plans, a cure will simply bring those suffering from arthritis to a state of social normality. Curing arthritis in the elderly, then, indeed falls within the bounds of medicine to provide.

This way of using the social norm criterion to justify a cure for later-life arthritis invites two alternative rejoinders. On the one hand, because of arthritis's prevalence in those over sixty-five, the range of life plans in society does not, in fact, include the possibility of people continuing to practice law, climb mountains, drive trucks, or design clothes – free of joint pain – into their later years. Indeed, Norman Daniels allows that "for each age (stage of life), there is a normal opportunity range."⁸ Because of arthritis's normality in later life, all life plans would in some way incorporate that fact. On the view that it's the task of medicine to bring people to the social norm, understood as the capacity to pursue a societywide range of life plans, there would be no call on medicine to deliver a cure for arthritis to those over age sixty-five.

On the other hand, suppose that the defender of the "socially normal" approach wants to insist that pain-free joints are socially normal, even for a person over sixty-five. After all, they would be necessary for people to continue pursuing a societywide array of life plans – lawyer, engineer, student of Russian literature, oil-rig worker – to the maximum possible. But then on the same argument, a pill that increased IQ to 300 – or life span to 200 – would be a cure, not an enhancement, since it too would be necessary for pursuing any number of life plans to the maximum. Few proponents of the social norm view, however, would want to deem such innovations as anything but enhancements. But if they are enhancements, then so is a cure for arthritis for those over sixty-five. And yet that's not what we want to think.

Georges Canguilhem, in his 1943 classic *The Normal and the Pathological* – a book that heavily influenced Michel Foucault's subsequent inquiries on similar themes – said that human beings are always "transcending the norm." Canguilhem's central insight was that the "momentarily normal [always itself includes] the possibility of tolerating infractions of the habitual norm and instituting new norms in new situations."[9] A philosophy that says that "cure is that which returns or takes us to normal" must, Canguilhem said, embrace the fact that it's normal for us always to be pushing the norm in the direction of enhancement.

It was a similar insight that led those advancing the social norm approach to reject (or modify) a competing alternative, the "biological norm" approach. According to the biological norm philosophers, the legitimate task of medicine is to restore a person to some notion of natural biological functioning. For example, it is the function of our legs to walk and run. So the notion of "legitimate" cure would embrace whatever restores or brings someone's legs to a point where they can execute that natural function. Yet as Dorothy Dinnerstein writes in refuting this claim, "[h]umans are by nature unnatural. We do not yet walk 'naturally' on our hind legs, for example: such ills as fallen arches, lower back pain and hernias testify that the [human] body has not yet adapted itself completely to the upright posture." To call an illness something "contrary to human biology is naïve," Dinnerstein says; "we are what we have made ourselves, and we must continue to make ourselves as long as we exist at all."[10]

Our biological functioning, in other words, is insufficient as a criterion for "cure." Legs that walk, jog, run a mile in four minutes, or run a mile in three minutes are (or would be) all engaging in their biological functions. Indeed, one could argue that if our criterion is biological functioning, then the faster the legs the better the functioning. New steroid treatment that enabled running a two-minute mile should therefore be deemed a cure, not an enhancement, even on the biological functioning criterion. This is simply another way of saying that biological functioning, in and of itself, tells us little about the line between cure and enhancement. We have to take into account the social roles we need to fulfill. Those roles require us – contrary, as Dinnerstein says, to what may be deemed purely natural – to walk and run on two legs. Our social roles also require not just vision, but the vision to be able to drive at night; not just opposable thumbs, but the manual dexterity required to write.[11] Any medical cure that stopped short of enabling those and countless other social activities – on the grounds that our biological functioning didn't strictly require it – would be deemed woefully inadequate. But once we acknowledge that social normality, not biological functioning or species normality, is the operative criterion, then we have to allow, somehow, for the inevitability that social norms will change and that medicine can legitimately be expected to play a role in such change.

Even the philosopher Christopher Boorse, who in a widely discussed 1975 article defined "disease" as a deviation from biological normality, then tightly circumscribed the relevance of that notion.[12] For he immediately went on to acknowledge that the role of medicine is in fact to cure not "disease" but "illness," which he defined as a falling short of social norms that may go well beyond mere biological requirements. But "[w]hy," as Lawrie Reznek asks, "draw a distinction between diseases and other negative medical conditions if no [practical distinction] is being picked out?"[13] And if we are going to acknowledge that medicine can legitimately take us beyond biological normality to social normality, we then have to confront the fact that we are always wanting, and legitimately so, to go beyond today's social norms, too. And so we cannot use them, either, as the basis for dividing cure from enhancement. Even Leon Kass and Francis Fukuyama, chair and member of the President's Council on Bioethics, respectively – though clearly drawn in principle to using a notion of social normality to draw the cure/enhancement cut – acknowledge how "fuzzy the boundary is."[14]

We meet with no greater success in attempting to make the cure/enhancement cut at the individual instead of the social level. Drawing a distinction between interventions that make the individual self whole (cure) and those that take the individual beyond whole (enhancement) is a vexing endeavor. For example, Erik Parens writes that "central to maintaining the idea of a self is the commitment to regard some of our actions and attitudes as justified by our reasons, not explained in mechanistic terms."[15] The implication is that a mild depressive who undergoes psychotherapy engages her mind in an effort to overcome her condition; hence any resultant improvement represents growth in her personal wholeness, not a violation of it. Prozac, by contrast, would bypass these intellectual processes, bringing improvements that are artificial ("mechanistic," and therefore enchancements), not real (appealing to reasons and therefore genuinely curative). But can we really equate the cut between making an individual whole and going beyond whole, on the one hand, with that between therapies that appeal to reason and those that work mechanistically, on the other? Prozac often cuts away neurotic encrustations on rational processes, while psychotherapy can frequently be mechanistic, subrational, in its workings.

Some commentators offer a different way of making the cut between cure – that which makes the individual whole – and enhancement, which takes him beyond whole. Such a distinction, they say, maps a deeper one between therapies that work externally and hence seem not to alter the individual – supportive shoes for runners, say – and those that operate internally and so seem to shift the shape of the self: steroids, for example. Yet we believe that whatever a student achieves on the Scholastic Aptitude Test (SAT) after having been tutored – thereby altering herself internally – is genuine, but whatever she might achieve by bringing a tutor, an external aid, into the test room with her would be artificial. We believe that whatever a baseball player achieves after having drunk coffee is genuine, but whatever he achieves after having taken steroids is artificial, although both operate on him internally. We believe that whatever a marathon runner achieves wearing air shoes is genuine, while whatever she achieves by taking a subway, as Rosie Ruiz famously did during the New York Marathon, is artificial, although both operate externally. As the psychiatrist Willard Gaylin has written, we must "re-examine the distinction between endogenous and exogenous" as a proxy for that "between artificial and natural." And when we do so, we will find that we are "further undermining some of the fragile distinctions that have supported us in the past."[16]

Listen, again, to Leon Kass thinking out loud during a 2002 President's Bioethics Council meeting. Kass begins by drawing a line between the antibiotic that allows a runner to throw off her infection and win a race – the achievement would genuinely be hers because she would have been made whole – and the steroids that would take her beyond whole, rendering her victory an artificial one. But he ends by arguing himself into acknowledging the incoherence of that very distinction: "[I]t's not so clear that [a steroid-assisted victory] would be the achievement of the agent. There's a certain line . . . where if you doped up several atheletes . . . what you'd really be praising would be the chemists rather than the [runner]. And I know what's coming next, because we're just bags of chemicals and it's very complicated."[17]

Cure versus Cultural Genocide

A second approach to the questions I pose in the opening paragraph would ask not "When does cure become enhancement?" but "When does cure become cultural genocide?" The idea here is that the deaf, or the obese, or the anorexic do not have medical conditions but rather are cultural groups. If they are so seen, then a cure could very well be a form of cultural genocide. As more and more deaf, obese, or anorexic people take cures, and as their numbers dwindle and then disappear, irreplaceable tiles in the multicultural mosaic will crumble. We will lose the culture of deafness, with its unique language; of obesity – would our culture not have been poorer without Falstaff, Fats Waller, Sydney Greenstreet, Santa Claus, or John Goodman?[18]; and of anorexia, which some anorexics describe as a religion and which others, anorexics and nonanorexics alike, have fashioned into the aesthetic of anorexic chic.[19]

Presumably, for a cure to amount to "cultural genocide," there must be a legitimate culture at stake. Those making a cultural genocide argument against cure, accordingly, expend enormous energy trying to show how the art and experiences surrounding their particular condition rise to the level of a full-fledged culture. But here, too, we run into problems of line drawing. The enterprise of weighing different conditions on some kind of scale of cultural substance – three points for a language, two points for a literature, four for a history of vicious oppression – is a perilous one.

We might, for example, venture that obesity is less a culture than blindness, because blindness has its own quasi-language, Braille, which – although it doesn't possess a unique grammar – does have its own singular symbology. Yet many obesity "activists [steadfastly] liken . . . medical efforts [against obesity] to genocide."[20] As early as 1977, Hillel Schwartz reports in his history of overweight in America, "a member of the Los Angeles Fat Underground wrote in an open letter to a doctor: 'You see fat as suicide, I see weight loss as murder – genocide, to be precise.'"[21] If "everyone who wanted to be thin could get thin by taking a pill," Richard Klein writes in his celebrated 1996 book *EAT FAT*, then "[m]aybe in this decade, maybe in thirty years, a final fat solution will be found. To my mind, postmodern fat becomes a cultural problem at this moment . . . when it may be at the point of becoming extinct."[22]

Or one might suggest that blindness has evolved less of a culture than deafness. After all, the deaf community has its own full-fledged language, with its own symbology *and* grammar: American Sign Language (ASL). That seems to be the view that Carol Padden and Tom Humphries take when they say that "[t]he term 'disabled' describes those who are blind or physically handicapped . . . not Deaf People."[23] Deafness is "not a disability," Edward Dolnick writes; "[i]nstead . . . deaf people . . . are a subculture like any other. They are simply a linguisitic minority . . . and are no more in need of a cure for their condition than are Haitians or Hispanics."[24] Deaf activists, the political scientist David Ingram notes, "have been maintaining for some time that ASL is the equal of any linguistic culture, its lack of literature notwithstanding"[25] (Ingram must be referring to written literature, since "the literature of American deaf culture, told in ASL, consists of history, tales, legends, fables, anecdotes, plays, jokes . . . and much more.")[26] And so, on this reasoning, devices such as cochlear implants get viewed "as cultural genocide, an attempt to decrease the deaf population and ultimately eliminate it."[27]

Yet in the eyes of others, "blindness," too, seems to have all of the same "qualities of a subculture."[28] Braille might not have its own grammar as does ASL, but then again, ASL hasn't evolved a written literature. If we accept the project of classifying cure as cultural genocide by gauging the extent to which the particular condition in question has evolved the traits of a culture, then whatever protection the culture of deafness deserves, what blind activists have for decades called the "[c]ulture of blindness" merits the same.[29]

One might say that while deafness embraces a language, blacks have uniquely borne the burden of "systematic and organized discrimination" and that therefore "a practice of altering . . . skin colour is [particularly] disturbing."[30] But there are members of the deaf community who claim that "[f]rom the deaf point of view, the notion that [cochlear] implants are beneficial 'is both inappropriate and offensive – as if doctors and newspapers joyously announced advances in genetic engineering that might someday make it possible to turn black skin white.'"[31] Others argue that cosmetic "surgery to bring a woman's body in line with prevailing standards of female beauty – liposuction, cheekbone surgery, rib extraction, breast augmentation – is on a moral par with surgery to make a black person resemble a white one."[32] And consider this statement: "'I am . . . invisible . . . simply because people refuse to see me . . . . When they approach me, they see only my surroundings, themselves, or figments of their imagination – indeed, everything and anything except me . . . .' So wrote renowned novelist Ralph Ellison about being black . . . But his eloquent description applies equally well to Fat Chicks."[33]

Carl Elliott is quite right: "If stigma is a form of oppression, then in America no group has a monopoly on oppression."[34] There is simply inveterate disagreement here, within and between groups harboring different conditions, but no overarching "intergroup" principle with which to draw the line between cure and cultural genocide. Are we going to say that a condition has generated a culture – and that cure therefore becomes cultural genocide – simply when some members harboring the condition say so? If not, what principles could we possibly use to decide – language? literature? a history of oppression? – given that each group seems to be asserting its own?

Reversing Our Lenses

I believe that those who seek to draw cure/enhancement and cure/genocide cuts are pursuing the right projects. But each of the two endeavors suffers from lack of an ultimately persuasive argument on which to make the desired cuts and hence to draw the final limits to medicine. Nor have the two cuts been brought together under a common framework. In this book, I suggest a way of remedying this situation by exploring what might happen were the two debates to exchange focal points.

To explain: Philosophers of the cure/enhancement cut preoccupy themselves with both a societywide question – what is the social norm of noses, mental states, or body size, and what goes beyond the norm into enhancement? – and individual-level issues – how do we decide when we've made an individual whole, or when we've gone beyond whole into enhancement?[35] Difficulties arise because the social norm itself is always moving in the direction of enhancement. And trouble emerges because the criteria that we use to determine what makes an individual whole – and what goes beyond – are, as Gaylin says, "fragile"; they often fail to make the cut in ways that accord with our intuitions. But these are not the only problems with the ways in which the social-norm and individual-wholeness criteria typically get applied.

The societywide question – what is the social norm? – tends, naturally enough, to elicit societywide answers: "To be sick" – to harbor a condition requiring cure – "is to have aberrant characteristics of a certain sort which society as a whole evaluates as being bad and for which that society assigns a sick role," says Robert Veatch. "Disease is the aggregate of those conditions which, judged by the prevailing culture, are deemed painful or disabling," claims Lester S. King.[36] As Norman Daniels argues, such statements mean that a condition is a medical one if, in looking across society as a whole, we see that it impairs the pursuit of a wide range of possible life plans, from lawyer to teacher to butcher to baker to computer programmer to executive producer.[37] Blindness and deafness, for example, would seem to qualify. "A sense capacity like hearing is plausibly considered a general purpose means, useful in nearly every life plan," Dan Brock writes, noting that "from some radical positions in the disability rights movement, even the loss of hearing is not a harm," but concluding that we "can . . . set aside that kind of a radical challenge."[38]

The individual-level question, for its part, would seem to direct us to the individual level for an answer. To use individual-level criteria to determine whether a treatment would be a legitimate cure – to determine, in other words, whether that treatment would make any given individual whole – it would seem to follow that we should consult the "specific abilities or capacities whose value and importance depend on the particular plan of life of the person who either has them or loses them."[39] One individual, Brock says, might "have no desire to play music or athletics," and would see medical innovations to enable people to play the cello like Yo Yo Ma or basketball like Michael Jordan as mere enhancement. But for another, the "capacity to play a musical instrument or to excel in athletics" may be precisely what he needs to feel "whole."[40] And so, if we are operating at the individual level, then in classifying a treatment as either cure or enhancement, we would have to determine whether it would make *that particular individual* whole. What would be enhancement for you or me might be a cure for an aspiring Yo Yo Ma or Michael Jordan, to say nothing of Yo Yo Ma or Michael Jordan themselves.

Just because the cure/enhancement questions get posed at the social and individual levels, however, does not mean that the best answers are to be found at the social or individual levels. At the social level – where we determine what's normal by looking at what is necessary for a societywide range of life plans – Brock suggests that we would deem the inability to hear to be a medical condition. Yet this seems too hasty. The fact is that a significant strand in the deaf community, and not just a radical fringe whose views we can set aside, disagree with Brock, insisting that hearing is unnecessary for a great many life plans. According to Candy McCullough, who with her partner unleashed controversy in 2002 by choosing a deaf sperm donor in the hope of producing a deaf child, "[h]earing status does not define success. Deaf professionals work as doctors, lawyers, therapists, professors, engineers. Like any good parents, we want our children to have better lives than we do. We just don't think that having hearing is a prerequisite for that."[41] On the flip side, many black Americans would argue that white racial features *are* a prerequisite for achieving a society-wide range of life plans in America today. Possibly unwrinkled skin is as well. Without at this point taking a position on these questions, I simply want to note that the societywide approach is too blunt to capture all the moral intuitions that many would want to see recognized in any valid cure/enhancement principle. If cure is "whatever is necessary to bring someone to a social norm," and if we then make the required determination by looking at features and functions that seem necessary for a wide range of life plans in society as a whole, we may get conclusions that aren't sufficiently nuanced. In some cases, those conclusions might also be torqued by prevailing social prejudices.

By the same token, though, if we deem cure to be whatever is necessary to make an individual whole, and accordingly make the required determination by looking to the individual level, then the medical system will fall hostage to innumerable individual idiosyncracies.[42] In advancing an individual-level answer to the question "what makes an individual whole?," Edmond A. Murphy declares himself "in favor of a policy of pursuing the individual best for each person," because "the optimal is a vastly more complex matter to define in a population than in an individual."[43] Surely, though, the medical system cannot be responsible for making an individual whole if what makes that particular individual whole is whatever he claims is necessary for the pursuit of his life plans, be it the capacity to play concert cello or excel at professional athletics. "[M]edicine can't just do things that are 'idiosyncratically desired.'"[44]

In Part 1, I look anew at the troubled notion that cure is what takes us to a social norm, and in Part 2, at the equally uneasy assertion that cure is what makes an individual whole. But instead of attempting to flesh them out at the social or the individual level, I do so from an intermediate perspective – that of the group harboring the condition in question.

Specifically, in Part 1, I argue that we can find and provide a cure for a condition when the group of people harboring it, from their own perspective, could legitimately deem that condition to fall below a social norm or (to take account of the fact that norms are always changing) if they could legitimately deem others to have gone beyond the norm to reach a social ideal. And in Part 2, I argue that a cure avoids the tag of enhancement if the group harboring the condition could legitimately deem such a cure necessary to make individuals whole.

Of course, the key is what is meant by "legitimately," and I shall argue for particular approaches in Parts 1 and 2. But what matters for our purposes here is that there exists an advantage to using a group perspective to determine what social normality and individual wholeness may mean. It avoids the one-size-fits-all approach of looking at the societywide level – where the concerns of large numbers of members of recognizable groups such as blacks or the deaf may not adequately be taken into account – while avoiding the pitfalls of allowing every individual a veto over what constitutes a medical condition.

When it comes to the cure/cultural genocide cut, by contrast, the problem is precisely that philosophers and activists focus on the group. To determine whether cure would be cultural genocide, any particular analyst will measure the substance of different groups' claims to have evolved a culture against whatever principle for determining cultural status the analyst happens to prefer: one that says that a history of oppression matters, for example, or that the presence of language is definitive. From the perspective of whatever groups fare poorly in the analysis, however, any such principle will always be contestable.

But that's not the only problem. Another is that this way of proceeding puts the cart before the horse. It says, "Let's assume that a cure would destroy the particular life experiences associated with a given condition – obesity, say, or deafness – along with the language, literature, music, dance, and theater interpreting and expressing those experiences. The question then is: Do those experiences and art rise to the level of a genuine culture that deserves protection?" But why not instead say, "Let's assume for the moment what we can't settle anyway: that the experiences and art associated with obesity or deafness or mild depression or any such condition rise to the level of a genuine culture. Still, would cure, even if everyone took it, necessarily destroy that culture?"

In other words, in the question "would cure be cultural genocide?," let us focus on the "genocide," not the "cultural." Even if blacks were deemed to have evolved a richer culture than the deaf, that wouldn't necessarily mean that more of black culture would vanish with Jerome McCristal Culp's imagined Michael Jackson pill than deaf culture would disappear with an advanced generation of cochlear implants. What, in this context, should we make of Onyekachi Wambu's observation that "[b]lackness . . . has floated free of its moorings in pigmentation" or of Ralph Ellison's claim that the "values and lifestyle [of] most American whites are culturally part Negro?"[45] Or of William Osler's aphorism that "half of us are blind . . . and we are all deaf?"[46]

In Part 3, then, I turn away from the attempt to weigh each group's claims to culturehood. Instead, I make the assumption that every member of a group harboring a particular condition – deafness, obesity, plain facial features, and the others – would take a cure, assuming that one could be legitimately offered on the criteria set forth in Parts 1 and 2. That would be the worst-case scenario from the perspective of those concerned with genocide. I then ask what would be lost culturally. Not, of course, to the group, which would no longer exist. Rather, to society as a whole – those who never harbored the condition – and to the individuals who formerly comprised the group, but who no longer harbor the condition. Is it possible, in other words, that anorexic or blind or mild depressive culture, whether or not it rises to some threshold level of cultural richness, could live on post-cure in society as a whole? Could it live on in those who had never harbored the condition but who might value or embody, in the ways suggested by Ralph Ellison and William Osler, its various cultural characteristics? And is it possible that the individuals who took the cure – who formerly harbored the condition – could or would conserve enough of its cultural substance to provide for their own personal continuity and identity? In Part 3, I suggest that the cultures surrounding each of the conditions offer cues to help us answer these questions.

Such an approach, for which I will argue in Part 3, has more in common with a liberal than a group-rights perspective on cultural value and preservation. On this liberal understanding, the question of whether any particular group survives over time – be it the deaf, the obese, Tibetan Buddhists, or Brooklyn Jews – is immaterial. But whatever culture the group may have evolved – its music, its dance, its cuisine, its thought, its way of life – is of value, and of value not only to the group but to society as a whole. Pierre Trudeau famously advanced this form of cosmopolitan liberalism. All members of any society, Trudeau said, can learn and love aspects of the cultures associated with any of the particular groups within it – the French language, Chinese history, Mayan art, or

Jewish mysticism – and thus keep them alive.[47] Even if a condition disappears because everyone harboring it opts for a medical procedure, that need not stop nonblacks who love rhythm and blues, or nondeaf people intrigued by ASL, or the nonobese who venerate Falstaff from nurturing these cultural traditions. After all, they never had the condition to begin with. Even if a group disappears due to mass exit enabled by medicine, it is thus possible that its culture will continue to live on in society as a whole, depending on the extent to which nongroup members in the rest of society have come to adopt its central motifs.

Trudeau's liberalism would have us look to the rest of society, to those who never harbored a condition, and at their needs for cultural richness to see if they might nevertheless keep a condition's culture alive. A different liberal understanding, one that Will Kymlicka has pioneered, would have us look to the individuals who formerly harbored the condition, but who are now cured, and at their needs for cultural continuity. On this liberal understanding, the question of whether a group per se survives remains immaterial. But whatever culture it has evolved will persist in being of value to the individuals, even if they wanted to be cured, who formerly harbored the condition and comprised the group. An individual's culture – the experiences and the artistic interpretations of those experiences that come from his being deaf or obese or neurotic – structure his identity. "Liberals should be concerned with the fate of their own cultural structures," Kymlicka says, "not because [cultures] have some moral status of their own, but because it's only through having a rich and secure cultural structure" that individuals "can make sense of their lives."[48]

If a significant portion of an individual's cultural resources and touchstones evaporated, assuming that's what a cure would mean, the result would be disorienting and destructive. But even if the groups "the obese" and "the deaf" disappear because everyone takes the cure, the cultural substance of those conditions might well live on in the individuals who harbored them. Suppose, for example, that the culture of obesity (or at least that of Fat Chicks) very substantially consists of plays, novels, and conversations focused on the competing role demands placed on women. Then there's no reason to think that much if any of it – and the ways in which it structures and gives meaning to women's lives – would disappear if obesity were entirely wiped out. Many of the cultural riffs Rosanne Barr makes by reference to her body size are made by Sandra Bernhard without any similar reference.

Such survival, however, is only a possibility, not a certainty. Suppose that cure not only disintegrates the group but also eliminates all traces of its culture from society as a whole, from those who never harbored the condition but who may well have valued the diversity its culture provides. And suppose that cure wipes out all vestiges of that culture from the lives of those individuals who formerly harbored the condition, but who continue to require its cultural substance to maintain their personal identities. Then we might indeed begin talking about genocide. At any rate, cure will have brought real cultural loss and cultural harm, whether we want to use the term cultural genocide or some other. The question, which I will look at in Part 3, is not whether a group's cultural riches and resources rise to some threshold level of cultural significance. Rather, it's whether the cultural riches and resources spawned by a particular condition are likely to survive the disappearance of the group harboring that condition: whether they're likely to survive in the individuals who formerly composed it and in society as a whole.

Here, then, is what I mean by suggesting that the cure/enhancement and cure/cultural genocide debates might usefully reverse their lenses or switch focal points: In Parts 1 and 2, I look at the cure/enhancement debate. For each of the eight conditions I mention in the opening paragraph, I ask whether cure would bring people to a social norm, bearing in mind that the social norm itself is always evolving toward a social ideal. And I ask whether cure would make an individual who took it whole or, alternatively, take him beyond whole. I will, however, answer these social and individual-level questions from the intermediate perspective of the group. What will matter is whether group members, in the case of each of the eight conditions, could legitimately perceive a cure as taking them to an existing, if evolving, social norm (Part 1) and/or as making an individual whole (Part 2). In looking at the group level in this way, I try to avoid the pitfalls involved in asking whether society, as a general statement, views a cure for the condition as necessary for someone to be socially normal, which is too one-size-fits-all. But I also try to elude the difficulties inherent in asking whether any given individual can deem a cure necessary to make herself whole, which would leave the medical system hostage to individual idiosyncracies.

In Part 3, I look at the cure/cultural genocide debate. I do so by leaving behind the group level, where the issue is whether those harboring any one of the eight conditions can legitimately regard their group as having evolved into a full-fledged culture with attendant group cultural rights. That much-debated question is ultimately irrelevant to the matters of whether and when cure can amount to a form of cultural genocide.

Instead, I ask whether cure, even if it destroys the group, will still leave significant vestiges of its culture alive. Possibly, in society at large, in those who never harbored the condition but who may value its cultural traits. And possibly, as well, within individuals who formerly harbored the condition but who continue to need its cultural strands to structure their identity.

By focusing on how the group perceives social normality and individual wholeness, and on how society in its entirety and individuals in plural embody the group's culture, I am able to draw some conclusions about the two cuts. And those conclusions differ from the ones to which we gravitate when the lenses aren't reversed. In Part 1, where I look at social norms, I argue that for seven of the eight conditions, a cure would be legitimate; but for one, it would constitute enhancement. In Part 2, where I look at individual wholeness, I likewise argue that for seven of the eight conditions a cure would be legitimate; but for one – a different one than in Part 1 – it can be enhancement. And in Part 3, I argue that for seven of the eight conditions a cure would not amount to cultural genocide; but for one – yet a different one – it would be.

The Eight Conditions

A word or two about those eight conditions: physical slowness for competitive runners, mild depression, black racial features, plain facial features, deafness, blindness, obesity, and anorexia. Some of them – mild depression, for example, or plain facial features – typically figure more in cure/enhancement debates. Others, such as deafness or obesity, tend more to provoke cure/cultural genocide debates. Even so, both debates can be made to lend themselves to all eight conditions. And so, I will look at all of the eight as I set forth my approach to the cure/enhancement cut, and likewise at all eight under the approach I propose to the cure/genocide cut.

Here is a related point, meant to reinforce a sense that there exists a relationship between the two debates and hence the eight conditions. At one level, all eight cases raise a question about the boundaries between a medical and a cultural condition. This is most obvious when it comes to those who harbor what would traditionally be deemed a medical condition – deafness and blindness, but also obesity and anorexia – and who are now arguing that it be treated as a culture. When it comes to the other four conditions – physical slowness, mild depression, black racial features, and plain facial features – there is a sense in which the reverse is the case. Those harboring them are seeking to treat, as medical, what more conventionally would be deemed cultural conditions. Blacks who seek surgery to pass as white are arguably asking to treat, as medical, issues that are better dealt with by changing prejudices deeply rooted in the culture. Likewise, mild neurotics who seek antidepressants arguably want to treat, through medicine, matters that are better resolved by combating cultural alienation, anomie, and materialism. Runners who seek steroids are opting to deal medically with obstacles that deserve, arguably, to be ameliorated instead by taking our everybody-loves-a-winner culture down a peg.

I have selected these eight cases not only because they provoke some of the most heated controversies over the boundaries of medicine, but also because, among them, they display fruitful points of both contact and contrast. Prozac for mild depressives often gets compared with steroids for runners, as cosmetic surgery for plain facial features does with similar techniques for black racial features; but, of course, there are also some critical differences. Blindness and deafness differ in many ways; the question will be whether those differences matter for drawing cure/enhancement or cure/genocide cuts. Likewise with obesity and anorexia. Yet although I focus on these eight, the approaches that I advance also lend themselves, as I will show in concluding, to other therapies that have recently been claimed by some to be cure, others enhancement, and still others a form of genocide – such as human growth hormone, IQ boosters, and Ritalin.

I will look at these eight conditions as they manifest themselves phenotypically. In doing so I define phenotype broadly, following Fukuyama, to embrace any kind of "physical appearance and features" or "mental [state] and behavior."[49] The question, in Parts 1 and 2, will be: What makes any particular phenotype a medical condition amenable to cure?

Some definitions of phenotype extend further to embrace everything that the person advancing them deems not strictly genotypic, that is, any characteristic of a person – including cellular, molecular, and biochemical structures – that can be affected in some way by the environment. But as Richard Lewontin and others argue, even genotype itself can be affected environmentally, and so it is fortunate that this debate doesn't concern us here. Instead, I am using "phenotype" to refer to those characteristics of a condition – such as its broad physical appearance and features or its mental states and behaviors, as Fukuyama says – that would matter to members of any group as they fashion their views of social norms and personal wholeness. Phenotypes, for my purposes, are thus simply "observed traits": observable, that is, in society and individuals by members of groups harboring the various conditions, not exclusively in biological labs by scientists. As Buchanan, Brock, Daniels, and Wikler say, "for each of us, it is the particular element of our phenotype, not every element of our genotype" – or, one might add, of our molecular or cellular condition – "that we take to be central to our conceptions of self and to our essence as an individual."[50] Such an understanding of phenotype is consistent with the way many philosophers and scientists use the term.[51]

This is not to deny that many, many medical conditions can be described at both phenotypic and subphenotypic – physiological, cellular, molecular, genetic – levels, nor is it to assert that there are any clear lines between such descriptions. For most medical conditions, this multiplicity of descriptions won't matter, since at whatever level you look, the condition will (on the arguments I make in Parts 1 and 2) legitimately be a medical one, or it won't. In some cases, though, the most phenotypic description of a condition – that is, the description least reliant on genotypic, cellular, or physiological observations – will conflict with more genetically, cellularly, or physiologically rooted conceptions. The significance of this will become apparent later.[52]

On the phenotypic approach I take, someone has black racial features only if, unmodified by cosmetics or hair styles, she looks black: You can see a "hint of Africa beneath [her] skin."[53] Even those who believe that genotypic notions of race are incoherent, whether they are thinking of the egregious "one-drop rule" or far more sophisticated notions based on population genetics, acknowledge that "[m]oving beyond race [genotypically] does not require [our] pretending that phenotypic differences do not exist."[54] Put another way, someone who has what are conventionally considered to be genotypically black ancestors, but who looks white, isn't passing for white (phenotypically).[55] For my purposes, she is white (phenotypically).[56] Of course, a person can also be black culturally, regardless of whether she is black phenotypically or genotypically (if the latter notion even has any meaning at all). But since one of the two main questions here is whether a Michael Jackson pill for black phenotypes would, if widely taken, be destructive of black culture, I stay with the phenotypic definition of the condition. And I note that when I refer to black racial features collectively with the other seven as "conditions," I mean conditions to be synonymous with phenotypes.

As for a phenotypically physically slow runner, I define him as one for whom there exist other runners, more naturally gifted, to whom he would always lose in competition, assuming that they all engaged in the same rigors of training, exercise, and diet. Obviously, on this definition, even very good runners – Olympic and world-class athletes – can be physically slow. But such scope is necessary to keep faith with the real issues posed by the use of performance boosters. They are live ones principally (if not exclusively) for accomplished athletes who are slower than just a few others, and not simply for the rest of us who are slower than many, if not most.

The cyclist Perolof Astrand captures what I mean by "physically slow runner" while talking of his own status in cycling: "I had done everything I could do to win the race including training over 500 miles a week in the months before, observing a strict diet, deploying weight training, utilizing massage therapists and trainers, and more . . . I was as strong and fast as I had ever been or would be. Nevertheless, it was apparent I was not going to win the race. Why? Because despite maximizing my [training, exercise, and diet], the upper ceiling of my physical nature had been reached and was still below that of the two riders ahead of me," who had trained, dieted, and exercised just as extensively.[57] Put another way, "naturally gifted" implies all those capacities that an individual can deploy without any stress or difficulty or exertion – without training, diet, and exercise. It is in these capacities that the physically slow runner is comparatively lacking.

As for obesity, anorexia, deafness, and blindness, each term will apply to a phenotype if it would be diagnosed as such by most physicians. I recognize that a range of phenotypes – from total to legal blindness, for example – fall under each of these rubrics, but that won't pose an issue in what follows. What's controversial, at least for my purposes, is not the (factual) question of whether any given person is obese, anorexic, deaf, or blind, but the (normative) issue as to whether those conditions, as conventionally understood, can legitimately be seen as medical ones.

As for those with "plain facial features," a term that I am using for want of a better one, they are people seeking cosmetic surgery. "Cosmetic" means that I am setting aside reconstructive surgery, which is reserved for those who are uncontroversially regarded as having a medical condition: people with burns, serious scars, port-wine stains, or those whose features are more aptly described as disfigured or even ugly rather than plain. "Facial" means that I am also setting aside cosmetic surgery for other parts of the body, such as breast enlargement or liposuction. And "features" underscores the fact that cosmetic facial surgery is generally sought for a particular feature or features – nose, eyes, lips, skin – that the individual concerned believes needs it, and not for a face in general.

As Kathy Davis writes in her study of cosmetic surgery patients, "many of the women I spoke with were not particularly critical of their appearance in general . . . They could cite numerous features which they 'wouldn't change for the world' . . . It was only this one particular body part – this nose or these [eyes] – which was problematic . . . which . . . 'ruined the rest.'"[58]

Finally, in defining mild depression, I will follow Peter D. Kramer's *Listening to Prozac* in applying that term to "the diverse syndromes," those less severe than clinical depression, "that respond to new medications," in particular selective serotonin reuptake inhibitors (SSRIs) such as Prozac, Zoloft, and Paxil. In characterizing those syndromes, Kramer goes on to say, "a good case can be made for the return of 'neurosis,' a catchall category for serious minor discomfort related to depression and anxiety."[59] Or, as the reporters Connie Strong and Terence Ketter put it, we are talking here about "moody and neurotic, mild non-clinical forms of depression,"[60] not major or bipolar clinical forms of depression. Accordingly, I will take the terms "neurotic anxiety," "neurotic moodiness," or "neurotic depression" to be synonymous with "mild depression." And, by a cure for mild depression, I mean a treatment that does what Prozac does, according to Kramer, when it works well: substitutes for the psychotherapeutic treatment of neurotic anxiety, moodiness, or depression.[61]

Whatever Prozac does when it *doesn't* work well – sometimes it has no effect, and at other times it has too much effect, allegedly becoming a "happy pill" that allows those taking it to feel blissful even under unwarranted circumstances – the cure for mild depression that I imagine (call it "super-Prozac") would simply eliminate neurotic responses of various sorts. It would still allow those taking it to react with nonneurotic, that is, appropriate happiness or unhappiness to the genuinely good or bad qualities of whatever life presents to them. Mild "depression entails a distortion of perception – the sufferer sees life as more bleak than it is," Kramer says, and so antidepressants, when they work as they should, merely "make a depressed person once again responsive to reality." When that reality happens itself to be bleak, the person on Prozac, like all "normal people," will and should "experience pain." That shows that they are "merely in touch with reality."[62] "Mild depression," Andrew Solomon says in his memoir of depression, *Noonday Demon*, "is too much grief at too slight a cause."[63] Prozac, when it works as it should, doesn't erase the grief; rather, it allows the grief to become proportionate to the cause.[64] Criticisms of Prozac for being a "happy pill" are more appropriate for narcotics.

Accordingly, my imagined super-Prozac – which simply works as Prozac should without the side effects, unreliability, or over/undershooting – would not make a person "happy," as Jonathan Glover says in discussing the same topic, "even in the face of a world that deserves a more complex emotional response." It would preserve "his legitimate despair," ensuring only that "in the normal run of things, [his] moods are roughly appropriate to the things that happen to [him]."[65] Almost the entire psychotherapeutic enterprise presumes the coherence of such a distinction between neurotic and appropriate unhappiness. While there are those who question it, they are, as they acknowledge, questioning the meaning and possibility of psychotherapy itself. The debate that they have provoked lies too far afield for me to get into here; so, as with the profession, I assume a distinction. Super-Prozac – my imagined fail-safe version of Prozac – is, then, a drug that unerringly replaces "neurotic unhappiness" with (at the very most) what Freud called "ordinary" or "normal" unhappiness, not unwarranted bliss. It simply does what psychotherapy claims to do. There is a huge debate over whether Prozac is an enhancement, even assuming that it is a treatment only for neurosis, not ordinary unhappiness, and I operate within that debate.

I will refer to people who have any one of these eight conditions as "harboring" the condition. If they can legitimately seek a cure on the criteria I set out in Parts 1 and 2, then I will say that they can legitimately view theirs as a "*medical* condition." That is, they can view it as one for which medicine, assuming our fantasy of unlimited financial capacity and technological facility, would have to devote resources for the development and distribution of a cure – as long as, additionally, there would be no cultural genocide involved (Part 3). In using the term medical condition, I will stay away from words such as "illness," "disease," and "disability," which have many different meanings for many different people.[66] And by referring to those with any given one of the eight conditions (e.g., the deaf, anorexics, the mildly depressed) as a group or a community, I don't mean to suggest that they participate in any organized structure, although they may. Rather, I mean that through their common condition they form a recognizable category, about whom we should have no more problem talking collectively than we do in referring to gun collectors or dairy farmers or Greek Americans as groups.

The three terms in the pair of cuts I will be making – cure, enhancement, and cultural genocide – have all caused me problems because none of them is neutral. To designate the means for eradicating a particular condition a cure seems, on the one hand, to already suggest that the condition concerned is a medical one, when of course, in this inquiry, that's precisely the issue to be determined. Yet on the other hand, words like "treatment" or "therapy" lack cure's connotation of actually eradicating a condition, as opposed to simply managing it. Generally, I will rely on the context to make clear whether I am referring to cure simply as a means of eradicating any condition – as, for example, when I say "In this case, a cure would be a form of enhancement" – or when I mean it to suggest "legitimate cure," a means of eradicating what can legitimately be seen as a medical condition.

I will assume, again following almost everyone else who has looked at the philosophical issues of cure/enhancement, that the imagined cures are safe, painless, and bereft of side effects.[67] I will also assume that, no matter what the metabolism or physiology of the particular individual who takes it, any such cure will immediately, completely, and permanently eradicate her phenotypic condition.[68] Of course, some cures – cochlear implants for the deaf, steroids for the physically slow, Prozac for the mildly depressed, Botox for the wrinkled – have already been developed, but they work imperfectly and selectively. I will borrow from the debates that they have provoked, but my discussion imagines the development and insurance coverage of cures that work perfectly and permanently for everyone with the condition.

Also, although I describe conditions themselves at a phenotypic, not a biochemical, cellular, or genetic level, I will – again following common practice – draw no distinction between cures that may be genetic, hormonal, cellular, pharmacological, or surgical. I don't need, in other words, to get very specific about the kinds of cures that a world of unlimited technology would furnish. True, in a sense, my project here focuses very much on the meaning of cure, since its two tasks are to draw lines between cure and enhancement and between cure and cultural genocide. But that is just another way of exploring how to determine whether any given phenotypic condition is a medical or a nonmedical one and whether, if that phenotypic condition disappears, there would be an unacceptable cultural loss. Nothing, for the purposes of my argument, hangs on what specific form a cure might take, with two exceptions. First, the discovery of a cure might (as some argue it often does) itself be what makes us want to deem a previously nonmedical condition to be a medical one. Second, the nature of the cure itself might have its own consequences in

causing cultural loss beyond whatever cultural consequences the phenotype's disappearance might bring. I will save the first of these questions
for Part 1; here I will say something about the second.

I have claimed that, for my purposes, a cure could take any form:
genetic, cellular, pharmaceutical, surgical. In principle, it could also take
a more broadly social form. If, for example, we resolved the tension
between competing social expectations placed on women, then we would
arguably cure some cases of compulsive eating and hence phenotypic
obesity. Yet (and I will say more about this in Part 3), while such social
expectations may well cause many cases of obesity, they also cause much
of the culture of obesity: the politics, the solidarity, the pride, the humor,
the literature, the memoirs. A more broadly social cure could actually
have far greater adverse cultural consequences – could come closer to
cultural genocide – than one that confined itself to phenotypic obesity
but otherwise left the underlying social forces intact.

I don't want to categorically rule out such "social" cures; they fall,
after all, under the ambit of public health, into which the domain of
medicine currently blurs. In our actual world of technological bounded-
ness, medicine arguably has to widen its institutional boundaries. It has
to enlist any broader social tools it can get – including those that fall
not just in the domains of environmental science or occupational safety
but wider political and social change – to erode the phenotypes it is
fighting.

This would seem to be Rachel Cottam's position in urging that it comes
very much within medicine's role to attack (here I continue with the
example of obesity) the phenotype's social causes. There is, Cottam writes
in *The Lancet*, "a more disparate malaise, of which overeating and obesity
could be symptoms," but which "[f]ew doctors have felt themselves qual-
ified, or willing, to explore," namely, that "many people are living at a
feverish pitch . . . . [M]edicine [has to] consider the ways human beings
often inflict damage in their relations with themselves, and how medical
practice can protect against this. Doctors cannot shirk their engagement
with ethics and philosophy . . . . Can the realities of the growing problem
of obesity bring about a broadening of medical focus and a concomitant
change in practice at all levels? We might have been slow off the mark
here, but if our approach remains the same – finding problems in the
medically objectified body without considering the confluence of self and
society . . . that could facilitate ill-health – we will surely miss other crises
in the making."[69] Medicine must, Cottam concludes, ease "the pressure
points . . . in our culture."[70]

My own view – and in a backhanded way I think that Cottam's argument shows this – is that however "broad" medicine's "focus" should be in our current situation, it would narrow in an ideal world, one without technological limits, to the elimination of the phenotype of obesity itself. It would then allow matters of culture to remain within the sphere of the "ethicists and philosophers," the artists and writers, the polemicists and critics, and the "self and society."

Here, then, I simply want to emphasize an observation that stands at the background of what follows. Given our assumption of technological boundlessness, the cures we imagine would and should confine themselves as closely as possible to surgically eradicating the phenotype while leaving intact any broader social behavior that may have caused it. Not that such behavior merits being left intact, just that, in an ideal world, it would as much as possible be left alone by medicine. In the presence of a cure for phenotypic obesity that our imagined limitlessness on medical technology allows, such broader social behavior would no longer be a medical concern, but a matter of other kinds of social policy. From the perspective of those formulating such social policy, one could then debate whether and how (say) the competing demands placed on women should be rebalanced on the cultural, social, and moral merits, without having to place a concern for phenotypic obesity in the scale. From the perspective of medicine, as it becomes less technologically bounded, it actually becomes more institutionally bounded – much more surgical and focused – as a social practice.

It is precisely to give each such cure the greatest benefit of the doubt – to put it on its strongest footing – that I am going to assume that it focuses as much as possible on the phenotype itself, not on eradicating its social-behavioral causes. There will, as Part 3 shows, be enough problem with the cultural damage that simply eradicating a phenotype itself – mild depression, anorexia, obesity – might cause, without having to reckon with the cultural impact of a cure that veers into the social causes of those phenotypes. For these reasons, my approach is sympatico with observations, such as Y. Michael Barilan and Moshe Weintraub's, that "[m]edicine aims . . . to find the best-localized and specific intervention . . . Medicine strives to find procedures that have the least possible repercussions in the wider bio-psycho-social circles."[71] Certainly, that should be its aim if technological constraints are no longer an issue.

I'll take this opportunity to stress that there is a profound difference between a "social cure" for a condition, say obesity, and the "social accommodation" of that condition. A social cure would fight cases of phenotypic obesity through an attack on its social-behavioral causes; it would involve, among other things, our reconciling women's conflicting social roles or eliminating poverty. The social accommodation of obesity, by contrast, would require us to reframe our attitudes toward the phenotype by celebrating fat culture or to reform the environment by altering airplane seats. The idea of a social cure views obesity as a medical condition to be eradicated. The idea of social accommodation views it as a culture to be protected.

Or consider mild depression. In his contribution to a recent collection of essays on Prozac, Tod Chambers expresses the hope that America is "a nation that . . . treasures the intellectual, aesthetic or religious offspring of the spiritual struggle" that depression, melancholy, and alienation provoke.[72] Such a hope, says Peter D. Kramer, another contributor, represents "the valorization of sadness." It leads to the social accommodation of depression, to its being given breathing space, to our extending understanding and latitude to the melancholic. It prompts us neither to cure his condition nor harry him for displaying his anomie and angst, but rather to value the cultural richness – the intellectual, aesthetic, and religious treasures – that his phenotypic condition brings to all our lives. Yet another contributor to the volume, however, seems very set on eradicating depression, not medically but through a social cure: by attacking the social behavior that causes it. Instead of "changing those [depressive] persons who do not meet dominant expectations" via drugs – that is, instead of curing the phenotype directly – "we might," Erik Parens writes, "change those expectations and the society that produces them" and thereby diminish anxiety, sadness, and alienation.[73]

Parens's advocacy of a social cure for depression definitely does not share in the "valorization of sadness" that lies behind Chambers's arguments for the social accommodation of depression. After all, Parens wants to get rid of depression by social means, while Chambers wants to accommodate or valorize it by social means. Possibly the two views can be reconciled if what Parens wants to cure is neurotic (inappropriate) depression and what Chambers wants to accommodate is ordinary (appropriate) unhappiness. But if so, then Prozac – which both Chambers and Parens criticize – would seem to be the solution, not the problem. Or as Elizabeth Wurtzel puts it: After taking Prozac, "my improved affect did not in any way sway me from the basic philosophical conviction that life, at its height and at its depth, basically sucks."[74]

Let me now turn from these considerations about cure to some surrounding the term, "enhancement." For some writers, the word carries a positive connotation. To enhance something, even if doing so is not necessary, is at least to make it better.[75] My use of enhancement is meant to imply nothing of the sort. It simply means a cure for a condition that, on the analysis I offer in Parts 1 and 2, cannot legitimately be deemed a medical one. For example, I might conclude that surgery or a Michael Jackson pill for black racial features is an enhancement. That wouldn't imply that a black person who undergoes such enhancement is improving herself. And I will take this opportunity to note that the issue of blacks seeking surgery to pass as white is a significant one; as Awa Thiam said in the 1990s, skin whitening is "the black disease of the second half of the 20th century."[76] In this context, Thiam's use of the word "disease" is worth keeping in mind: It describes not the condition, but the cure.

As for "cultural genocide," the term causes me, and presumably will cause many readers, discomfort in connection with cures for deafness, blindness, obesity, or anorexia. Unlike situations in which there can be no controversy over the use of the word genocide, in these cases the motive governing those being accused of the genocide is a benevolent one, a therapeutic one. That cuts only so much ice, however, given that the benevolent impetus to cure – *furor therapeuticus* – has been responsible for some famously horrific episodes in the history of medicine.[77]

Another, and more critical, distinction between the use of cultural genocide here and elsewhere is that here, the mechanism does not involve people being slaughtered, but rather their deliberately deciding to undergo a medical procedure. But even so, there are complications. Deaf or obesity activists claim to be seriously aggrieved by their fellows who seek to, or try to, desert them by pursuing cures for their condition. So, in a far from satisfactory fashion, I have tried to give their due to those who have introduced the term cultural genocide into the debates I am analyzing by using the term myself, except in contexts where I simply am not comfortable doing so. In that case, I rely (sometimes in tandem) on synonyms such as "cultural loss" or "cultural harm" or "disappearance." I suspect that there will be readers who will bristle at what they see as my use of euphemisms, just as others will bridle at my invocation of what they would deem an unnecessarily provocative term.

Finally, I want to bracket out two issues – equality and autonomy – from discussion. Critics often argue that if we pursue cures for plain facial features or physical slowness, or for mediocre IQ or shortness, then those who can afford them will gain an unfair advantage over those who cannot. I exclude this concern by assuming that public health insurance will cover any treatment that, on the arguments set out in Parts 1, 2, and 3, can be understood as neither enhancement nor as genocide, but as a cure for a legitimate medical condition.

Critics, though, also argue in the alternative. They worry not only about the possibility that few will have access to a cure, but also about the possibility that everyone will. "Suppose it becomes much more common to have cosmetic surgery performed," Nils Holtug says; "[t]hen people will benefit less from such surgery, because much of the comparative advantage will be gone."[78] In other words, those with average noses will get beautiful noses, but (so the worry goes) those who already have beautiful noses will gain spectacularly beautiful noses. Hence a great deal of expense will have gone into leaving the social order exactly as it was. But I am assuming that a cure will be made available only to those with the phenotypic condition indicated: those with plain facial features, not those with beautiful facial features.

True, if we make a cure available to the plain-featured, and everyone in society accordingly becomes beautifully featured, the result might be a constriction in cultural diversity. I address that issue in Part 3. But doing so is clearly not pointless. It wouldn't simply ratchet up the same ranking of beauty to a higher level. Some individuals – those with plain noses – would clearly enjoy a competitive gain, even if, as a result, noses themselves ceased to be a source of competitive advantage. True, as Gregory Stock says, "the gifted [i.e., the beautifully nosed] of today ultimately may not welcome such a leveling, because it would diminish [their] edge . . . and make society very competitive, even for the best endowed."[79] But wouldn't that be a good thing?

As for the issue of autonomy, it's often asserted that a particular condition does not merit a cure – and, certainly, not a publicly provided cure – to the extent that it was freely, autonomously, or voluntarily chosen. Some people believe that the obese could control their weight if only they so chose,[80] or that anorexia "begins with a deliberate choice,"[81] or that if someone is mildly depressed or neurotic, he himself is responsible since he could snap out of it if he simply made the choice to do so. These claims, however, are all eminently contestable scientifically.[82] And at the deepest level, they sink into what G. A. Cohen has called the irresolvable "morass of the free will–determinism problem."[83] If the extent to which a condition is freely chosen is pivotal to ascertaining whether we have any obligation to cure it, then we are unlikely to make much progress. More important, many would want to offer a cure for anorexia even if it were freely chosen, and not for big noses even if they aren't freely chosen.[84]

So I set the "choice" issue aside. None of the arguments that I make in what follows relies on any assumption, one way or the other, about whether individuals choose and can control, do not choose and cannot control, or partly choose and partly control, their conditions. Hence, while I investigate the border between a medical condition and a culture, I do not explore the so-called border between a medical condition and a sin or moral deviancy, a border that gets drawn according to where any given analyst believes determinism ends and free will begins.[85]

Some philosophers examine issues similar to the ones that I am discussing in the context of embryo selection or germline engineering. There the question is whether a parent should be able to control a child's skin color, athletic ability, mental states, or physical appearance. It is not whether (what is at issue here) a person should be able to medically alter his own skin color, athletic ability, mental states, or physical appearance. Some of this embryo/germline discussion is relevant to my considerations, and I will draw on it. But it also raises issues that pit autonomy against not determinism but paternalism: issues that, again, lie afield of my concerns.[86] For that reason, my entire discussion can be taken to concern itself with adults – when I speak of "society," I mean "adult society" – and not children.

In all of what follows, I am going to take very seriously Thomas Murray's observation that, in the kinds of debates I am examining, we can draw lines based only on "complex practical understandings" of the conditions in question.[87] And we can do so only for a particular place and time: in this case, America (or perhaps pluralist democracies more generally) here and now. As Jonathan Glover wrote in his 1984 *What Sort of People Should There Be?*, "[s]ome of the values that will figure prominently here might have meant little to a medieval European, and may mean little now to people in China or Japan. And even among the likely readers of this book, although I hope there will be understanding of its values, it would be unrealistic to expect general agreement."[88]

My focus, accordingly, will home in on contemporary social practice and argument. I hope to persuade readers that my approaches to the cure/enhancement and cure/genocide cuts are worth pursuing. But, following Glover, I do not expect – nor, for the sake of establishing the validity of those approaches, do I require – any reader to agree with

all the ways in which I apply them to each of the eight conditions. If I
characterize deafness, say, or obesity in a way that you don't accept, our
disagreement may well be over the characteristics of deafness or obesity,
not over the principles I am advancing to draw the cure/enhancement
and cure/cultural genocide cuts.

My method will be John Rawls's famous "reflective equilibrium." I will
examine the worlds of practice and argument surrounding the eight
conditions and draw out of them principles that I think will make the
cure/enhancement and the cure/genocide cuts. I will then (or simultaneously) do the reverse: apply those principles back to the world of
practice and debate. In some cases, those principles will show certain
practices to be wrong and certain arguments to be mistaken. In others,
though, the better path will be for me to conclude that the principle is
wrong and needs correcting. With as few iterations as I can possibly manage, I will try to reach a reflective equilibrium between philosophy and
practice, between our moral intuitions and the principles I advance for
drawing cuts between cure, enhancement, and genocide – and hence for
determining the final limits to medicine.[89]

1

Between the Normal and the Ideal

When it comes to determining whether a condition is a medical one, philosophers such as Leon Kass or Christopher Boorse advance an essentially biological approach. They want us to look to the biological norms of the human species – our genetic, cellular, and organic functioning – for the foundations of what medicine should and should not do. Their understandable concern is that without such a biological anchor, we would have no grounds for refusing someone like Dartmouth Medical School professor Joseph Rosen, who ended a medical conference some years ago by "pounding the table . . . and announcing that, were he given permission by a medical ethics board, he would try to engineer a person to have wings."[1]

But as many critics have urged, and as I too argue in the Introduction, there is a serious weakness in the biological functioning approach to species normality. Unless we at the same time consult social norms, it tells us very little. Perhaps, as a proposition of biological functioning, our legs aren't even meant to carry us upright, as Dorothy Dinnerstein suggests. Nor would a reliance on natural biological functioning seem to allow medicine to concern itself with the vision sufficient for night driving. But once we admit that medicine's task is to take us to whatever happens to be socially normal, we then have to accept that the social norm itself is always evolving. The question would seem to be this: Can we devise a way of drawing the cure/enhancement cut so as to place any future means of eradicating arthritis inside the domain of legitimate medical cure while relegating the eradication of our winglessness to the realm of mere enhancement? In the first three sections of this part, I suggest a means of doing this by looking at both social norms and social ideals in particular ways.

Those particular ways are shaped by a further fact. While an approach that looks at social norms (and ideals, about which more shortly) is superior to an approach that relies on biological norms, it too – absent further modification – runs into difficulties. Certainly, those who advance the social norm approach voice a concern worth heeding. Unless we define conditions as medical only if they impair the pursuit of a societywide range of possible life plans, the medical system will fall hostage to individual idiosyncrasies, responsible for developing cures to enable this person to play professional basketball or that person to sing at the Metropolitan Opera House.

But there is a difficulty, too, with adopting a societywide perspective on social normality; there is a difficulty, in other words, with deeming social normality to be whatever society as a whole believes it to be. It's too one-size-fits-all. Sometimes, as well, it can fall prey to social prejudices. The question is: Can we can find an approach to social normality that accords due consideration to the views of those deaf people who deny that hearing is necessary for a societywide range of life plans, or to those many people with wrinkled skin who believe that smooth skin is, without having to deem a medical condition to be whatever any given individual says it is? In the final section of Part 1, I look in detail at a perspective intermediate between society as a whole and individuals one by one: that of the groups harboring each of the eight conditions. And I suggest that we can indeed find legitimate group perspectives, perspectives that members of groups can legitimately take, to the issue of whether their condition is socially normal and/or related issues having to do with the pertinent social ideal.[2] It is those perspectives that, I argue, should determine what counts as a medical condition.

The Problem with Canguilhem

Begin by defining a social norm for anything – weight, nose size, skin texture, content of melanin in the skin, mood, speed, sight, hearing – "not as a fixed point, but as a range of variations" around the "statistical mean, [median] or mode."[3] And let us define a social ideal for the same things as "an object of general desire, possessing value which appeals to the mass of the population": the most desirable range of weight, nose size, skin texture, racial features, mental states, seeing and hearing capacity, whatever they may be – not whatever they should or should not be as an ethical matter, but whatever they are as a sociological matter – in a particular society at a given time.[4]

Leon Kass, Frances Fukuyama, and others resist the idea of using medicine to assist perfectly normal people to reach an ideal: That is what they mean when they consign a treatment for a given condition to the class of mere enhancement. But as Georges Canguilhem pointed out, unless any given time period's social norms are set in stone, they can change only as individuals begin to depart from them in the direction of the ideal, thereby ultimately embodying that ideal in a new norm, even as the old norm becomes abnormal.[5] This raises the question of what medicine's role in such an evolution should be.

What Canguilhem's observation calls to mind are scenarios like this: In 1850, it was normal for nearly all of an adult's teeth to display signs of decay. Cure, at that time, would have been limited to the removal of a completely rotten tooth and possibly its replacement by a false one made of ivory, porcelain, gold, silver, wood, or animal bone. In that era, the kind of dental work that we now deem routine for adults – fluoride treatments, scaling and flossing, cavity-filling, and root canal surgery to prevent or correct that normal decay – would (even though some of these techniques were available in rudimentary form) have been enhancement. And, of course, very few, if any, adults would have achieved an ideal of no tooth decay whatsoever.[6]

But over time, thanks to changes in nutrition, vitamin intake, water quality, education, and personal hygiene, more and more adults would have begun to control and reduce their tooth decay.[7] As the years passed, this process would have rendered abnormal the very worst cases of decay among adults, which had formerly fallen within the bounds of social normality. At one stage, dental techniques to prevent or correct these most serious cases of decay would have ceased to be enhancement; they would, instead, simply have become necessary to bring those with this newly abnormal condition up to the evolving norm. With the further passage of time, as more and more adults reached the long-standing ideal of actually being totally decay-free for portions of their adult lives – due to continued improvements in nutrition, water quality, and personal hygiene – that venerable ideal would have embarked on the road to becoming the "new normal."[8] As a result, fluoride treatments, scaling, cavity-filling, and root canal surgery for any adult whose teeth were not decay-free would now have become cure, no longer mere enhancement. Even if "decay free" was still closer to being the ideal than the norm, the fact that more than a few others had attained it would justify curing those with some decay.[9]

Then, at one point – perhaps the point we are at now – a new ideal would have begun to emerge: the ideal of having not only nondecayed but perfectly white teeth. As long as relatively few adults manage to attain that ideal, any cure for discolored teeth will remain an enhancement. But as more and more do attain perfectly white teeth – by giving up smoking, brushing with whitening toothpaste, renouncing tea and coffee, and the like – that ideal will embark on the road toward becoming the norm, turning dental tooth whitening into a legitimate cure.[10]

A believer in biologically defined norms would object. After all, she would say, a person can't eat – a basic biological function – with decayed teeth. Curing this person would always have been legitimate. But a person can eat with discolored teeth, so curing him will always be enhancement. Here again, though, there is some sleight of hand in the biological-norm position. In fact, a person *can* eat with decayed teeth, even badly decayed teeth, just not as well as with nondecayed teeth. So what we're talking about couldn't be a biological norm, but a social norm – a norm that at any given time sets an expectation as to how well one should be able to chew one's food. And once we talk about social norms, we have to take into account the possibility that those norms could evolve to include pearly white teeth.

This kind of dynamic – on which what used to be normal becomes abnormal, what used to be ideal becomes normal, and a new ideal appears over the horizon – describes the evolution of many cures and conditions but certainly not all. Sometimes, for example, there is backsliding: Currently, the social norm of weight is moving not toward but away from the social ideal. And ideals themselves can shift back and forth like shuttlecocks, as ideal body size in Western societies has over not just centuries, but within decades, gone from smaller to bigger to smaller.[11] Sometimes the issue is not so much that a particular dynamic differs from the one that Canguilhem's approach implies as that there is no dynamic at all. Contemporary society considers schizophrenia abnormal, neurosis normal, and (a fair case can be made on criteria that I shall discuss shortly) nonneurotic self-esteem ideal; yet it's not the case that at one time schizophrenia was normal and garden-variety neurosis was the ideal. Here, no Canguilhem-style dynamic ever really commenced. Conversely, while at one point, scurvy fell within the bounds of normality and not having scurvy was ideal, now not having scurvy is normal but also ideal.[12] The ideal didn't move on to some new notion of the optimal absorption of vitamin C by the body, although it perhaps might some day.[13] But, for the moment, the dynamic has stopped.

All of these complications have to do with one particular aspect of the Canguilhem-style scenario: the dynamic aspect, the part that describes the movement of a condition through time. Neither norm nor ideal always moves continuously forward in the same direction, as the cases of obesity and body size show. Sometimes they never really begin to move, as with schizophrenia. Sometimes they finish moving, as with scurvy. But I think that we can still rescue something absolutely crucial from Canguilhem for the purposes of making the cure/enhancement cut. For although the Canguilhem-style scenario doesn't describe movement through time in a way that's always accurate, it does show us what has to be the case at any point in time for cure to be legitimate. The scenario that Canguilhem's analysis suggests might fail dynamically, but we can refurbish it to apply statically.

On this refashioned approach, those with a particular condition would have no justification for deeming it to be a medical one – cure would be enhancement – if, at any given time, the condition fell within the current social norm and few if any had attained the current social ideal. This snapshot would resemble either the very beginning or the very end of the cycle that Canguilhem's analysis implies. Think of the situation in which substantial tooth decay for adults is normal, while few or none have yet reached the ideal of having no decay. In such circumstances, taking measures to absolutely eliminate tooth decay would be enhancement. Or think of the moment when being decay-free has become the new normal, but few if any have attained the newly emergent ideal of perfectly white teeth; here, treatment for discolored but otherwise nondecayed teeth would be enhancement.

If, however, those harboring a particular condition can legitimately view it as falling outside the norm, regardless of whether anyone has reached the ideal state, then they can reasonably ask to be brought at least to that norm. In addition, if they legitimately deem themselves to be normal, but equally legitimately deem more than a few others to have reached the ideal, they can ask to be brought to that ideal. These snapshot situations resemble middle ranges in the Canguilhem-style dynamic. Where the very worst cases of decay have become abnormal, treating those cases would be cure, not enhancement. And even as "some decay" remains the norm, if more than a few have already reached the decay-free ideal, then treating those with only some tooth decay would not be enhancement. It would be only fair and, certainly, legitimate cure.

We can, in other words, cut the Canguilhem-style dynamic up into static slices. In each, we can determine whether a cure would be enhancement even if we don't accept that, over time and for any given condition, those slices connect together or lead one to another in any particular way, still less the particular way that Canguilhem's analysis suggests. We are led to this template by the pitfalls of the biological approach, the weakness that Canguilhem detected in the social norm approach, and the problems in Canguilhem's own suggestive analysis.

All of which begs the question: How, in specific terms, do we know when it's legitimate for group members to view their condition as socially abnormal? And how do we know when it's legitimate for them to deem others to have reached the social ideal? Our concern here, as I said in the Introduction, lies not with whether society as a whole – on the basis of whether a condition promotes or inhibits a societywide range of life plans – stamps that condition as normal, ideal, or neither. Rather, our concern is whether members of the specific group in question can legitimately view their condition as falling outside the social norm and/or believe that nongroup members have actually attained a social ideal. In that case, cure wouldn't be "mere" enhancement. But if group members cannot legitimately view their condition as falling outside the social norm, and if they cannot legitimately deem others to have attained the social ideal, then the case that cure is really enhancement becomes a strong one.

Norms

How should we assess such legitimacy? Begin with the task of determining social normality, following which I will turn to the question of social ideal. When it comes to the legitimacy of group members' views as to whether their condition falls within the bounds of social normality, it should matter whether – with respect to their phenotype – society as a whole distributes itself according more to a bell curve or to a skewed curve. A bell curve, shaped smoothly as it is, can allow for legitimate disagreement as to where to draw the cutoff of normality, since the curve itself suggests no obvious "ranges of [normal] variation."[14] The bell curve "has no landmarks," as Edmond A. Murphy puts it, rendering "arbitrary" any "classification in the sense that there is no criterion, intrinsic or extrinsic . . . that helps [us] say where" the lines of normality should be drawn.[15] On a bell curve, the mode, median, and mean all congregate at the same point – the peak of the bell – rendering them useless for suggesting any broader or distinctive ranges of normality, hence leaving open any number of legitimate possibilities for describing such ranges.

Attention spans, for example, distribute themselves on a bell curve.[16] This allows Francis Fukuyama to pronounce, legitimately on the approach that I am advancing, that the vast majority of the population – even those diagnosed with attention deficit disorder (ADD) – actually fall "into the tail of a … distribution of normal behaviors."[17] Fukuyama looks at the bell curve and draws the cutoff of normality so that, say, only the 2 percent of the population with the lowest attention spans are abnormal. Others, though, look at the same curve and, with no less although certainly no more legitimacy, mark the cutoff of normality at various higher points to render abnormal millions of adults and tens of millions of children.[18] When Len Barton writes that there are no "absolutes or clear dichotomies … which presume [that] we can distinguish between normal and abnormal," he is thinking of the bell curve, which allows for any number of conceptions of normal range, each no less legitimate than the others.[19] Likewise for Abraham Rudnick, who says that "[a]ccording to the medical conception, it is unclear whether [many conditions are] a pathological phenomenon or a normal variable."[20]

Nor are standard deviations of much help in precluding debate over the cutoff of norm on a bell curve. "Our conception of the degree of severity that gives rise to a disability is constantly changing," Theresa Glennon notes; "[f]or example, the definition of mental retardation has changed from one standard deviation from the norm to two standard deviations – instantly lowering the number of mentally retarded people."[21] Glennon's remark exemplifies a much-discussed problem: the arbitrariness of using standard deviations to describe normal ranges on a bell curve. The Food and Drug Administration (FDA), to take another example, has decided that human growth hormone can be given only to children more than 2.25 standard deviations below the average height for their age and size – in other words, to the shortest 1.2 percent.[22] It's not clear, however, why the cutoff should be 2.25 as opposed to 2.15 or 2. Indeed, some doctors offer human growth hormone treatments when a "child [is only] one or two standard deviations below normal height."[23]

Some believe that the bell curve renders the very idea of social normality incoherent, since it can't be specified. And it's true that if we expect a univocal, societywide answer to the question of whether any particular phenotype is socially normal, then whenever the phenotype falls on a bell curve, any such answer will be an arbitrary one. Another possibility, though, would be to take a group-level, not a societywide perspective. It would simply be to say that for a condition that falls on a bell curve, members of the group harboring it can legitimately view their condition as either socially normal or socially abnormal. Any group member can legitimately view her condition – no matter where it falls outside of the mean/median/modal point – as abnormal, though it would be just as legitimate for her to view it as normal.

This is obviously a very latitudinarian view of legitimacy, but I don't think it's possible to say more. Person A might believe that noses above the 60th percentile on a bell curve of nose size are abnormal, while B believes that any nose above the 70th percentile is. Who's to say who's right – or that in placing abnormality at or above the 80th percentile, C is mistaken, or when he places it at or above the 90th, D is? As I will show in due course, though, this openness does not come at the cost of an inability to make any plausible overall pronouncements about whether members of a group can legitimately demand a cure.

It's true that persons E and F might disagree as to whether their particular condition is abnormal not because they draw the cutoff of normality at different points on, say, the spectrum of nose sizes, but because their particular nose sizes themselves fall at different points. E's nose size might fall in the 65th percentile, and he thinks of his nose as normal. F's, somewhat larger, might fall in the 75th percentile, and he thinks of it as abnormal. And perhaps this is precisely because both actually agree on the cutoff of norm: that it's around, say, the 70th percentile. Their jointly drawing the line of normality at the 70th percentile, however, would simply be one entrant in a much larger debate in which others perfectly legitimately draw the line at 60, 80, or 90 – all of which the bell curve allows. More important, person G could just as easily see her 65th percentile nose as abnormal and seek the cure, while Person H could equally readily view his 75th percentile nose as normal and not seek a cure: just the reverse of E and F.

Sometimes, of course, those falling on both sides of a bell curve can legitimately describe their condition as abnormal, but in other cases only those falling on one side can. This difference depends on where the ideal is located, something that I shall explore momentarily. But here, suffice to say that if the ideal takes the form of a golden mean – noses shouldn't be too large or too small – then those whose noses fall on either side of the bell curve can deem their noses abnormal. If, however, the ideal takes the form of a pole – say, the capacity to pay complete and sustained 100 percent attention – then those who fall on the side of the bell curve closer to the ideal could not deem their condition abnormal, though it might still be less than ideal.

Christopher Boorse, acknowledging that it "is safe to begin any discussion of health by saying that health is normality," then goes on to criticize the idea of normality as a range around "statistical means," noting that "many deviations from the average – e.g., unusual strength or vital capacity . . . are not unhealthy."[24] True. But while any given person might legitimately place unusually impressive strength or vitality outside the normal range on a bell curve, such strength or vitality would fall on that side of the bell curve closer to the ideal, not farther from it. Indeed, they may even comprise the ideal. So, for purposes here, I do not class them as "abnormalities."

Of course, not all curves distributing the population with respect to a condition are bell curves. Many are skewed in one direction or the other. And, by comparison with a bell curve, a skewed curve – one in which mean, median, and mode all differ – is itself more suggestive of particular cutoffs of normality. The mode on a skewed curve falls at the peak of the hump, while the median and the mean each fall on that side of the mode nearer to the tail. Any given point on the hump will thus be closer to one of the three – the mode, the median, or the mean – meaning that the borders between the ranges around each of the three can be given definition.[25]

Even so, if a group member's condition falls at any point anywhere on the hump of a skewed curve, he can still, on the approach that I am arguing, legitimately deem it either normal or abnormal. On the one hand, it would be legitimate for him to regard a point anywhere on the hump as normal, since it would fall within the range of at least one of the three markers – mode, median, or mean – that signify normality. On the other hand, it would also be legitimate for him to deem any point on the hump abnormal, since it would fall outside the ranges of the remaining two markers. On the curve distributing weight over society that skews toward overweight, for example, the modal weight will be greater than the mean weight. A person whose weight fell at a point nearest the social mode, but who deemed normality to fall closer to the social mean, could legitimately view her weight as abnormal.

If, however, a group's condition falls not on the hump at all but on the recognizable tail of a skewed curve, it conclusively lies outside the norm.[26] For group members to view their condition as normal would, on the framework that I am advancing, be illegitimate. The condition would uncontroversially be a medical one. So, for example, no one could legitimately deem her cystic fibrosis normal; a cure for cystic fibrosis could not be enhancement. This does not mean that people with cystic fibrosis can be forced to take a cure; no competent adult can be. Any adult who refuses a cure, however, is not entitled to any continued social accomodations that merely substituted for a cure: accommodations meant to make life more commodious for those afflicted with cystic fibrosis only until science discovered how to eradicate it. She would be entitled only to those accommodations that cystic fibrosis legitimately might command as a culture, and the nature of the arguments she would need to make remain to be considered in Part 3.

A couple of points of clarification before looking at some examples: When I refer to the "group of those harboring a condition," there is a sense in which I am not taking any specific position on how such a group may be defined. For example, on the bell curve from severe depression to mania, the group conventionally called mild depressives would be thought to consist of those on the "depressive" half of the curve who are not severely depressed, that is, not too close to the severe depressive pole. The category of mild depressive would also, of course, exclude anyone anywhere on the entire half of the curve that faces the manic pole. For reasons I have just argued, mild depressives so defined could disagree about whether their particular point, or any particular point, within the mild depressive section of the bell curve is normal or abnormal. But, also for reasons I have just argued, individuals whose phenotypes fell anywhere else on either side of the bell curve outside the median/mean/modal point – whether they are conventionally grouped as severely depressed, hypomanic, or hypermanic – could consider themselves either normal or abnormal. The bell curve suggest no cutoffs.

Or take another example. On what I will argue is a skewed curve distributing sight over society – with the hump much closer to 20/20 vision than to blindness – the group conventionally called "blind" falls on the tail. The blind are thus unequivocally abnormally sighted, unequivocally possessed of a medical condition. But individuals falling on the hump of the skewed curve distributing sight over society could also view themselves as a group capable of demanding a cure. They could do so if, for example, their particular level of sight fell in a range around the social mean, but they deemed the norm to center around the (higher) mode.

A group, then, can occupy any section of either a bell or a skewed curve. If it occupies the tail of a skewed curve, its members would have to view their condition as abnormal; if it occupies the half of a bell curve closer to the socially ideal pole (about which more soon), its members would have to view their condition as normal. Otherwise – if the condition fell anywhere on a bell curve or on the hump of a skewed curve – they could legitimately view their condition as either normal or abnormal. When it comes to defining the eight groups in what follows, I will use the descriptions I set out in the Introduction, some of which (the blind, the deaf) are conventionally set by medicine and others of which (slow runners) I have established for purposes of discussion.

A second point: No individual can be forced to take a cure. But where the condition falls on the tail of a skewed curve and is therefore unequivocally abnormal, as with cystic fibrosis, those who don't want a cure have no legitimate reason to confront or criticize those who do. They bear an obligation not to challenge other group members who might in fact want to take advantage of a medical cure. The condition is unambiguously a medical one.

When, however, we are talking about a bell curve, those who don't want to take a cure will also legitimately be able to view their condition as a normal one, as anyone anywhere on a bell curve can do. And hence – say we're thinking of the bell curves distributing small-to-large nose sizes or depressive-to-manic mental states – they may reasonably challenge and engage those who view the exact same condition, the exact same point on the bell curve, as abnormal and seek a cure. And, of course, those who get challenged can reasonably argue back; a legitimate and continuing group debate can take place. For such conditions there can be legitimate disagreement, a legitimate ongoing exchange, among group members as to whether their condition is a medical one. Ultimately, though, it is up to each group member to decide for himself whether or not his condition is socially normal or socially abnormal.

Homosexuality, Pregnancy, Death, and Atheism: Are These Medical Conditions?

Before turning to the question of social ideals, let me try out the framework I am advancing for social normality on a handful of conditions other than the eight of central interest. Is homosexuality, for example, abnormal and hence a medical condition? After all, aren't gay men located on the tail of a curve of male sexual orientation skewed heavily toward the "sexually oriented to women" end?

On one view, perhaps so. But suppose that, instead of using a curve distributing sexual orientation over men, we consult a curve distributing sexual orientation over adult society as a whole. Yes, on the spectrum from "sexual orientation to men" to "sexual orientation to women," when applied to men only, we get a skewed curve with the tail falling rather markedly on the "sexual orientation to men" end. But if we apply that spectrum not just to one sex or the other but to society as a whole, we don't get a skewed curve. Some argue that in fact we would get a bell curve. On this view, very few of us are exclusively sexually oriented to one gender or the other; more of us combine sexual orientation in various ways, with the highest concentration of the population (whether we know it or not) in the bisexual middle. In this case, given that bell curves themselves suggest nothing about where to draw the bounds of normality, it would be quite legitimate to view sexual orientation to men – whether experienced by men or women – as normal.

There is, of course, an alternative to this notion that when we distribute sexual orientation over the population as a whole, from sexual orientation toward men to sexual orientation toward women, we get a bell curve. It is that if we are going to distribute sexual orientation over the entire population, the resultant curve will be a bimodal one. A large group in adult society is sexually oriented more or less exclusively to men, another large group is sexually oriented more or less exclusively to women, and then there is a valley of bisexuality in between. The symmetry of this distribution across society – the fact that each of the two "humps" is itself a bell curve – suggests, in its own way too, that homosexuality can legitimately be deemed perfectly normal. After all, on this bimodal distribution representing sexual orientation across adult society as a whole, gay men simply form part of the hump representing those who are sexually oriented to men. And every person, man or woman, whose sexual orientation falls on this hump, being as it is one of but two in the bimodal distribution, can legitimately deem his or her condition normal. I think that this difference over which curve to use in assessing the normality of homosexuality – one distributing sexual orientation across men only versus one distributing sexual orientation across the entire society – captures, in its essence, the debate that exists in America over the question.

Abortion provokes the same kind of debate over which curve to use. On the one hand, most women give birth. When we distribute "being pregnant during one's lifetime" across women, we get a skewed curve in which the modal, median, and mean woman all have been, are, or will be pregnant at one or more points during their lives. Facing such a curve, it would be hard for a pregnant woman to argue that her condition is abnormal and that pregnancy is therefore a medical condition requiring cure.

But, on the other hand, this particular curve is not the only one that's pertinent to assessing the normality of pregnancy. There is not only a curve that distributes pregnancy-during-lifetime across all adult female members of society, but one that distributes pregnancy at any one time over all adult members of society, both men and women. Pregnancy, of course, is a dichotomous condition. There are only two options, not-pregnant and pregnant, and so I am using the word "curve" in its notional or stylistic sense. And it is this curve – "either pregnant or not" distributed across the entire adult population – on which pro-choice advocates have, in effect, been asking America to focus. It happens, of course, to be skewed toward not being pregnant.

On this societywide curve, pregnancy – especially if one defines normality as a range around the social mode, which is not being pregnant – can legitimately be deemed abnormal. After all, the modal position would be the one occupied by the greatest number in society. And all men as well as many women – in other words, a majority of adults–aren't pregnant at any given time. A normal range viewed as centered narrowly around the mode would render abortion, on the approach that I am arguing, a legitimate cure. Of course, though, even on such a curve covering all adults and skewing toward not being pregnant, being pregnant can still also be deemed normal. Since no one can be a little bit pregnant, the person at the mean, among men and women as a whole, is simply pregnant.[27] So anyone who placed the socially normal range around the social mean would regard being pregnant as a perfectly normal condition.[28]

The fact that homosexuality or pregnancy can be viewed on different curves at the same time introduces yet a further consideration into the analysis that I am proposing, and I will raise this "multiple curves" possibility where relevant in what follows. It will, however, pose an issue only when, as with homosexuality or pregnancy, the curves in question fall into conflict, with one of them skewed and the other bimodal, or one of them skewed one way and the other skewed the other way, and the like. For example, noses can fall along a bell curve from aquiline to snub, but also along a bell curve from narrow to wide. Skin can fall along a bell curve from dry to oily, but also along a bell curve from loose to taut. There are multiple curves in these cases. But they do not complicate the notion that those seeking cures for problems of their noses or skin, whatever curve they use, can legitimately view their conditions as abnormal, since bell curves themselves are silent about normality's bounds. Likewise, the phenotypic manifestation of late-stage cancer – its characteristics as observable to those harboring the condition – fall on the tail of a skewed curve. And so do its various subphenotypic manifestations, its cellular aspects as observable in a lab. The condition is abnormal, no matter what curve one consults.

With homosexuality and pregnancy, however, there is what I would call a "conflict of curve." And, I now want to argue, in each case one of the two curves is preferable. Specifically, the proper curves to consult here are the ones that distribute the phenotypes "sexual orientation" or "pregnancy" across adult society as a whole. Curves that distribute sexual orientation across men only, or pregnancy across women only, require our smuggling notions of normal biological functioning into our definitions of medical condition. They require us to base our definition of medical condition on the idea that there is, or should be, a difference in the sexual orientation of men and women, and in the child-bearing activities of men and women, such that separate curves make sense. And this, as gay rights activists routinely point out, is to presume that sexual orientation serves the biological function of procreation and not (as well) broader social functions of emotional expression, relationship-building, recreation, and pleasure-seeking. It is, as abortion-rights activists continually observe, to assume that women fill a particular biological role in procreation and not (as well) broader social roles of leadership, entrepreneurship, romantic partnership, or career-building.

Let me pursue this further by focusing on the case of homosexuality (and gay men in particular). I am not in any way denying that presumptions on which it's normal for men to be sexually oriented toward women have validity as biological propositions; that is, given certain observations about biological functioning. I'm simply claiming that, when there's a conflict of curve for the purposes of determining a medical condition, the ones that are less encumbered by biological notions of normality are preferable. The point, after all, is to determine what *social* normality is, and that's what a curve distributing sexual orientation over *society as a whole* tells us. In fact, the societywide curve captures both social and biological notions of normality. It reflects the fact that it's normal to be sexually oriented to men whether you're a woman or a man. The separate curve distributing sexual orientation exclusively over men reflects only the biological notion, on which it's normal to be sexually oriented only to women. Given that social and biological conceptions of normality differ in this case, it's inapt to determine social normality in ways that are shaped at the get-go by a biological notion of normality, that is, on curves distributing sexual orientation over men and women separately.

Yet although we are concerned with social normality, not biological normality, it is not *society's* views of what's socially normal, normal for the widest range of life plans in society, that counts. As I argued in the Introduction, that approach is too one-size-fits-all. If a societywide range of life plans includes pursuing careers in the military or the clergy, or marrying, then in America homosexuality would be abnormal even today. Instead of society's views of the matter, what should count is whether the group itself, gay men themselves, can legitimately view their condition as socially normal. I am arguing, in effect, for a kind of inversion here. Instead of society as a whole determining normality by looking at curves distributing sexual orientation over each gender group separately, the group in question – gay men – should determine their normality by looking at a curve distributing sexual orientation over society as a whole. Doing so, gay men can perfectly legitimately deem their sexual orientation to be socially normal.

To make some prior assumption about a person's natural biological functioning, in this case his sexual functioning, and on that basis to construct the curve on which a medical condition is to be determined, is to get ourselves into a position where some phenotypes might be normal for one person but not another based on his genotype. We would, however, never say that phenotypic cystic fibrosis is normal, or deny that it's a medical condition, for those with the cystic fibrosis gene. Nor, then, should we say that phenotypic sexual orientation toward men is abnormal, or claim that it's a medical condition, for those with an X and a Y chromosome.[29]

Put it another way. It is, in fact, possible to construct a societywide curve on which homosexuality is *abnormal.* On this particular societywide curve, though, the poles wouldn't be simply "sexual orientation to men" and "sexual orientation to women," which would give us a bimodal distribution. Instead, one pole would be "sexual orientation toward men if you're a woman" plus "sexual orientation toward women if you're a man" (straights), and the other would be "sexual orientation toward men if you're a man" plus "sexual orientation toward women if you're a woman" (gays). Such a curve would be a societywide one, but it would be skewed in the direction of straights, making homosexuality abnormal.

In fact, though, this curve is simply what one would get by combining the two curves segregated by gender. One of those curves, recall, distributes men over the spectrum from sexual orientation toward women to sexual orientation toward men. And the other distributes women over the spectrum from sexual orientation toward men to sexual orientation toward women. The very ideas of "straight" and "gay," then, bundle two phenotypes, sexual orientation and gender, on the basis of a biologically rooted notion of which sexual orientation normally goes with which gender. They are less "purely phenotypical," less reliant on exclusively observable traits, than are the two phenotypes unbundled: sexual orientation and gender. And, of course, both of those curves would be distributed bimodally across society as a whole, meaning that anyone anywhere on either curve could regard him/herself as normal.[30]

As I argued in the Introduction, in determining whether a condition is a medical one, our focus should remain as close as possible to the level of the phenotypical as defined by Fukuyama: the condition's "physical appearance and features," its "mental [state] and behavior," and any other traits that would be observable to those harboring it. Hence, when there's a conflict of curve, the proper ones to consult would be those that come closest to the purely phenotypic rather than to the biologically – cellularly or genotypically – bundled, inflected, or configured. In this case, we should go with the bimodal curves distributing the phenotypes of gender and sexual orientation separately, on one of which it is socially normal to be a man and on the other of which it is socially normal to be sexually oriented to men.

One might reply that, simply as a phenotypic proposition – without dragging notions of biological functioning into it – when you look at the world around you, you notice that most men are sexually oriented to women. But that doesn't make straight a phenotype any more than the fact that most people have knees and noses makes "knee-nosedness" a phenotype. Or, more to the point, it makes straight a less purely phenotypic concept than gender and sexual orientation taken separately.

All of which implies that it's perfectly legitimate to view homosexuality as normal, as not a medical condition. In the same way, it's perfectly legitimate to regard pregnancy as abnormal, as a medical condition, since the better curve is the one distributing "pregnancy at any one time" across the entire population, not "pregnancy during lifetime" across women alone. That, of course, doesn't settle the question as to whether abortion is morally justified any more than noting that kidney failure is a medical condition settles the question of whether kidneys should be bought and sold. But it does shield against one arrow in the pro-life quiver.[31]

We might approach the phenotypic consequences of aging in the same way, as a conflict of curve. On the one hand, let us stipulate that there is a bell curve distributing, say, muscle strength over society as a whole, from low to high. Those on the lower half could view their muscle strength as either normal or abnormal. Those on the higher half, by contrast, could not view their condition as abnormal, assuming that the social ideal of muscle strength is to be found at the pole on the high end. Now think of a seventy-year-old woman. Her muscle strength would almost certainly be located on the lower half of the bell curve, say at the 10th percentile, and she could, legitimately, view her condition as socially abnormal.[32]

She could ask to be brought to a social norm of muscle strength that she identifies as, say, a range within 5 percentiles of the modal median mean point in society as a whole. That range, presumably, would be populated largely by thirty-five to forty-five-year-olds.

But, on the other hand, we might construct separate curves – and they too would be bell curves – of muscle strength for each age group. The normal ranges for seventy-year-olds would then differ from those for forty-year-olds. Say that on the bell curve confined to the seventy-year-old bracket, our seventy-year-old woman fell in the higher half. If this were the curve that mattered, she could not view her muscle strength as abnormal and demand a cure, even though her condition would fall on the lower half of the muscle-stength curve distributed over society as a whole.

The problem with curves broken down by age group is that they come closer to importing biological notions, notions of cellular aging, into the description of phenotype than does a curve distributing muscle strength over society as a whole. They presume that there should be, or that there is, some difference in the muscle strength of seventy-year-olds and forty-year-olds. Such a presumption may, of course, carry great weight as a biological proposition. But for the purposes of determining what is and isn't a medical condition, when there's a conflict of curve, the one least tied to genetic, cellular, or broadly biological notions becomes preferable. A separate curve of muscle strength for seventy-year-olds assumes that phenotypically weak muscles should be considered normal, and hence not a medical condition, for those whose cells are of a certain age. But that would be like arguing that phenotypic cystic fibrosis is normal, and hence not a medical condition, for those with the cystic fibrosis gene. To bundle phenotypes such as weak muscles together with wrinked skin and brittle bones into a single phenotype called "aging," such that each is normal when found with the others, is to create a phenotype on the basis of biological notions of normal functioning. It is to create a phenotype based on the species-level utility of older generations dying off to make way for the new. Declining muscles, however, are far from socially functional.

True, society itself, at the moment, might determine social normality by distributing muscle strength across curves divided by age group. We might, as a society, have decided that the notion of a "societywide range of life plans," which medicine can be made responsible for enabling, should decrease in scope as age mounts. Life plans for forty-year-olds might include week-long hikes in the mountains, whereas those for seventy-year-olds would not. We could, as Norman Daniels says, "make the normal opportunity range relative to age."[33] But, I am arguing, instead of society as a whole determining normality by looking at the bell curves distributing muscle strength over each age group separately, the group in question – seventy-year-olds, say – should determine normality by looking at the bell curve distributing muscle strength over society as a whole. On such a view, a seventy-year-old can legitimately deem her declining muscles socially abnormal, and hence a medical condition (although, since bell curves themselves suggest no cutoffs of normality or abnormality, she can just as legitimately view her declining muscles as socially normal).

"A man of 60 should be considered normal only if he has the same blood-pressure and blood-cholesterol as a healthy man of 25," as Marc Steinbach has written; "[t]he fact that in his population group [a] 'healthy' [man] of 60 [might] have an increased blood pressure may reassure him but should not mislead the physician.... There should be only one set of normals – namely, the values characteristic of young adults between 20 and 30 years."[34] To group people by the age of their cells – to use their cellular age as a basis for determining what's normal for a particular group – is invidious. It would prohibit scientists from curing prostate cancer in men over seventy-five on the grounds that for men of a certain cellular age or condition, that cancer is normal.[35] It may be normal for those with aging cells to find that they get phenotypically expressed in weak muscles, but weak muscles are not normal for society as a whole. In the same way, while it may be normal for a cystic fibrosis gene to get expressed phenotypically in cystic fibrosis, cystic fibrosis is not normal for society as a whole. And while it's abnormal for someone with an X and a Y chromosome to phenotypically express in sexual orientation toward men, sexual orientation toward men is normal for society as a whole.

The approach that I am advancing thus allows dwindling muscles, decrepit bones, and wrinkled skin to be medical conditions, no matter what a person's age. So, then, would it not follow that death itself can be viewed as a medical condition? This question isn't answered simply by saying (as I am) that it's legitimate for the aged, as for everyone else, to demand cures for fatal conditions such as cancer, kidney failure, or vascular disease on the grounds that these conditions are all socially abnormal. "Even if individual cures were developed for all diseases," the science writer Andrew Pollack says, "neither life expectancy nor maximum life span would rise much, though more people would come closer to achieving the maximum. To have people live to 130 or 150 would require slowing aging."[36]

But I am, as noted, also taking the position that it's legitimate for us to cure the phenotypic manifestations of aging – declining muscles, brittle bones – since such conditions, too, can legitimately be regarded as socially abnormal. Conceptually, though, it's possible to believe in curing the phenotypic manifestations of aging while still denying that death itself is a medical condition for which we should seek a cure. Testament to this possibility can be found in the idea, perhaps vain on technological grounds but not incoherent on conceptual grounds, of "squaring the curve": of figuring out ways of enabling us to live a completely healthy life to an old age – with full muscle strength and smooth skin – and then die without any period of decline.[37] So the question is this: If all the phenotypic conditions that kill people can legitimately be deemed medical ones, and if all the phenotypical manifestations of age can too, then (separate question) what about death itself?[38]

We might say that death is not a medical condition since everyone eventually dies. It's neither abnormal to die nor, for that matter, has anyone ever reached a social ideal of not dying. But the approach I'm advancing couldn't exclude death from being a medical condition on those grounds. After all, everyone also eventually gets colds, or mildly depressed, or coronary atherosclerosis, and yet we consider them medical conditions.[39] And everyone eventually gets weak muscles, wrinkles, and frail bones, yet I am saying that it's legitimate for those harboring them to deem these conditions medical ones.

Weak muscles, wrinkles, and frail bones can be deemed medical conditions because what matters is not how many of us across society (i.e., all of us) have the genotypic, cellular, or biological capacity to manifest them over time. What matters is how many of us across society (a minority, hence their abnormality) are manifesting them phenotypically at any one time. My concern lies not with processes but with states. Yet if our focus rests more properly on states than on processes, it would then seem that death, too, would have to be considered a medical condition. While everyone in society will eventually die in time, such that the process of dying is normal, no one in society is in the state of being dead at any one time. Death, it would seem, is utterly abnormal after all. So isn't death therefore a medical condition?

Again, though, we have a conflict of curve. It's true that, looking across society as a whole, it's utterly abnormal to be dead; and, we might add, everyone has reached the ideal of being nondead. That makes it seem, on the approach that I am advancing, that death is the medical condition *nonpareil*. And yet, this is the wrong curve. Since it's utterly abnormal to be dead, and since all of us have attained the ideal of being alive, if death is a medical condition, then it's one that nobody could ever get. The quality of not being dead is what defines the population to begin with, and so it couldn't be an attribute distributed across that population in the same way that height or nose size or wrinkles or muscle strength could be. Or put it another way. If we expanded the relevant population to include the dead, then not only would being alive become abnormal, but so would almost any condition we deem healthy.[40]

I believe the preferable curve is one that distributes not death but life span over the population. While anyone, no matter how old, can legitimately argue that it's normal, across society as a whole, to have the muscle strength of a forty-year-old, no one can claim that it's socially normal to be 140. It simply makes more sense to say that no one alive is in the state of being 140 (and hence that such a lifespan would be abnormal) than to say that no one alive is in the state of being dead (and hence that death is abnormal). And so, above and beyond any attempt to deal with socially abnormal conditions such as cancer or declining muscles, which might indirectly extend the life span in limited ways, medical efforts directly devoted to extending the life span would not be called for on the approach I am advancing. They would constitute enhancement.

Let me pose one other query about medical condition and social abnormality before we move on to the matter of social ideal. On the approach that I am arguing, can minority religious beliefs – beliefs that fall on the tail of a skewed curve – ever be a medical condition? Can someone regard her atheism, say, as abnormal, hence a medical condition, and so demand a medical cure to bring her to the norm (of, let us say, Christian belief)?

No. Consider an analogy with Prozac or, more to the point, with a super-Prozac that unerringly cured mild depression. The point of such a drug, as I suggested in the Introduction by citing the observations of Peter D. Kramer, Jonathan Glover, and others, is not to make people happy, or even euphoric, all the time no matter what happens to them. The idea, rather, is to liberate people from reacting dourly, darkly, or anxiously no matter what happens to them, freeing their minds to react appropriately to whatever events, good or bad, life throws at them. Getting rid of mild depression doesn't mean replacing it with perpetual happiness – that's not the alternative – but rather with a diversity of moods, sunny or dark, that take their coloration from whatever life presents to us. As Peter D. Kramer says, "[w]e do not expect the medication to work directly on the cognitive component" of depression – whatever unhappiness comes from life's realities should not be expunged with a drug – "just as we do not imagine there is a pill for, say, atheism or chauvinism; that sort of imagining would violate the rule that the drug we have in mind is a good deal like Prozac."[41]

Kramer paves the way for a direct comparison between a pill for mild depression and one for atheism, or chauvinism, or any other belief system. For any such drug to fall within the legitimate province of medicine, it would have to free the individual not from atheism per se, any more than a cure for mild depression would free a person from unhappiness. Instead, it would attack neurotic hyperrationalism, say, or the weight of a rote skepticism developed years ago and never challenged, or any other mental blocks or emotional inhibitions that may have precluded the individual from responding spiritually or religiously to experiences for which such reactions would be appropriate. The drug would free her to revise or criticize her atheistic views on an ongoing basis as she encounters new experience.

Such a cure, consequently, would not replace her atheism with a belief in God any more than super-Prozac would replace mild depression with happiness. It would not, as Kramer says, work on the cognitive content of a person's religious beliefs. Instead, it would allow the cured individual to react in a spectrum of ways that now varied as widely as did her experiences. It would give her the possibility of responding with a spiritual warmth to the kinds of experiences that appropriately elicit such warmth while not in any way precluding the possibility of her reacting with the feeling of an empty universe to events that appropriately elicit that kind of reaction. Out of such experiences, she could develop and continually review and reconstitute her views of God's existence.

To say that a reaction is appropriate to an experience is by no means to say that it is the only one appropriate to that experience. The matter of appropriateness – of whether any given experience is one for which a numinous religious feeling is an apt reaction or, on the contrary, one for which an existential chill is more suitable – is a matter for which there is no one answer. Now able to stand back from and open-mindedly scrutinize her beliefs, a cured person could very well react with existential melancholy to the same sunset that elicits a religious affirmation in the next person. Or she might respond with an affirmation of God's existence in the light of a sad event that drains such a belief from others.

Belief in God may well be distributed over society on a curve skewed away from nonbelief, but the ability to be spiritually moved, the tendency toward skepticism, the aptitude for rationalism, the capacity for soulfulness, and like characteristics are all (I would stipulate) distributed on bell curves. Hence any individual can deem his particular positions on any of these curves as normal – or not. In other words, he can deem any particular reaction along any of these dimensions to any particular life event as appropriate – or not.

The correct curve, then – at least insofar as determining a medical condition is concerned – would thus not be the one distributing atheism over society. True, that curve may well be skewed toward believers. But if it's not the correct curve, then abnormality, let alone medical abnormality, is not an appropriate designation for atheism. Instead, the correct curves would be the bell curves distributing skepticism, rationalism, soulfulness, openness, reflectiveness, and the like over society as a whole. Any individual falling anywhere on any of these curves could see her condition as normal and not seek a cure; such an individual would not be deemed to have a medical condition. Just the same, however, any individual could see some or all of her particular dispositions, no matter where they fell on such curves, as abnormal, and seek a cure to bring herself within whatever range she deemed normal. Whatever changes to her belief in God then occurred, they would happen only as a result of such cures.

None of this is to say that cures for various degress of rationalism, skepticism, and the like would survive either the individual authenticity or the cultural genocide concerns set out in Parts 2 and 3. My point simply is that such cures would not constitute enhancement on the criteria of interest here in Part 1. Anyone could legitimately view his own position on the relevant bell curves as falling outside the normal range of rationalistic or skeptical or soulful or open-minded tendencies and regard medicine as a means of bringing himself within that range. And, of course, he could legitimately see things otherwise. If there is an argument against medicine providing such cures, it would have to be that they violated a criterion of individual genuineness by implanting an artificial trait (Part 2) or that, as more and more took them, they would begin to inflict an intolerable cultural loss (Part 3).

Always assuming that there are no technological or financial limits to medicine, I have "road-tested" my suggested approach to "social normality" on conditions as various as homosexuality, pregnancy, aging, death, and atheism. I hope to have shown that it generates conclusions that are intuitively acceptable. But to return to the main path: Social normality, I am arguing, should get determined by looking at whether phenotypes distribute themselves on a bell or else a skewed curve across society as a whole. On a bell curve, where median, mean, and mode congregate at one single point and the curve itself remains silent on the question, members of the group harboring the pertinent condition can legitimately disagree as to whether it is normal or abnormal (unless the group falls on the side of the bell curve closer to a polar ideal, about which more momentarily, in which case they cannot deem their condition abnormal). If the curve is a skewed one, a group on the tail cannot claim that its condition is normal. Groups whose conditions fall on the hump, however, can still legitimately disagree as to whether their phenotype is normal or abnormal, depending on whether they carve the range of normality around the median, mean, or mode.

Ideals

But there is also the question of whether others have yet attained the social ideal. If only a few have, then the situation resembles the very beginning stage of a Canguilhem-style dynamic: a stage like the one where, in the nineteenth century, few had yet attained the social ideal of decay-free teeth. Or where, more recently, few had attained the social ideal of perfectly white teeth. A cure that brought individuals to such an as-yet virtually unpopulated social ideal would be enhancement. But suppose that the social ideal has been reached by more than a few, as in the mid-stages of a Canguilhem-style dynamic. Then it would be legitimate, even for those who view their condition as normal, to demand a cure that would bring them to that ideal, an ideal that some number of others – even if not enough to have yet made that ideal into the "new normal" – would have attained.

At one point, then, a social ideal can be sufficiently populated that those outside of it can legitimately ask medicine, on simple grounds of fairness at a time of limitless resources, to take them there. But at what point? Here, I am going to follow the logic of something I noted previously in discussing social normality. When it comes to determining social normality on a bell curve, the curve itself is of no help in suggesting a place for drawing the cutoff. Accordingly, I argued earlier, anyone outside the mean/median/modal point may view her condition as abnormal, although, of course, she just as equally need not. The question now has to do with social ideal. And along similar lines, I would say that anyone whose condition falls outside of a populated social ideal, even if that ideal is conceived as a single point populated by only one person, can legitimately ask medicine to bring her to it. To say that 5 percent or 2 percent or 1 percent of the population must have achieved that social ideal before others can claim medical means to get to it themselves is, I believe, as arbitrary as saying that a person must deem herself to fall on the lowest 5 percent or 2 percent or 1 percent of a bell curve before claiming medical means to get to normality.

To begin to apply this understanding of an already-reached social ideal, consider that any such ideal can take one of two forms. It can either be a golden mean located somewhere between the two poles on the spectrum encompassing society's range of relevant characteristics or it can be located at one of those poles itself. Consider the spectrum of mental states that range from depression to mania. For the purposes of determining social *normality*, group members would consult the bell curve distributing society as a whole over such a spectrum.[42] For the purposes of determining the social *ideal*, group members would look to a golden-mean range somewhere between the two poles of depression and mania, since neither pole is considered socially ideal. This is not to deny that there can be disagreement within the group as to where between the poles a golden mean might be located. Certainly, any group member need not locate it where any other group member does. Nor need he place it at the midpoint or the average; he might well deem it to be closer to the mania than to the depression pole. That's why it's a *golden* mean, not just a mean.

But as long as it is a golden mean, there can be no legitimate disagreement as to whether (wherever any group member locates it) others have attained it. Ideals that take the form of a golden mean are always populated, since they necessarily overlap the curve distributing characteristics over society as a whole, whether it is bell-shaped or skewed, at a populated range. Even those who believe that their condition falls within socially normal bounds can, legitimately, seek a cure to bring them to a golden-mean socially ideal range, since an ideal so conceived is always populated.

Now consider the other kind of social ideal, the sort that takes the form not of a golden mean but of a pole. Think of IQ, and assume for the moment what is of course controversial, namely, IQ's legitimacy (in the way in which Richard Herrnstein and Charles Murray argue it) as a measure of human intelligence. The bounds of social *normality* would be located on the bell curve distributing IQ across society. The range for the social *ideal* would be found not at a golden mean but at the pole on the upper side. An ideal that takes polar form, however, admits of disagreement as to whether anyone has attained it. The highest known IQ is 298. Anyone who draws the polar cutoff to include that point – even those who believe that their IQ falls within normal bounds on the bell curve – could legitimately ask medicine to bring them to it.[43]

But because a polar-type ideal range does not in and of itself suggest a cutoff as to where it begins, some might draw it so as not to embrace even the very high end of the current population but rather to lie still further beyond. Some people – those who talk of a therapy that will bring human IQs to 400 – are aiming for a polar ideal range that no one has yet attained, one entirely off the chart of the current curve distributing IQ across society.[44] And, on the approach that I am advancing, they have no call on medical science to provide a cure that will take them there.

The question, again, would not be whether society itself has fixed either a polar or a golden-mean social ideal at particular set ranges. There is no singular social view of the social ideal, only views taken by members of the group harboring the condition concerned. The question would be at what ranges group members can legitimately locate such an ideal. One mildly depressed person might identify the golden-mean ideal mental state as closer to the depressive pole, another as closer to the nondepressive pole. But since any golden-mean ideal is already populated, each can seek a cure to take her to the social ideal as she identifies it. One person with an IQ of 110 might identify the polar ideal cutoff at 135 (for her the polar ideal range embraces the top 5 percent of the population) and seek a cure that takes her there; another might seek to go all the way to the highest populated polar point of 298. But those who draw the cutoff for a polar social ideal so as to exclude anyone in the current population – an IQ of 400, say – cannot ask medicine to bring them there. Any such cure would be enhancement.

One important loose end: In their recent book *The Pursuit of Perfection*, Sheila M. Rothman and David J. Rothman dismiss the philosophical enterprise of trying to make a cure/enhancement cut. Because of "the difficulties of drawing a hard line between cure and enhancement," they say, "[o]nce you accept the moral legitimacy of an effort to cure, it becomes very difficult to build an argument for the moral illegitimacy of the effort to enhance."[45] History, they say, "is filled with examples of cures turning into enhancements. Hormone replacement therapy began as a cure for the acute symptoms of hot flashes and anxiety that sometimes accompanied the passage to menopause; later it became an intervention to keep skin supple and improve memory in postmenopausal women. Plastic surgery was developed to rehabilitate soldiers injured and maimed in World War I; the same techniques were later applied to the lined face and the small breast. Advances in the treatment of Alzheimer's disease may someday produce memory enhancement for the normal population."[46]

Whereas I am speaking about enhancement turning into cure over time, as what was once an unrealizable ideal becomes realized and then normal, the Rothmans seem to be speaking of the reverse dynamic: cures turning into enhancements.

What accounts for this difference? What I think accounts for it is that, despite dismissing the cure/enhancement differentiation as incoherent, the Rothmans in fact assume a particular, and unargued, distinction between the two. On it, hormone therapy for hot flashes, or plastic surgery for disfigured soldiers, or treatment for Alzheimer's disease constitutes cure, while hormone therapy to create supple skin, or plastic surgery for wrinkles, or Alzheimer's drugs to improve normal memory are enhancement. If that's indeed how the cure/enhancement line should be drawn, then there is a sense in which cures do become enhancements over time.

But the Rothmans make no argument for that line and indeed go on to dismiss the very possibility of such a distinction. On the arguments I've been making here, what the Rothmans deem enhancement – such as treatment to make skin supple in post-menopausal women, or Botox for sixty-five-year-olds, or drugs to improve normal memory – can in fact be deemed cures, not enhancements. And if cures are understood more broadly in the way for which I've argued, then society has indeed shown itself more than able to withstand the conversion of cures into enhancements. We've been very good about dismissing, outlawing, ridiculing, and refusing to fund – as lying beyond the limits of medicine – IQ enhancement that would take us to 400. The same with wings for human beings, or steroids that would bring athletes into realms of achievement that no person has yet attained, or drugs that make people euphoric in a way they couldn't possibly be without the drug. Enforcement is another matter, but line drawing is not a problem when the cure/enhancement cut is made in the way I am arguing it should be made. Enhancement, here, is whatever takes us to an unpopulated social ideal.[47]

Each of the eight conditions that I will shortly examine lies along one or the other of the two kinds of curve, bell or skewed, for determining normal ranges and lends itself to one or the other of the two locales – golden mean or polar extreme – for determining ideal ranges. Depending on this underlying configuration, I will argue, disagreement can be more or less legitimate, within any given group, over whether its condition falls within the bounds of social normality and over whether others have actually attained the social ideal – in other words, whether their condition is a medical one. I will test my approach to legitimacy against actual arguments made by those harboring each of the eight conditions – arguments as to where each falls with respect to social norm and social ideal – and show that what people harboring a condition tend to believe largely accords with what I would argue is legitimate. In seven of the eight cases, I will suggest, group members can legitimately regard their condition as a medical one; society, therefore, must pursue a cure. One of the conditions, however, is not a medical one, and the request for a cure would be illegitimate.

I am obviously granting a rather large scope to declare a condition a medical one. My approach would entitle members of any group who can legitimately view their condition as socially abnormal to demand a cure that would make them normal. It also would allow group members who legitimately believe that nongroup members have reached a populated social ideal – regardless of whether those group members believe that their condition is normal or abnormal – to demand a cure that would take them to that ideal. And so one might ask: Because I am imagining unlimited resources, such that we don't have to weigh whether cancer is more serious than physical slowness, and because I am imagining that a cure for any condition *can* be developed, wouldn't the reach of medicine, on the approach I am advancing, expand limitlessly?

No. For in one critical sense, the approach I am recommending does place a cap on what medicine can be expected to do at any one time. Those who might differ from the approach that I am advancing, and who would prefer to use a "firm" biological definition of normality, understandably fear the possibility that without the biological anchor, the notion of cure will become untethered from any standard. Once we renounce the biological-norm approach, even given its flaws as described in the Introduction, then – so the worry goes – there would be no principled way of denying requests for treatment that would make people eight feet tall or give them an IQ of 400. There would be no way of saying "no" to a Joseph Rosen when he proposes to engineer a person to have wings. The retort by Lester S. King – that "[o]ne person might desire to be eight feet tall," or have wings for that matter, "yet the majority of people do not"[48] – is scarcely reassuring. After all, the majority of people could change their view.

I deal with this fear by requiring that the social ideal in question be a populated one before those harboring a condition can legitimately seek to be brought to it. Being eight feet tall or having an IQ of 400 may well be an ideal. Perhaps the majority of us, even now, would desire those states. But since no one has yet reached those points – since they don't fall within a *populated* ideal range – medicine cannot be asked to find a cure that would bring them about. Any such procedure, in other words, would be mere enhancement.

There is a notable tendency for writers and critics to acknowledge, in passing, the difference between a populated and a nonpopulated ideal but then to ignore what I believe to be its significance. Sheila and David Rothman, for example, say that "enhancement looks beyond the normal, aiming to put the individual at the far end of the curve, or better yet, off the curve,"[49] as if the two projects – at the far end of the curve and off the curve – necessarily lie equally outside the realm of medicine. Cass R. Sunstein makes much the same elision, only for him, the two projects lie equally within the realm of medicine. "Suppose that medical technologies could make ninety five percent of Americans as healthy, physically and psychologically, as the most healthy Americans now are," Sunstein writes; "[t]hat would seem to be an extraordinary advance that would greatly reduce human suffering.... Would it be wrong to use technologies that would make all of us as healthy as, say, the top one percent? . . . But now suppose that biotechnology could move people well beyond the top one percent – that it could make people healthier than anyone is today ... what would be wrong with it, if we were not causing harm to anyone or discriminating against anyone?"[50] On the approach that I am advancing, however, there is a distinction between a legitimate cure that enables people to reach an already populated social ideal, and mere enhancement that takes them beyond.

There's an important implication here: A cure cannot, itself, be what has enabled people to populate an ideal. It cannot be, since it's people having already reached the ideal that justifies a cure in the first place. For example, "[c]hanges in diet ... can in a few generations change the ideals in regard to stature."[51] Suppose that, over a long period of time, and due to alterations in diet, many people became nine or ten feet tall, and a range around eight feet came to be seen as the populated golden-mean social ideal. Those who didn't fall within that range could then ask for a cure to take them to it. But, on the scheme that I am proposing, no one could develop a cure that would make people much taller, dispense it widely, and then point to a newly populated ideal of eight feet as a justification for the cure. When people claim that their condition falls short of an ideal that others have attained, and hence ask for a cure, those others have to have attained it without the cure, via some other means of human development. And this places a firm cap on what falls under the responsibility of medicine at any one time. As it so happens, in the cases that follow, wherever a group can legitimately claim the social ideal to have been attained by others – whether it's perfect sight or an ideal nose or Freudian ordinary (un)happiness – significant numbers have attained it without having been medically cured.

There might be a final, buried issue here about the boundaries of medicine, so let me bring it to the surface. The World Health Organization (WHO) once advanced a very broad – and controversial – definition of health as "a state of complete physical, mental and social well-being." Such a notion might well embrace (at least it seems not to exclude) many a polar ideal state that no one has yet realized, such as an IQ of 400.[52] The role of medicine being to bring about health (technology and resources permitting), it then follows that those who accept the WHO definition of health tend to embrace a very wide notion of cure. Such a notion would embrace all manner of social policy from nutrition to pure food laws, child care to education, occupational health to environmental policy. More exactly, anyone who accepts the WHO definition would deem all these enterprises to come within the ambit of medicine, defined broadly to include anything that might fall under the contemporary rubric of public health.

But we have to be careful. For if that's what medicine is, then we could not devote the resources to nutrition, education, or environmental policies necessary to increase IQ over time to (say) 400 until that ideal had become populated by *yet other means*, means that we could classify as beyond even this wide swath of medicine, as beyond cure. The notion that an ideal must have been attained by nonmedical means before medicine can act pushes, on the approach that I am arguing here, against the WHO definition, thus naturally limiting medicine's proper domain.

Such pushing comports with a claim I made in the Introduction. In an ideal world in which medicine's technological limits vanish – medicine is able, let us say, to develop a pill that eradicates phenotypic obesity – medicine's institutional limits will grow more significant. Prior to the cure's development, medicine (via public health) would have endeavored to fight the phenotype by, among other things, combating broader social forces that contribute to obesity: poverty, lifestyle, conflicting demands placed on women, and the like. But if and when medicine is able to strike the phenotype surgically without having to erode it indirectly and incompletely by battling broader social forces, it can then leave those fights, worthy as they are, to other social institutions: government, nonprofits, churches, grass-roots politics, social criticism, media, and the arts.

Yet there would be a reverse dynamic at play helping to ensure that the realm of medicine doesn't inordinately constrict. If we excluded too much from the domain of medicine, then medicine would not be able to act whenever new ideals became populated by nonmedical means. Suppose that, in a world in which medicine faces no technological limits, a scientist tries to game the system by describing as nonmedical a lab-synthesized chemical that would bring IQ to an as-yet unreached ideal of 400. Since, according to him, the chemical is a nonmedical product (say he identifies it as a nutritional supplement, not a drug), it can, the scientist might say, immediately be used to take people to 400. After all, on the criteria that I am suggesting, it is only medical cures that have to wait until people have attained an ideal by nonmedical means, and this *is* a nonmedical means.

Society, however – through its regulatory apparatus – would have little reason to go along with this, to allow the chemical to be the means whereby people first came to populate a social ideal of 400 IQs. For if the chemical is defined as nonmedical, as falling within the domain of a social institution other than medicine, then it would carry an unwelcome implication. Because medicine would be obliged, in an era without limits, to give anyone a socially ideal phenotype that others have achieved, medical science would then have to come up with something else that would create an IQ of 400.

More particularly, medicine would have to come up with something else that operated even more directly on the phenotype than this nutraceutical, since medicine is that which operates more surgically on a phenotype than other social institutions: those charged with environmental protection or workplace safety or nutrition, the category into which the scientist is trying to place his invention. If the chemical is to be placed on the nonmedical side of the line, and the medical is that which operates even more directly on the phenotype than the nonmedical, there would be no room for medicine at all here. And so there would be a strong incentive, for society, to coalesce around the idea of defining as medical any lab-synthesized means of creating an IQ of 400, including the scientist's chemical. But then – even if we had the resources and the technical knowledge – we'd have to wait to develop or distribute it until a significant number of people attain an IQ of 400 without it. If, indeed, they ever do.[53]

As long as we have incentives not to define medicine too widely – else we'd have no nonmedically attained ideals of the sort that we need in order to justify cure – or too narrowly – else we'll have no medical means available to meet any nonmedically attained ideal – we needn't worry about the borders of medicine on the approach that I am arguing. There most certainly are some. This is not medicine *sans frontieres*.[54]

In sum: I am here advancing an approach that, first and foremost, aims to avoid the difficulties inherent in the biological notion of normality. Instead, the approach I am advocating looks to social normality but then modifies the social-norm notion in two ways. First, it tries to elude the major problem surrounding the usage of *social* in the social-norm approach: namely, that a medical condition is what hampers a societywide range of life plans, which is too one-size-fits-all. Instead, the approach I am advancing argues, we should look at whether members of different groups can legitimately view their condition as socially normal or abnormal. And, second, the approach that I am suggesting tries to escape the problems entailed in focusing exclusively on *norm* in the social-norm approach, which is that it seems to freeze normality at what's normal now. Instead, the approach I am outlining takes into account not just social normality but social ideals.[55] I have suggested principles for using the concepts of social norm and social ideal to classify conditions as medical ones, which I will now apply to the eight of central interest.

The Eight Conditions

Begin with the condition of being plain-featured. I use the term "plain" as distinct from "ugly" or "disfigured," since the latter connote a need less for cosmetic than for reconstructive surgery.[56] When it comes to the social norm of noses, say, or skin, what is critical is that these facial features get distributed – along a spectrum from small to large noses or loose to taut skin – throughout society on bell curves. Here, there can be legitimate disagreement as to how widely or narrowly to draw the cutoff of norm, how big one's nose or how loose one's jowls have to be for them to qualify as abnormal, since the curves themselves are silent on the matter.

And, in fact, whether in their own memoirs or in the writings of those who study them, those with plain facial features bear witness to the legit-imacy of such disagreement. Some avow that their large noses or wattled chins fall outside the bounds of social normality – and so seek a surgeon's intervention. Each of the women that Kathy Davis discusses in one part of her study of cosmetic surgery "drew the conclusion that her prob-lem was different than the normal difficulties women have with their appearance – more serious, or more limiting, or simply of a different order altogether. . . . It wasn't about beauty, but about wanting to become

ordinary, normal, or just like everybody else."[57] "[M]any women," Medard
Hilhorst affirms, "ask for surgical corrections not by referring to an idea
of perfectness or beauty, but to their idea of 'normality.' "[58] A typical
postsurgery comment: "Now I look like a normal person."[59]

But there are also other cosmetic-surgery seekers who, just as insis-
tently – and legitimately – believe that their large noses and wattled skin
fall within the social norm. They recognize, Nils Holtug writes, that they
are pursuing surgery "to improve normal features,"[60] to "transcend . . .
the normal," as Sander L. Gilman says.[61] Instead of feeling like an "out-
cast from more ordinary looking people," Kathy Davis reports of one
cosmetic-surgery seeker, "Diana discovered," by looking around her cosmetic surgeon's waiting room, that her condition was "normal."[62]

Why is someone who accepts that her condition is normal not bolt-
ing, but rather continuing to sit patiently in a cosmetic surgeon's waiting
room? She must believe that although she has reached a social norm, others have reached an ideal; that she is in a situation resembling the mid-
cycle snapshot of a Canguilhem-style dynamic. Indeed, when it comes to
the question not of whether one's nose, skin, or lips fall within the bounds
of social normality, but whether others have attained ideal noses, skin,
or lips, there are fewer grounds for dispute. That's because socially ideal
noses or skin assume the form not of a pole but of a golden mean, a range
somewhere between the smallest and the largest noses (in proportion to
a given face) or between the loosest and the tautest skin. Such a range
will necessarily be populated.

And, in fact, whether in memoirs or in studies, candidates for cosmetic
surgery seem universally to express a belief that there are at least some
others in society who have achieved the ideal skin, nose, lips, or eyelids.
All have in mind for themselves a realizable – because realized – social
ideal. Surgeons, Richard Simpson writes, "now refer to each body part by
the name of the celebrity who is seen to have the ideal one." A poll "names
the ideal nose as Nicole Kidman's," Simpson continues; "its perfection
comes from its averageness. . . ."[63]

Note that this achievable golden mean for any given facial feature
doesn't have to be an exact midrange on the spectrum of small to large
noses, say, or of taut to loose skin. Skin that is about 75 percent taut might
be considered the social ideal; looser and you look flabby; tighter and you
look skeletal.[64] Socially ideal skin might in fact assume a golden mean
on more than one spectrum, not only the one between loose and taut
but also the one between dry and oily. Nor need this socially *ideal* skin –
this golden mean between loosest and tautest – fall within what any given

person regards as the social *norm* of skin. Nor must it center around the mean/median/modal position on the bell curve distributing actual skin types in society over the range from taut to loose.

In fact, there need be no agreement on where the ideal range is located, only that it lies somewhere between the polar extremes of loosest and tautest and is therefore populated. Some psychologists, for example, believe that the golden-mean social ideals for various facial features actually do range themselves around the mean/median/modal points on the bell curves distributing those features across the population; that people perceive the most beautiful facial features to be those that are in fact the most average.[65] Other psychologists claim that people identify the golden-mean social ideal to be a slight distortion or "exaggeration" of average features.[66] But there is no disagreement with the notion that ideal facial features occupy some sort of golden-mean range on the spectrum of existing facial features – and therefore that many have attained them.

There is, of course, a difference between any particular socially ideal feature – whether skin, nose, or eyelids – which is best understood as occupying a golden mean on the spectrum from loose to taut, say, or large to small, and socially ideal features when aggregated into an overall notion of facial beauty, which would form a pole on the spectrum from ugly to beautiful. A polar ideal admits of disagreement as to whether anyone has attained it: as to whether it begins at a point past where the spectrum of actual beautiful faces ends or whether it will include some of them. Accordingly, while Wendy Chapkis believes that certain icons have attained an ideal beauty – "the beautiful woman," Chapkis writes, "remains a symbol of the ideal against which [all women] will be judged"[67] – others, such as Naomi Wolf, declare that "ideal beauty is ideal because it doesn't exist."[68] This disagreement is legitimate because ideal beauty occupies a pole on the distribution from ugly to beautiful, while ideal noses occupy golden means on their respective distributions of small to large or snub to pointy.[69]

In his fascinating discussion of apotemnophilia, the desire to have a limb amputated, Carl Elliott makes a series of rhetorical statements meant to show that, once we allow various other kinds of cosmetic surgery, we will have no grounds to deny that amputating an apotemnophiliac's limb is a legitimate medical procedure. Elliott's examples come from nonfacial cosmetic surgery, but that difference doesn't matter here. He argues as follows: If "[y]ou can pay a surgeon to suck fat from your thighs, lengthen your penis, augment your breasts, redesign your labia, even (if you are a performance artist) implant silicone horns in your forehead or split your tongue like a lizard's," then "[w]hy not amputate a limb?"[70]

The approach that I am advancing suggests the following answer: When it comes to thighs, penises, breasts, and labia, whose sizes each array themselves on bell curves, it's entirely legitimate for people to disagree on the bounds of normality. Many can, and many will, legitimately view the conditions – the sizes – of their thighs, penises, or breasts as abnormal.[71] But the desire for horns and split tongues would have to be assessed on a skewed curve, on which the vast bulk of us do not have those phenotypes. In fact, it would be *having* horns or a split tongue that would fall on the tail of the relevant skewed social distributions and would, therefore, be abnormal. Not having horns or a split tongue is socially normal, not abnormal, and hence cannot be regarded as a medical condition.

Elliott later states that "[i]n the same way that a person might want to have healthy tissue removed through breast-reduction surgery, so an amputee wannabe wants to have healthy tissue removed through amputation." But socially ideal breast size assumes a golden mean in the population distribution, with reference to which some women can legitimately feel too large. The socially ideal number of limbs, by contrast, assumes a pole in the population distribution, and those with two limbs – including "amputee wannabes," as Elliott calls them – have already attained it.

Mild depressives, like the plain featured, face a bell curve for determining normality – or, really, many bell curves – along with ideals that assume the form of golden means. The neurotic mental states that I am classifying under mild depression distribute themselves across society (as do facial features) according to bell curves, from sadness to euphoria, or from anxiety to tranquility, or from solemnity to extreme gregariousness and the like.[72] "The number of people with different neuroticism scores," F. Kraupl Taylor writes, "is normally distributed."[73] Bell curves offer no suggestions, in and of themselves, as to where the cutoff of the norm should be drawn. Hence, there is legitimate room for the wide disagreement that characterizes the mild-depressive "community" – those who lie on the sad or anxious or solemn sides of these curves – on the question of whether their conditions, their neuroses, are normal or not.

On the one hand, many mild depressives – notionally looking at the bell curves distributing various moods over the population and seeing people who seem better able to cope – legitimately believe that their condition doesn't make the cutoff of social normality. When it comes to mild depressives, Peter D. Kramer writes, the point of "Prozac [is to] give

[them] access to pleasures identical to those enjoyed by . . . normal people in their ordinary social pursuits."[74] It's a staple for those writing about their experiences with Prozac to make declarations such as "I felt – and the stab of recognition was wonderful after so long – completely normal."[75]

But, on the other hand, the bell curve allows mild depressives, just as legitimately, to view their condition as already normal. "[T]ransient episodes of anxiety, sadness, or elation," Peter Whybrow writes, "are part of normal experience."[76] Many "psychological traits are assumed to fall into a 'normal' distribution, with most of the cases in the middle and a few at the extremes," Abraham Maslow and Bela Mittelmann wrote decades ago; "[t]hese extremes, which constitute only a small percentage of the population, are arbitrarily lopped off and labeled 'abnormal' [while] the far larger clustering around the middle" – including those who are merely mildly depressed – "is arbitrarily called 'normal.' "[77]

Of his patient Tess, Peter D. Kramer writes that "she was never euphoric or Pollyannaish"; in "mood and level of energy, she was 'normal.' " But, following a course of Prozac, "her place on the normal spectrum changed . . . from 'serious,' as she put it, to 'vivacious'."[78] Tess, Kramer is saying, could legitimately regard her initial condition, her neurosis – her solemnity – as normal. But then if Prozac would simply be moving her, as Kramer acknowledges, from one point within what could legitimately be described as the normal range to another, how could such a cure be justified?

It would be justified only if that second normal point (say, vivaciousness) fell, unlike the first (solemnity), within what Tess could legitimately deem to be a populated social *ideal*: a golden-mean range somewhere between extreme solemnity and extreme vivaciousness. Unlike for those using narcotics or hallucinogens, the ideals for mild depressives taking Prozac do not assume polar form, such as extreme vivaciousness or euphoria or placidness. Rather, the aimed-for ideals occupy ranges around golden means: Freud's ordinary (un)happiness, reactions to events that are neither inappropriately sad nor inappropriately euphoric, inappropriately anxious nor inappropriately tranquil, inappropriately solemn nor inappropriately vivacious. Thus Peter Kramer describes the "social ideal" – one that he believes Prozac furnishes – as occupying a position (and, of course, not necessarily the midpoint) between the dysphoric and the euphoric, between depression and mania.[79] A golden-mean social ideal, such as this, is one that mild depressives can legitimately perceive at least some others, and perhaps many others, to have reached.[80]

Both the plain-featured and the mildly depressed, then, face bell curves for ascertaining the pertinent social norms, and they face golden means for locating the related social ideals. That implies, on my argument, that members of each group can legitimately perceive their condition as lying outside the bounds of social normality and/or that others have attained the social ideal. And, in fact, this seems to be how many actually do perceive things. It is thus legitimate for members of each group to regard their condition as a medical one and to ask for a cure – although, of course, it would be equally legitimate for them to regard their conditions as normal and not seek a cure.

Now, what of obesity and anorexia? Start by looking at them together, since they both concern weight. The bounds of socially normal weight, to begin with, would have to be plotted on a skewed curve. That's because an increasing number of Americans are overweight to the point where their numbers are beginning to dominate comparable ones for underweight and especially for anorexia. According to the U.S. surgeon general, the proportion of overweight and obese people in the United States was 65 percent as of 2001. Although a distinction gets drawn medically between "overweight" and "obesity" – overweight is a Body Mass Index (BMI) of 25 to 29.9; obesity is a BMI of 30 and over – we can set aside that differentiation for our purposes. Anyone who can legitimately deem his weight to be abnormally heavy – as falling outside a legitimate conception of the bounds of social normality – would, whether he is technically overweight or technically obese, be entitled to view his condition as a medical one.[81] As British obese (now overweight) activist Shelley Bovey says, "I'm still a fat woman [although] I may have lost weight.... I don't think it matters whether you are 19 1/2 or 12 1/2 stone [her current weight]."[82] So I will use the terms "overweight," "obese," and "fat" interchangeably; in other words, I will use those terms in much the same way as do those overweight, obese, and fat people participating in public debate.

As for the socially ideal weight range, it would have to be a golden mean somewhere between overweight and underweight. It doesn't matter that people may disagree as to where precisely that ideal is located. Some might use as a criterion the ideal BMI range (19 to 24.9) drawn from government guidelines. Others might leaven that standard with a notion of contemporary sexual attractiveness.[83] Either way, it's closer to the thin than to the heavy end of the spectrum. As Deborah Sullivan notes, the "ideal body," occupying as it does a golden mean between underweight and overweight, is now "much thinner than the population [norm]," which skews heavy.[84] But as long as it's located somewhere between the poles of emaciation and corpulence, the socially ideal weight range will legitimately be held to be populated. Given that there can be disagreement over where a golden-mean ideal range lies anyway, it may be seen by some to embrace "slim" and by others "*zaftig*" at the same time.

So this is the structural background for anorexia and obesity: a skewed curve distributing weight across society for the purposes of determining social normality and a golden-mean social ideal. This background determines the legitimacy, and also (it would seem) the actuality, of views in both the obesity and anorexic communities as to whether their weights are included in the social norm and whether others have achieved a weight that's socially ideal. Consider obesity first. Among the obese, there is ripe division as to whether their condition falls within the socially normal bounds of weight. Some fat people believe that those bounds exclude the overweight. Although "we have an overweight majority," Susan Bordo writes, they "acknowledge that they are not 'normal.' "[85] But others – many of them associated with the fat-acceptance movement – insist that it is a "myth ... that fat people are abnormal."[86] Of the actress Sara Rue, Alessandra Stanley reports that she "resent[s] being described as plus-sized or full figured; 'I consider myself normal' she said."[87] Because "fat is what most of us are becoming" – because the curve is skewing heavy – there is now, Richard Klein says in *EAT FAT*, a "wide range of healthy [i.e., normal] body sizes," including the obese.[88]

Such disagreement over the normality of obesity is perfectly legitimate: With its separation of median, mean, and mode, a skewed curve itself offers at least three distinct alternatives for centering a conception of the normal weight range. Those fat people who view obesity as socially abnormal might, explicitly or implicitly but certainly legitimately, be thinking of a range around the social mean: a BMI close to (say) 26 or 27. By contrast, those viewing obesity as normal might, but in any case legitimately could, be thinking of an area around the social mode: a BMI closer to (say) 28 or 29.[89] Nils Holtug sums up the legitimacy of disagreement over obesity's normality: "[T]he concept of normal is vague. Is excessive fatness normal? How fat would one have to be, exactly, for it not to be normal?"[90]

When it comes to the question of whether or not any others have attained a socially ideal weight, the obese community is equally riven. But how so? After all, when an ideal range takes the form of a golden mean, as it does with body weight, it should be uncontroversially populated.[91] And indeed, many in the obesity community – generally, those who also happen to believe that their body sizes lie outside the social norm – do believe that others have attained a socially ideal golden-mean body size. Typical comments: The "ideals ... that have been presented to most of us in this society are thin and attractive women. They are the ones to emulate."[92] "Falling short of the cultural ideal ... the ideal of the thin, contoured body ... generates shame."[93] In believing that others have attained an ideal state even as they view themselves as abnormal, this segment of the obese community sustains a worldview on which cure would be no mere enhancement. Rather, it would be a deeply wished-for – and justified – medical treatment.

But it must be acknowledged that there exists another view of "ideal" in the obesity community. Those who hold it generally comprise the same subgroup who, when it comes to the matter of social norm, believe that obesity in America today is socially normal. And they don't deny that others have attained the *social* ideal. It's just that for them, the social ideal is irrelevant because they posit a competing group ideal, on which the fatter the better. It is a group ideal because, as those who advance it themselves insist, only the obese qualify for it. There's no illusion that it is (or expectation that it will become) an ideal for society as a whole. This group ideal of weight, obviously, is not a golden-mean one – as is the social ideal of weight – but a polar one, encompassing a range at the far heavy end of the weight spectrum; it "celebrate[s] large women [and men] in particular."[94] Those fat people who favor it – who believe not only that their weights are socially normal, but that those weights meet the only ideal that matters to them, the fatter the better group ideal – are about as far away from wanting a cure as possible. For them, obesity is at least a lifestyle, if not a culture.[95]

I am not going to pass judgment on whether or not, on the approach I'm advancing, it's legitimate for a group's members to posit their own group ideal to counter other group members' legitimate sense of the social ideal. There is, however, no reason for medicine, underwritten as it is by social resources, to help group members reach a group ideal. In any event, the question here is simply whether a significant number of fat people could legitimately view their condition as a medical one and ask for a cure. And the answer to that – an affirmative one – depends on the fact that fat people can legitimately (as indeed many do) view their condition as falling outside the social norm and/or believe that others have achieved the social ideal. The possibility that other fat people can legitimately view their condition as falling within the bounds of social normality, and care more about a group than a social ideal, doesn't undercut this claim.

I do, though, want to tie up one loose end having to do with the obese group ideal of the fatter the better. It is a group ideal, not a social one, because those who fall outside the obese community are not expected to aspire to it. Some of the other groups we are discussing also harbor group ideals. In the case of the deaf, for example, there exists a group ideal according to which if you're deaf, the deafer the better. Many deaf activists, in particular those who favor learning ASL to better communicate within the deaf community, hold this view. What makes it a group ideal is that those who hear are not expected to aspire to it.[96]

Yet unlike with the obese, this deaf group ideal gets challenged not just by a social but by another, competing group ideal: If you're deaf, the less deaf the better. This view rejects sign language (manualism) in favor of learning lip reading or speech (oralism), the better to communicate with the nondeaf community. While this latter group ideal is derived from a perceived social ideal – hearing is ideal – it nevertheless remains a group, not a social, ideal. One can achieve the group ideal of being an oralist deaf person and still remain a long way from the social ideal of hearing. So within the deaf community, one group ideal – the deafer the better – gets challenged by another group ideal – the less deaf the better. For the deaf, there is thus no singular group ideal to counterpose to the social ideal.

This is not so with obesity (or, as we shall see, with anorexia). While there is an obese group ideal of the fatter the better – just as there is a deaf group ideal of the deafer the better – there is no competing obese group ideal of the less fat the better, while there is a deaf group ideal of the less deaf the better. Why so? Because in the case of the deaf, the *social* ideal – perfect hearing – is a polar one, located at the very opposite end of the social distribution from deafness. This is why it's possible to have a distinct deaf group ideal of the less deaf the better, distinct because it comes nowhere near the social ideal of being an actual hearing person. But the social ideal of weight is a golden mean. If an obese person follows the creed of the less fat the better and loses weight, then she'll bump up against that golden-mean social ideal – slim-but-not-emaciated body size – much, much sooner than an oralist deaf person who follows the creed of the less deaf the better will run into the far-away polar ideal of perfect hearing. There is no room for a group ideal of a "thin fat" person, as there is for an "oralist deaf" person.[97]

For my purposes, this means that there is a single group ideal of weight for the obese – the fatter the better – available to challenge the social ideal of weight for the population as a whole. This is not so for the deaf, where there are two competing group ideals – the more deaf the better, the less deaf the better – that together create considerable ambiguity as to what is ideal for the group. In 2001–2, Shelley Bovey, a noted writer on obesity, lost 100 pounds and, while still overweight, was no longer nearly as overweight as she had been. By her own telling, she found herself criticized by "an encroaching neo-fascism that said you must be proud to be fat." There was no countervailing subgroup within the fat community that hailed her attainment of a competing fat group ideal. If anyone congratulated Bovey, it was for moving toward a social ideal.[98]

What of anorexics? The fact that the social distribution of weight is so skewed toward heaviness suggests that anorexic weights are uncontroversially abnormal; it also suggests that members of the anorexic community would be justified in so viewing them. More emphatically, it would be illegitimate for anorexics to view their weight as normal. And yet, as is well known, a large proportion of anorexics actually do just that. Many an anorexic, as Hilde Bruch says, will mount a "vigorous defense of his emaciated body as not too thin but as just right, as normal."[99] Such views, as most anorexics who hold them ultimately or even simultaneously realize, amount to a "perceptual distortion."[100] In fact, however, since anorexics must locate the social norm on a curve that skews heavy, those who view their weight as falling within the socially normal range can even see themselves as overweight. Many women with anorexia, as Rita Freedman writes, nurture "the belief that one is too heavy even when one's weight is within normal range."[101]

Though their belief that their weight falls within the range of social normality is distorted, these anorexics – I'll discuss a second subgroup momentarily – tend accurately to see the social ideal of weight as a golden mean. Perhaps they place it on the slim side of the spectrum, but certainly not at the pole of extreme thinness, emaciation. Indeed, they are constantly feeding their families and friends to ensure that those others don't become too thin.[102] These anorexics do not aspire to emaciation; it's just that they don't see themselves as emaciated. Thus, they fail to seek a cure. Instead, because they mistakenly deem their weight to be socially normal, and since social normality falls on the heavy side of the social ideal, they feel they have to starve to reach that ideal.

Such perceptual distortions, however, should not obscure the fact that a second subgroup of anorexics in fact do clear-sightedly view their condition as abnormal. And legitimately so: They are fully cognizant that they lie on the tail of a social distribution curve of weight that skews toward the heavy, with all of the curve's markers for possible ranges of normality – mean, median, and mode – on the distant other side. Anorexics who view their weight as abnormal tend to participate in on-line pro-anorexia chat groups, where their self-description as falling outside the norm is everpresent. "I know I exceed normal limits," says one posting.[103] "[I am]

not . . . normal," says another.[104] " '[N]ormal' people . . . think that seeing ribs poke through your skin is disgusting. . . . " or "[we are not] normal persons" say still others.[105] Cynthia Billhartz of the *St. Louis Post-
Dispatch* excerpts this statement from one site: "If you . . . just want to
look a bit better in a bikini, go away. . . . Better yet, eat moderate portions of healthy food and go for a walk. However . . . if your relationships
with food and your body are already beyond 'normal' parameters . . . then
come inside."[106] The scare quotes testify that while the norm in question
is the perceived social norm, that's not all that matters. There's still the
question of ideal.

Though this subgroup views its condition as socially abnormal, its members generally don't seek a cure. That's because, unlike the first subgroup,
they turn away from the socially ideal weight – a golden mean – toward
a polar group "ideal [of] extreme thinness,"[107] an "emaciated ideal."[108]
It is a group ideal, not a social one, because only anorexics need (so to
speak) apply. It is, as one "pro-ana" website puts it, for the "chosen, the
pure, the flawless."[109] So polar is this ideal range that those anorexics
who focus on it disagree as to whether anyone has actually attained it.
Even "Kate Moss is fat," according to one posting;[110] another allows that
"I want [Christina Aguilera's] body" but then adds, "well, maybe weigh
5 pounds less than her."[111] And so they egg each other on to go further
and further in the direction of this polar group ideal, to "think things
like 'I can lose more than her' or 'I can be thinner than her.' "[112] "[N]ot
only is 'ideal' shape . . . unattainable for all but a tiny, freakish few," Mary
Ann Sighart writes of this polar anorexic group ideal, "but perfection is
unattainable for all."[113] Consider the tension in this statement: the ideal
is attainable for a tiny few but also unattainable even for them.

This is the ambiguity of the polar-style ideal; even one and the same
person can view it as attained, yet unattained. So although they understand that their weight places them well outside the social norm, this
second subgroup of anorexics does not seek a cure. Instead, they turn
away from the governing social ideal – the golden mean between corpulence and emaciation that countless others have attained – and embrace
their own attained yet unattained polar group ideal. Instead of trying to
gain weight, they starve.

In her memoir of anorexia and bulimia, Marya Hornbacher identifies herself as a member of this subgroup. In saying that she had to
overcome "the part of [her] that wanted to be normal," Hornbacher
acknowledges that her anorexia located her well beyond the social norm
of weight. In addition, Hornbacher recounts, she resolutely pursued an
attainable-yet-unattainable polar group ideal, patting herself on the back

and "humming all day long, remembering that once upon a time my ideal weight had been 84, and now I'd beaten even that."[114] It is to such anorexics that Roberta Pollack Seid's wistful comment is best directed: "There is a golden mean. We need to find it again."[115]

It is only when this second subgroup of anorexics – those who know full well that their weight falls outside the social norm – jettison their polar group ideal in exchange for the golden-mean social ideal that they seek a cure. And it is only when the first subgroup – many of whom help friends and family to reach the socially ideal golden mean – recognize that their own weights are actually socially abnormal that they seek a cure. When both of these types of anorexics do seek a cure, they do so with eminent legitimacy. Occupying as they do the tail of the skewed curve on which the social norm of weight must be determined, and facing a golden-mean socially ideal weight range, anorexics can legitimately see their weight as socially abnormal while believing many others to have reached the social ideal. On those grounds, they have a medical condition. They can legitimately seek a cure, whether it be one that brings them to the social norm or to the social ideal, and society must offer it.

I earlier defined a slow runner as someone for whom there are always other runners capable of beating him, assuming that he and they all engage in the same rigors of training, exercise, and diet. In effect, this means that even very good runners, such as those who come in twentieth or twenty-fifth in the Boston Marathon, can be slow runners. But that does not mean that they can claim a cure on the grounds that they are socially abnormal, only on the grounds that they may fall below a populated social ideal.[116]

Running speed distributes itself across society on a bell curve.[117] Those who fall on the low-speed half can legitimately regard their running speed as socially abnormal and seek a cure, although they can just as legitimately view their speed as socially normal, since bell curves fail to suggest cutoffs as to where the social norm begins and ends. As various articles in *Runner's World* are always reassuring the reader, it "is normal" if, "[w]hen you run, you get out of breath"; "feeling fatigue for the first mile ... is normal," and so are numerous other failures that the slow, nongifted runner's flesh is heir to.[118]

Those who fall on the high-speed half of the bell curve – those who come twentieth or twenty-fifth in the Boston Marathon – cannot, by contrast, regard their running speed as socially abnormal, since they fall on the side of the bell curve closest to the polar ideal. But they can still call themselves slow runners, and many in effect do, precisely because the social ideal of running capacity takes a polar form at the high end of the spectrum. Hence, even runners on the faster side of the bell curve – as long as their view of the ideal assumes a polar range that human beings have already attained – could legitimately ask to be brought to that state. When the runner Keith Brantly says, of the top tranche of runners in the 1994 Boston Marathon, that "[t]hese are guys who can run a world record,"[119] he is imagining a populated social ideal, one that he and other runners could legitimately seek medical assistance to reach.

Someone else, though, contemplating a different version of the polar ideal of human speed – after all, polar ideals themselves suggest no cutoff as to where they begin or end – might have in mind a range that nobody has yet attained. This kind of runner aspires to be "better than the best," to "do something that's never been done."[120] The "ideal from which the image of the athlete derives its seductive power," Mary Tiles writes, "is one [that] can transcend [current] physiological limitations. . . ."[121] No one, for example, has reached the ideal of running a marathon in two hours, one minute, and forty- seven seconds, which the sports researcher Elmer Sterken argues is theoretically humanly possible.[122] There can, however, be no call for a cure to help marathoners reach such an ideal. It is a range toward which runners will move only when one, and then another, transcends current physical limitations by dint of training, effort, nutrition, and exercise. For the moment, it remains for all runners to attain on their own without aid a of cure, and hence it cannot justify a cure. And in the light of such an unattained ideal, all runners – no matter how fast or slow – are equal in at least one respect: None has yet reached the degree of perfection it represents.

Slow runners, then, fall into two classes. But in both, they can legitimately regard their condition as a medical one. If, falling on the low-speed half of the bell curve, they see themselves as abnormal, they could seek a cure that would bring them at least to what they see as the norm; if in addition they had in mind a populated version of the polar ideal, they could legitimately ask to be brought there. Slow runners who fall on the high-speed side of the bell curve couldn't view their condition as abnormal, but they could legitimately ask for a cure to bring them to a populated version of the polar ideal. Such a cure would not be mere enhancement.

True, the bell curve and the polar ideal allow as well for the opposite conclusion. Slow runners on either side of the bell curve can legitimately view their running speeds as normal; in addition, they could deem the only polar ideal range worth caring about to be one that no human being has yet attained. Instead of taking a cure, those runners can avail themselves of whatever social accommodations the group can justifiably claim: "environmental" accommodations that might give slower runners their own leagues or "attitudinal" accommodations that would require a ribbon for everyone who enters a race, thus recognizing that all runners are equal in that none are ideal, all are imperfect.[123] But such claims are not at issue here, since they have no bearing on the legitimacy with which other slow runners can seek a cure.

The idea that it is legitimate for members of the group "slow runners" to view their condition as a medical one – that it is legitimate for them to view cure *as* cure and not enhancement – will raise an eyebrow in some quarters. But bear in mind the following: First, if we intuitively resist the idea that slow running is a legitimate medical condition, we may have good reasons for doing so, but those reasons might well have to do with considerations other than those that rely on the social norm/social ideal criteria. Another set of criteria having to do with individual wholeness and genuineness, which I will explore in Part 2, might actually come closer to capturing what it is that bothers us about the idea of a cure for slow running. In other words, it might be legitimate for medicine, on social norm/social ideal criteria, to bring slow runners to the level of a Carl Lewis but not, necessarily, on criteria of individual genuineness or wholeness.

Second, we might have some lingering sense that a world in which all runners run at the social ideal would be one in which races wouldn't be worth running, since everyone's phenotypic abilities would then be equal. But if and as runners are brought to the (already-attained-by-others) social ideal of phenotypic running ability, one or another athlete will then light out for a new ideal, via the ardors of training, diet, and exercise, thereby leading the pack and thus distinguishing himself.[124]

Nevertheless, there is a nettle to be grasped here for those who instinctively rebel against the idea that slow running ability is a medical condition. I am, recall, assuming that resources are unlimited. I am arguing that if members of any group can legitimately view their condition as falling outside the social norm, then they can ask for a cure to bring them to that norm. And, I am also arguing, if members of that same group can legitimately deem others to have achieved the social ideal, then – whether they see themselves as normal or not – they can ask for a cure to bring them to that ideal.

If it's legitimate for a twenty-year-old slow runner to claim that his condition is a medical one, then it should be legitimate for an eighty-year-old slow runner to do so. I can find no principle – except for that of triage, which I am assuming away via my stipulation of unlimited resources –

to place a cure for twenty-year-olds' slow running within the limits of medicine but not a cure for eighty-year-olds' slow running. As I argued earlier, it would be wrong to use biological – cell-based – notions of age to segregate society into groups according to which certain phenotypes (of physical speed) are permitted as normal for one biologically determined age (or gender) group but not another. Indeed, even now, and within any given class of ability, older runners routinely beat younger ones and women beat men, complicating any simple equation between age/gender and some notion of normal phenotypic speed.[125] Is it fair that athletes, having devoted their lives up to age thirty training as runners, must then give up that career because of the dictates of their declining physical capacities? Don't we wish that "Michael [Jordan] could play basketball until he were not forty but eighty?"[126]

Thus far, we have looked at slow runners, whose condition falls on a bell curve for determining the social norm of running speed and who face a polar-type social ideal of running speed. We have looked at the obese and anorexic communities, whose conditions fall on a curve skewed toward overweight for determining the social norm of body weight and who face a golden-mean social ideal of body weight. We have also looked at the plain-featured and the mildly neurotic, whose conditions, for the purposes of determining social normality, fall on bell curves describing the distribution of features from (for example) big to small, or neuroses from sad to euphoric, and who face golden means for locating the attendant social ideals. Now, finally, we turn to the last possibility: groups whose conditions fall on a skewed curve for the purposes of determining social normality and who face a polar form of the social ideal.

Consider blindness and deafness. When it comes to social normality, it matters that the abilities to see and hear are distributed across the population according to skewed curves. Blindness, which ranges from totally blind to legally blind, and deafness, which ranges from a loss of anywhere from 50 to 110 decibels, occupy the tails of curves skewed heavily toward the capacities to see and hear.[127] While blind and deaf people claim to be normal as individuals, or to lead normal lives, I have not found any who assert that they have normal sight or hearing. Their location on the tail of a skewed curve would, according to the criteria that I am advancing, preclude their doing so legitimately.

So, for example, in his history of blindness in America, Floyd Matson declares that the "blind can live normal, fully productive lives," adding that "I was raised as a normal person who cannot see."[128] For some blind activists – who, along Matson's lines, describe a blind individual as "basically a normal person who cannot see" or as able to engage in "the normal activities of living"[129] – the normality of blind individuals and their lives is already a fact. For others, it may depend on further social efforts to "normalize" the blind person; to make her a fully functioning member of society; to enable her to work, move around, tend to her domestic needs, raise a family, socialize: all normally. But even these writers, who eloquently argue that the blind can live normally, acknowledge that the blind do not see normally. Naomi Schor speaks bluntly of the blind as not "normally sighted";[130] Robert Amendola says that when it comes to sight, the blind are "below normal."[131]

Reasoning about normality flows along similar channels in the deaf community. Sharon Duchesneau and Candy McCullough, the deaf couple who in 2002 sparked international controversy by seeking a deaf sperm donor, "resent the implication that to be deaf is to be inferior to someone of normal hearing."[132] Such a statement is worded so as to avoid implying that the deaf *hear* normally. Sentiments of this sort, as Beryl Lieff Benderly says, deny "that a deaf child cannot act normally ... in some other way than auditorily." They also, however, affirm "that the very basis of cognition in a world without meaningful sound is – has to be – different" from that of the "normally hearing."[133] Many a deaf or blind writer claims that even now, with proper accommodation, he can be a normal person leading a normal life. None claims that he thereby will have socially normal sight or socially normal hearing. That's because blindness and deafness occupy the tails of skewed curves distributing sight and hearing over the population: curves skewed heavily toward those who can see and hear.

When it comes to the social ideal of sight and hearing, it matters that both ideal hearing and ideal sight take the form not of golden means but of polar ranges. Accordingly, there can be legitimate disagreement among the blind and the deaf as to whether anyone has actually ever attained truly ideal sight or hearing. Some, certainly, believe that ideal sight or hearing is simply that which the most keen-sighted or most keen-eared possess – 20/10 vision or hearing loss of zero decibels – and they can legitimately ask to be brought to that level. The blind memoirist Rod Michalko goes so far as to say, simply, that "the ideal actor is someone [who] can see."[134]

Others, though, may just as legitimately believe that no one really has attained ideal sight or hearing – that the polar ideal of sight or hearing actually lies beyond the spectrum of current human attainment – and they rest content in not pursuing what they view as an illusion. "[B]lindness in this context symbolizes the very real dangers that confront every individual," Michael E. Monbeck writes, "and that every individual should strive to admit and come to terms with in his own life. . . . These are, specifically, that we all have our 'blind spot,' are 'in the dark' about many things . . . that we have eyes, but cannot see . . . ."[135] This kind of claim helps animate those in the blind community who oppose, or at least are ambivalent about, a cure. After all, if each of us is blind to some extent – if we each fail at some level to deeply perceive whatever is before us – then even those who see best cannot claim to be anything but minuscule degrees closer, compared with the blind themselves, to the distant polar ideal of *truly* seeing. There should be nothing in the situation of the sighted for the blind to covet, for there's nothing ideal about it. The same can be said of deafness.

In sum, both blindness and deafness, occupying as they do the tails of skewed curves, are abnormal, and the blind and the deaf can certainly ask for a cure to bring them to social normality. Whether others have attained ideal sight or hearing – an ideal that occupies a polar position – is a matter of debate. But certainly, those blind or deaf people – indeed, those normally sighted or normally hearing people – who draw the polar cutoff to include 20/10 vision or hearing loss at zero decibels, perceptual states that many have attained, can ask to be brought there, too, by a cure.

Finally, consider whether American blacks could legitimately deem black racial features a medical condition and the Michael Jackson pill legitimate medicine. Could black Americans view phenotypic black racial features as falling outside the social norm and/or believe that others, in particular those with phenotypic white features, have attained the social ideal? At one level, they clearly could. The norm of phenotypic racial features would have to be located on a skewed curve, one on which "white racial features" occupies the hump in white-majority America, and "black racial features" falls on the tail.[136] And, indeed, many writers, black and white, describe black racial features as falling outside a social norm. "In this society," Theresa Glennon writes, "it is considered 'normal' to be white – and being anything other than white is therefore necessarily a departure from this norm."[137] "[W]hiteness" in America, Michael Eric Dyson says, has been "made to appear normal. . . ."[138] In his memoir *White Lies*, Maurice Berger quotes two eighth-grade African-American students who had been asked, in a 1994 survey of racial attitudes in the schools, what it would be like if they could suddenly become white. "I would be normal," both said.[139]

As for a social ideal of racial appearance in America, those black writers who believe that there is one – not, of course, that there should be one – definitely do not see it as a golden mean. If there is a phenotypic racial ideal in America, it is not to be found somewhere between black and white in the domain that has variously been called light brown, colored, gray, high yellow, coffee, or mulatto. Rather, it is a pole at one end, the white end of the spectrum on which racial features are distributed.[140]

Of course, to be a "light-skinned" black – coffee-colored, light brown, high yellow – may well be to have attained a group ideal. Some black women, as Vivian Owusu says, believe that "the lighter" a black woman "you are, the better you are."[141] But this light-skinned group ideal gets challenged by a competing dark-skinned "black is beautiful" group ideal – by a "rejection of all but the most jet-black and the kinkiest-headed as beauty symbols"[142] – just as oralism (the less deaf the better) gets challenged by manualism (the deafer the better) as a group ideal. There is, then, no unequivocal black group ideal available to compete with the social ideal, which, for those black writers who perceive one in America today, occupies a pole at the white end of the spectrum.

Polar ideals, however, necessarily allow for disagreement over whether others have actually attained them or not. For some black writers, the cutoff for a white racial ideal actually locates itself well beyond the pole occupied by even the "whitest" of actual phenotypes, such that no one has attained it. "[P]erfect phenotypic whiteness doesn't exist," Kim Shayo Buchanan writes; "this Nordic ideal is a cultural self-image that doesn't even reflect the way white North Americans really look."[143] But for a different group of black writers, the "white end" of the spectrum is an expansive place populated by people whose melanin gives them "Type 1" white skin. "[I]n American and European society," as Alvin Poussaint said in an interview with *Ebony*, "[w]hiteness is held in the greatest esteem."[144] Black Americans, Carl Elliott writes, "run the danger of constantly seeking an ideal of beauty that they will never quite reach," the implication being that others have reached it.[145]

Indeed, there's something particularly invidious about whiteness as a populated social ideal: It completely overlaps, and equates with, whiteness as the social norm. The curve for determining norm skews white, and the pole for locating the ideal is on the white end of the spectrum; norm and ideal meld. Consider, as a piece of testimony, Maurice Berger's musings upon viewing a composite white male face. It "is at once *typical* and *perfect*," Berger writes; "[m]odeled from an averaging of the measurement of thousands of 'native white' men gathered from many parts of the United States, [it] is a life-size composite of *ideal* data translated into three dimensions. A model of '*normal*' perfection...."[146] Consider, as a further piece of testimony for the claim that whiteness is viewed as both social norm and social ideal, the frequent use of the word "normative" by black writers to describe whiteness. The term suggests – and, in context, can clearly be seen as meant to imply – a conflation of what I have been calling norm and ideal. So, for example, Ruth Frankenberg writes that America "normativizes whiteness,"[147] and Birgit Brander Rasmussen states that "whiteness . . . appear[s] normative."[148] "Normative," when used in this way, seems to capture what Mary Tiles has in mind when she speaks of a "[s]lippage . . . between that which is usual and that which [it is thought] ought to be."[149]

It would seem, then, that black racial features fall on the tail end of a skewed curve for determining the social norm, and those black writers who perceive a social ideal place it at the distant polar end. On the approach that I have been arguing, then, couldn't black Americans legitimately view black racial features as a medical condition? After all, blacks in America can legitimately – and many certainly do – perceive their racial features as falling outside the social norm. And many legitimately can, and certainly do, perceive that white Americans have attained a social ideal of racial features. But I, and I assume all readers, would deeply resist the conclusion that black racial features can legitimately be deemed a medical condition requiring cure. I think, though, that another look at the approach that I have advanced can explain why.

In crucial ways, the question of black racial features resembles that of gays in America. For the purposes of ascertaining social normality, gays have found themselves placed on the tail of a societywide curve skewed toward "straight." And they have found themselves facing a distant polar social ideal of sexual orientation that also enshrines straightness. The concept of straight rests on a particular bundling of the two phenotypes "sexual orientation" and "gender," a bundling dictated by biological conceptions of normality, on which it is normal to be a man and sexually oriented toward women or a woman and sexually oriented toward men. But if we decouple the two phenotypes of gender and sexual orientation, and then distribute each over society as a whole, we get two bimodal curves, on which it is normal to be a man and normal to be sexually oriented toward men. These are the curves that the approach I am arguing would commend.

Much the same is true of black racial features, although there are some differences. I earlier said that a person is "phenotypically" black if he looks black, regardless of whether he is "genotypically" black (whatever that may mean). But even the phenotypic notion of black racial features in fact depends on what is (certainly for purposes of determining a medical condition) an inapt genotypically based bundling of various phenotypes. To designate kinky hair and dark skin and broad noses as black is to rely on a genotypically configured notion of phenotype, one based on the (contested) concept of an African genotype. And it is to do so when there is a conflicting, and less genotypically complected, way of conceiving the matter: as the distribution of phenotypes such as skin color, hair contour, nose shape, or lip size across society as a whole, each on its own distinct bell curve free from being bundled by any notion of racial genotype. To assume that a genotypically conceived group called blacks has to exhibit a particular collection of phenotypes – "dark brown skin, wooly hair, a broad nose, full lips"[150] – which places them on the tail of a curve skewed to the opposite bundling, is to smuggle genotypic notions into the description of phenotype. Only in a genotypically configured notion of "condition" must phenotypic darker skin, broader noses, and tightly curled hair somehow go together, something that is manifestly not so in the real world of actual phenotypes.[151]

Even many of those scientists who believe in the utility of genotypic conceptions of race accept that "black" and "white" wouldn't feature in the list; that there are, rather, scores if not hundreds of races (or "populations") on the most apt understandings.[152] Yes, it might be that certain skin colors and hair textures go together on average more than do others, but that is no reason to bundle them together as single phenotypes. Scandinavians combine blue eyes and blonde hair to a greater degree than dark skin is found with broad noses, but we don't consider Scandinavians a race.[153] The Hokkaido Ainu share more characteristics than do Asians as a whole, yet they are not considered a race; Basques share more than Europeans, and so if Europeans are a race, then "Basques are . . . a race as well."[154] To talk about a black phenotype and a white phenotype – of black racial features or white racial features – is, then, to use genotypic concepts to structure phenotypic ones. And this is something that the approach that I am advocating renders illegitimate whenever there is a conflict of curve, whenever an alternative curve (or curves), less genotypically influenced, suggests that the same phenotype(s) should be distributed differently.

There are a couple of key differences between the situations of homosexuality and race. First, as a biological matter, sexual orientation and gender do go together. There's a story about biological functioning that weds them; the point simply is that biological notions take second place when there's a conflicting, less biologically rooted way of looking at the matter. But when it comes to race, even as a biological matter, the very notion is much more problematic. Any arguments for grouping certain phenotypic "racial" characteristics together because it's biologically functional to do so – sun-protecting dark skin combined with "[f]rizzy hair allow[ing] sweat to remain on the scalp longer, [resulting] in greater cooling" – are virtually irrelevant today and certainly in America.[155] "Heterosexual" thus makes sense as a biological concept in ways that "black" does not.[156]

Second, think of the skewed curve distributing adults in society from straight to gay. On that curve, the categories of heterosexual men and heterosexual women – that is, the two categories created by bundling gender and sexual orientation together according to biologically functional criteria to make the pole "straight" – are both deemed socially normal. Gay men and lesbians, those who combine gender and sexual orientation in ways that are not similarly biologically functional – who form the "gay" pole – are, on this skewed curve, abnormal. But on the skewed curve distributing adults in society from white to black, only one of the categories bundling skin color, nose size, and hair texture according to putatively biologically functional criteria gets deemed socially normal: whites, whose skin color and air-warming narrow nostrils are arguably functional for northern climates.[157] Not only does the other putatively biologically constructed group, blacks, fall outside of the social norm, but so do all those who combine physical characteristics of hair, skin color, and physiognomy in varieties other than those dictated by (spurious) racial genetic criteria.

Once we jettison a genotypically configured notion of racial features for more purely phenotypic understandings of skin color, nose shape, or hair curliness, we will necessarily be talking about curves of a different shape. Once we distribute phenotypic hair across society on a spectrum from curly to straight, or skin on a spectrum from light to dark, or lips on a spectrum from thin to thick, we will see a series of bell curves – on which any point can legitimately be viewed as socially normal – not one single curve skewed toward something called "white racial features." And the social ideal, assuming that such a notion persisted, would in all likelihood shift from a pole called white racial features to a series of golden means.[158] Such means might not necessarily lie right smack in the middle of these various curves, but they would certainly not be found at the straight-haired or thin-lipped or narrow-nosed or white-pallored

extreme polar ends of these various spectrums either. The cover of
a September 1993 special issue of *Time* depicted "The New Face of
America": a composite ideal female face whose features are supposed to
represent the golden means on several spectrums: nose, hair, skin color,
lip thickness, and the like. The face is golden-skinned and full-lipped and
on all counts looks very different, and not only because of its sex, from the
composite ideal American male – averaged not from disaggregated facial
features but from bundled racial features – contemplated by Maurice
Berger.

If we were ever to rid what should essentially be understood as more
purely phenotypic characteristics of their genotypic baggage, then the
norm and ideal for racial features would simply become norms and ideals
for a number of different facial features. We would have moved into the
realm of non-race-charged cosmetic surgery, where any number of bell
curves for particular facial features combine with any number of golden
means. In this domain, anyone can legitimately view his features – from
kinky hair to straight hair, from thick lips to thin lips – as normal, since bell
curves offer no cutoff point. But equally, anyone could legitimately view
the same features as abnormal; those who draw the cutoff of normality
to exclude lips of their particular thickness or noses of their particular
width or skin of their particular darkness might legitimately seek cosmetic
surgery. Their doing so, however, would differ in no way from the typical
cosmetic-surgery situation in which, even now, many people draw the
cutoff of normality to exclude lips of their particular thinness or skin
of their particular wrinkledness or hair of their particular straightness
and who legitimately seek surgery or other medical treatments for it.
A person's seeking a cure for her thick lips or dark skin or wooly hair,
in other words, would not be tantamount to her viewing her race as
abnormal or a medical condition. We would have consigned that curve
to the ash heap of history. She would simply be viewing one or another of
her facial features, each on its own, as abnormal, as a medical condition
without any reference to race. That, I think, is something we can accept.
But, of course, we've yet to consider the question – and won't until Part 3 –
as to whether cosmetic surgery that might wipe from the face of the earth
certain skin colors or noses or lips would amount to cultural genocide.[159]

With some of the other groups under discussion, the conditions in
question can also be redescribed so as to be placed on more than one
curve: The difference, though, is that doing so creates no conflict of curve.
For example, blindness – which itself is located on the tail of a curve of
seeing capacity skewed toward the sighted – can be broken down and

its characteristics distributed on a number of other skewed curves: The majority of us have attached retinas, but there is a tail of totally detached retinas; the majority of us have a functioning optic nerve, but there is a tail-end minority who do not. One can describe blindness due to glaucoma at the phenotypic level as a loss of vision, at the neurological level as damage to the optic nerve, at the tissue level as deformed connective tissue of the lamina cribrosa, or at the cellular level as damage to retinal ganglion cells. No matter how you categorize it, blindness falls on skewed curves and is abnormal on each of them.

But with black racial features (as with homosexuality), there is a conflict of curve: The racial one is skewed, but the ones broken down by feature are all bell-shaped. I have argued that the curves broken down by phenotypic features should supersede the one where features are bundled on genotypic grounds. How to effect such a transformation of curves is a question that I won't explore here, except to note that doing so takes the entire issue of black racial features out of the reach of medicine and makes it a matter of social justice – of changing social attitudes to the degree necessary to alter the curves. This isn't a question of accommodating black Americans as a cultural group, about which I say more in Part 3. It's a prior question: the question of defining black racial features as *not* abnormal or nonideal – hence not even potentially a medical condition.[160]

In this discussion, I have come some distance from Canguilhem's approach, let alone Norman Daniels's view that a medical condition is one that makes it impossible to pursue a wide variety of life plans in a given society, let alone Christopher Boorse's claim on which a medical condition is some deficit in our natural biological functioning. A condition is a medical one, I am arguing, if members of the group harboring it can legitimately view their phenotypic condition as falling outside the social norm (in which case they can ask that a cure take them to that norm) or deem others to have reached the social ideal (in which case they can ask that a cure take them to that ideal). Such a situation – and it's a situation that applies in one way or another to seven of the eight conditions – would justify our funding a cure, assuming limitless financial resources and scientific competence. But even assuming limitless financial resources and scientific competence, it would not be right for us to provide a Michael Jackson pill for black racial features.

We have a conflict of curve here. And whenever the curve distributed over the more genotypically constructed phenotype designates a condition as abnormal, while the less genotypically configured one does not, then medicine is not the first recourse. Freeing ourselves from the bundlings imposed by the genotypically constructed phenotype is. Social change is. I believe that this way of making the cure/enhancement cut accords with our moral intuitions. Whatever differences there may be between them, the seven other conditions diverge in a fundamental way from black racial features.

2

A Visit to the Kantian Doctor

What of the claim that we know a cure to be mere enhancement when, on the best understanding, it instills a trait that is ungenuine, artificial, and inauthentic to the individual? And what of the corollary: that anything that an individual achieves as a result of such a trait shouldn't redound to her credit, because the trait is not genuinely hers? The runner on steroids or the mild depressive on Prozac courts unease as to whether her performance or personality really is her own: whether steroids and Prozac are less cures that make her whole, make her who she is, than enhancements that make her into something else.[1]

Though this question is posed about individuals, it cannot – I argued in the Introduction – be answered by individuals. Every person will have a different idea as to what is necessary to make her whole. Apotemnophiliacs, who will feel whole only once an arm is amputated, and aspiring major-league pitchers, who will feel whole only once their arms can throw like Kerry Wood's, will offer widely differing and unsatisfactory answers. Better that we should transcend the individual plane and examine this question at the group level. The question will be, what can we say of a group in general – slow runners, mild depressives, the plain-featured, the deaf, the obese, and the others – as to whether cures will make the individuals who belong to it whole or, alternatively, take them beyond whole, thereby becoming enhancements? But before looking at each group, we have to determine what exactly the concern is here.

Genuineness, Artificiality, Struggle, and Ease

Let us begin with what the concern is not. It is not that a four-minute mile or a nonneurotic temperament per se would be an artificial state for any person who has never attained it. Wholeness is not stasis. The concern is with means, not ends. One can attain such a new state, a Staff Paper for the President's Bioethics Council says, either through "artificial enhancement" – which for the Council means steroids, Prozac, and the like – or else through "genuine improvement." That means diet, exercise, and training in the case of physical slowness, say, or therapy, introspection, and maturation in the case of mild depression.[2]

Why should new physical or mental states born of exercise or therapy be deemed genuine and those born of steroids and Prozac artificial – mere enhancement? Let us rule out some possibilities by focusing on running, where the debate is most developed; I will then broaden my focus to take in the other seven conditions. One might claim that there's something more "natural" about exercise and diet; they work with muscle tissue and the cardiovascular system. But, as many have noted, this couldn't be the issue. After all, testosterone that athletes may take, or blood doping – in particular, in the form of reintroducing the runner's own banked blood into his body prior to a race to increase his red blood-cell count – involve wholly natural substances. And yet many deem them to be enhancements. They are thought to take a runner to a new level of achievement, but by artificial, not genuine, means, such that the new speed is not really his accomplishment.[3]

Steroids, others say, are "separate and external" to the slow runner.[4] They come at the runner from outside of himself. And, so the argument goes, it is precisely their external nature that implies that they take the athlete beyond his "whole," that attests to their status as not genuinely a part of him. But air shoes and running blocks are external to the runner, and yet aren't regarded as enhancements; rather, they are deemed necessary to help the runner exercise his genuine capacities. Some, in fact, argue that on the contrary, it's aid that's internal to the athlete that artificially distends his whole, while assistance that remains exclusively external allows that whole to remain untouched.[5] Consumed as they are internally, steroids, on this argument, internally distort and shift the shape of the self, of an individual's whole. Air shoes, then, are all right after all, since they do not interfere in any way with the individual's inner workings. Yet, so the retort goes, athletes take vitamins, protein powders, and caffeine internally without our viewing them as engaged in enhancement.[6]

In his recent book *Enough: Staying Human in an Engineered Age,* Bill McKibben suggests another possibility. "Say you've reached Mile 23" of a marathon, McKibben writes, "and you're feeling strong. Is it because of your hard training and your character, or because the gene pack inside you is pumping out more red blood cells than your body knows what to do with? . . . Right now we think of our bodies (and our minds) as givens; we think of them as us, and we work to make of them what we can. But if they become equipment – if your heart and lungs (and eventually your character) are a product of engineering – then running becomes like driving [in which] the skill, the engagement, the meaning reside mostly in those who design the machines."[7] The runner on steroids who wins a race, on McKibben's argument, hasn't himself won the race, because it is other identifiable human beings – his doctor or (more typically) his trainer – who have supplied the ingredient that allows him to win. His victory is a victory for the doctor or the trainer or, perhaps, the scientists who developed steroids, but not for the runner himself. The problem with this argument, though, is that coaches, dietitians, and sport nutritionists already have much to do with the athlete's "training and character"; yet we have no difficulty believing that whatever the runner attains with their assistance, he attains genuinely.

The President's Council on Bioethics advances another possible under-standing of the "difference between improvements made through train-ing and improvements gained through bioengineering." In its 2003 report *Beyond Therapy,* the Council says that "when and if we use our mastery of biology and biotechnology to alter our native endow-ments, . . . we . . . make improvements to our performance less intelligi-ble, in the sense of being less connected to our own self-conscious activity and exertion. . . . [F]rom the athlete's perspective, he improves as if by 'magic.'" Steroids represent "interventions whose relation to the changes he undergoes are utterly opaque to his direct human experience," unlike the processes of training and exercise, in which the entailed sweating and straining very much does enter his consciousness. With steroids, the runner "risks a partial alienation from his own doings, as his identity increasingly takes shape at the 'molecular' rather than the experiential level."[8]

There are problems, however, with this attempt to distinguish train-ing from steroids. An athlete is no more conscious of the ways in which training, exercise, or diet alter her body – the molecular processes at work do not enter her consciousness – than she is of the way in which steroids accomplish the same end. Nor is it clear why the principle that the President's Council advances wouldn't apply to, and hence put in question, a cure for cancer. Curiously, *Beyond Therapy* then goes on to acknowledge all of this, taking away what it has just given: "This is not to suggest that changes in the body produced through training and effort are not also molecular. . . . Neither are we casting doubts on efforts to improve the body by means that work on it directly; to do so would require us to cast doubts on all of medicine and surgery."[9]

Still others try to draw a distinction between cure and enhancement so as to mimic, at the individual level, the notion of a social ideal. Whatever takes an athlete to her own personal "peak" or "best," on this argument, allows her to operate genuinely and claim credit for her feats; whatever moves her beyond that personal best – such as steroids – takes her into the realm of the artificial. But such an approach falls victim to its own version of Canguilhem's observation, namely, that the individual's own peak will always be changing. "Athletes already engage in a multitude of practices designed to take them beyond [their natural peaks]," Michael Lavin points out, such as "Nautilus training . . . interval training, special diets" – all of which, those who view steroids as illegitimate are likely to acknowledge, are quite legitimate. It is difficult, Lavin concludes, to use the notion of "personal peak" to "sustain a sharp distinction between" cure and enhancement.[10]

Lavin's observation underscores a crucial point. In equating cure with interventions that do no violence to a person's genuineness, and enhancement with the artificial, we cannot be talking about the difference between something that restores the individual to a prior whole and something that takes him beyond. Wholeness, again, is not stasis. Rather, we must look for a way of distinguishing between personal change that is genuine and personal change that is artificial, regardless of the baseline at which the individual happens to be located when the change begins.[11] We should not be looking to equate genuine change with that which returns a person to some enshrined personal status quo and artificial change with that which takes him beyond that one particular point. We are seeking a principle, in other words, that draws the genuine/artificial cut so as to place the runner who changes his abilities via Nautilus training and aerobic exercise, who ingests vitamins and protein powder, who has a trainer and a dietitian, and who uses air shoes and running blocks, on the "genuine" side of the ledger. And, at the same time, such a principle would at least raise a question about the artificiality of the runner's abilities when the runner changes them through testoterone supplements, blood doping, gene packs, bioengineering and steroids.

Although it sometimes gets short shrift,[12] there is in fact a principle that can make this cut where all the others – natural/unnatural, external/internal, internal/external, personal responsibility/other responsibility, experiential/molecular, and personal best/beyond personal best – fail. Drugs that cure physical slowness or mild depression constitute "artificial enhancement," on this argument, because they make the process of acquiring new traits of physical speed or mental clarity too "easy." By contrast, genuine "self-improvement" – changing one's physical abilities through diet and training or one's mental state through therapy and introspection – entails "striving and struggle."[13] As Dan Brock says in the context of mild depression, "altering a fundamental character trait or psychological feature by a 'quick fix' of popping a pill seems to some people too easy and less admirable than changing that same trait or feature through hard-earned insight therapy."[14]

The question, of course, is: What lies behind this equation of genuineness with struggle and the corollary identification of the artificial with ease? Before I suggest an underlying principle, note that if we apply this distinction between genuine-as-struggle and artificial-as-easy to the runner, it seems to work well. True, the lines it draws may not be utterly sharp. But at least it allows us to array the various interventions on a spectrum – the spectrum from struggle to ease – that conforms to our moral intuitions about genuineness and artificiality. The interventions that we tend to accept as involving genuine improvement entail struggle – for example, Nautilus workouts, strict and unpleasant diets, and aerobic training. Or else they make possible much more struggle than they ease, as with air shoes and running blocks. Or at the very least they won't cause the athlete to let up on any amount of struggle or exertion: An athlete taking vitamins is still likely to struggle, exert, train, and exercise at least every bit as much as he did when not taking vitamins. All of these interventions – from training to proper shoes to vitamins to the support offered by a running block – could legitimately be deemed properly therapeutic, legitimately resident in the realm of cure, if cure is understood as that which allows for genuine improvement in performance.[15]

Those who oppose blood doping or bioengineering or gene packs or steroids, by contrast, can make a plausible (if, as we shall see, not wholly incontrovertible) case that these interventions will substitute for at least some element of struggle. By comparison with air shoes and vitamins, gene packs or bioengineering afford much more substantially the same kinds of results as exercise, diet, and training without requiring comparable struggle, strain, or exertion. And, by comparison with vitamins and air shoes, gene packs or bioengineering give the runner greater reason to ease up in certain ways, since he would not have to train or exercise as much as before to attain the same measure of success. His accomplishments will, or at least can, come to him somewhat more easily; hence they bid fair to constitute artificial enhancement.

What is the idea behind this equation of genuine self-improvement with struggle and the flip-side equation of artificial enhancement with ease? Though it seems never to be made explicit, what nowadays would be called a broadly "Kantian" view of the self seems to be at work. A person's core or genuine self, on this basic Kantian understanding, exists apart from her various attributes or traits. There is an "I" that would still be there even if I changed my job, my name, my religion, my politics, my athletic capacities, my facial features, my race, my temperament. This I, this genuine self – otherwise known as the "subject" – constructs my life. It does so by working over the years to improve some of those characteristics and attributes that constitute the rest of me, to discard others, and to preserve still others. When and as this genuine self does so – say it transforms my physical slowness into speed through diet and exercise – it transfers its own genuineness to the new attribute. That new trait of speediness becomes incorporated into my whole, part of my genuine self, not something beyond it, because it was attained by my self's own acts: its discipline, perseverance, and effort. Such acts of improvement require the genuine self – the subject – to struggle, certainly more than it would had the person attained the same traits through chemical or surgical means. As Michael Walzer says, it is characteristic of the "self that [it] struggles to realize itself."[16] Struggle, then, is the genuine self's mark of authorship. To the extent that the individual is successful in her struggle, she herself can take credit for her new trait because her genuine self, her subject, was the author of it.

   This Kantian "genuine self," going about its business of remaking various parts of the individual, is commonly connected to the idea not just of struggle, but of autonomy. Many Kantian philosophers accept the proposition that the genuine self, the subject, can freely choose, and not simply struggle creditably, to remake many of a person's characteristics and traits. These two claims, however, are detachable. For example, there is no consensus as to whether obese people really can autonomously or freely choose to overcome their obesity. There is agreement, though, that if an obese person is to do so herself, the task will involve struggle – difficulty, pain, effort – and this, a Kantian doctrine would have it, will engage the subject, the genuine self, more than would a pill. In the same way that we credit a trait to someone who struggled for it, whether or not she can be shown to have chosen to do so, we hesitate to credit a trait to someone who came by it easily, whether or not he chose to do so. Barry Bonds claims not to have intentionally used steroids when he applied creams his trainer provided. But whether he deliberately chose to do so or not has little bearing on whether we think his home runs are genuinely his.[17]

My approach, as I said in the Introduction, is to avoid making arguments that rely on any kind of assumption about choice and autonomy, whether it be that individuals have choice and autonomy, don't have choice and autonomy, or fall into some complex middle ground. So I will set Kantian concerns with autonomy and choice aside. I will, instead, simply explore how far the Kantian notion that genuineness entails struggle can take us toward making the cure/enhancement cut at the individual level by helping us define an enhancement as a change – a new individual trait or achievement – that is not genuine because it comes too easily.[18]

In doing so, I will not inquire as to whether the Kantian view is itself justified. That is an ongoing topic of philosophical debate. But, as I have suggested by looking at some alternatives in the case of running, the Kantian cut between struggle and ease is prima facie the best tool for making the cure/enhancement cut when that cut is understood as the distinction between providing for genuine and artificial individual improvement. And so I want to look closely at what it suggests about cures for each of the conditions under discussion. How, even on a Kantian view properly thought out, do we know whether or when a cure for obesity or mild depression or plain facial features or slow running would stray into the realm of artificial enhancement? And does this pervasive but unstated Kantian view ultimately make sense as a way of drawing the cure/enhancement cut at the individual level, the level of individual genuineness and artificiality?

A few preliminaries: By "struggle," I mean the most effective action that an individual can take to alter her phenotypic condition, as long as that action necessitates exertion or difficulty. In the case of the slow runner, for example, I have identified struggle with training, diet, and exercise, and the slow runner's phenotypic condition – her (meager) running ability – therefore consists of whatever she can do without struggle, without exertion or difficulty, without the benefit of training, diet, or exercise. The more such ability a runner has – I am now thinking of people whose running ability falls on the high end of the bell curve – the more "naturally gifted" she is. Santa Ana track coach Darel Newman captures this meaning when he says that there are "always going to be some kids that are so naturally gifted that they can go out and triple jump 45 feet or run a . . . [10.0] 100 without any real training."[19] As the champion sprinter Linford Christie puts it, "I managed to beat guys who were training regularly. My attitude was 'So why the hell do I need to train?' "[20]

To be a naturally gifted runner, however, entails not just being "given" or "blessed with" great muscle strength or a high capacity for oxygen uptake without having had to struggle for it. One is also gifted to the extent that one can acquire (more) such traits with less struggle than would be required of others.[21] A gifted runner, say a Linford Christie, boasts a high ratio of muscle growth or oxygen-uptake increase to unit of struggle – unit of training, exercise, sweat and strain – expended. Or switch the example from the physically slow to the obese. A person might have been blessed with a thin physique without having had to struggle for it. But he might additionally have been given an ability to lose a large number of pounds with little struggle, without having to diet or exercise strenuously, while for others, shedding the same amount of weight would require far more struggle. Or consider mild depressives. One, marshaling all his resources of maturity and self-understanding, might manage only to keep his substantial neuroses at bay during a first date. Another, more "naturally gifted" in the way I mean here and exerting the same measure of effort, will manage to curb his neuroses much longer.

Linford Christie's natural gift, we can assume, represents the populated social ideal of gifts in the realm of running (sprinting) ability. It represents the social ideal as achieved by humans thus far, to which, on the criteria set out in Part 1, medicine would have the obligation to bring any runner who so sought. Yet what if Christie, blessed with such socially ideal gifts, had maintained his youthful attitude of "Why the hell do I need to train?" What if he had remained content with whatever natural gifts he could muster by training minimally or not at all? Then he would have been beaten by at least some runners with the same or even fewer gifts who struggled more. As it happens, though, runners such as Linford Christie and Donovan Bailey "have put in endless training to go so far, building upon their birthright to improve their muscles' size, strength and short-term fuel supplies."[22] Anyone seeking to be brought to the populated social ideal would, on the criteria set out in Part 1, be medically entitled to the same gifts that Donovan Bailey has, but would then have to struggle as much as Bailey if he wanted to match Bailey's achievement.

With that in mind, let me set out the twofold structure of the Kantian approach. On the one hand, it is egalitarian, holding that no one's natural gifts – that which she has been given or can get with ease – should give her a leg up on others, and that cure is a legitimate means of righting such imbalances. According to this Kantian egalitarianism, just because someone is naturally gifted – can easily run a 10.0 100 meters, has a socially ideal body shape, or possesses beautiful facial features – she has no claim that others not match those gifts via cure. Medicine should provide it. On the other hand, though, the Kantian approach subordinates this egalitarian view to a genuineness proviso, according to which cure should never diminish a person's genuine, struggle-born achievement, whatever it may be. If it does, then that cure – no matter how equalizing – becomes an artificial enhancement. It becomes a means of doing more easily something that the subject had been accomplishing, via the struggle to train and exercise, or undergo therapy and introspect, with greater genuineness. Medicine should not provide it.

The egalitarian impulse flows from the Kantian's utter indifference between a trait that comes from a pill and one that comes from an innate natural gift; the genuineness proviso flows from the Kantian preference for a trait born of struggle to either of them. Consider: Since a natural gift comes easily, Kantians would view it – think of a sprinter's natural gift for running a 10.0 100 – in exactly the same light as they would view a pill that enabled a sprinter to run a 10.0 100. In each case, the trait in question, the ability to run a 10.0 100, is extrinsic to the genuine self: obtained by nothing that the subject itself did. Only traits that come by neither natural gifts nor pills but by struggle are genuine. Not that the Kantian is somehow opposed to traits that come either from natural gifts or pills. No person entirely makes or remakes herself through struggle. It's just that where a real alternative presents itself, a trait born of struggle is always preferable, because more genuine, than one born either of a pill or as a natural gift.

Because there's no difference between a natural and a cure-born gift, then, Kantian egalitarianism holds that anyone is entitled to the latter in order to match what others possess in the former. The Kantian genuineness proviso, however, slaps on a caveat. Since struggle-born traits are favored over cure-born traits, cure cannot be administered if it will diminish struggle, transferring traits or accomplishments that had been achieved genuinely by the subject, through struggle, to the realm of effortless (hence artificial) attainment via medical cure. But how do we determine whether a cure will erode the magnitude of traits and accomplishments that come under the domain of the subject? How do we tell whether cure would be a means of achieving with ease what the subject had attained more genuinely with struggle, as opposed to simply taking its place, like any natural gift, outside the subject?

For each of the eight phenotypes, two questions will be key. First, is it even possible for struggle to substitute for cure, at least to some extent? Is it even possible for an individual to struggle to overcome, or at least erode, his phenotypic condition? If not, then it would be inapt to describe a cure as supplanting a more genuine alternative for improvement, one that by comparison would make the cure appear to be mere enhancement. If struggle cannot in any way substitute for cure, then for a Kantian, cure (say, cured deafness) can be no more nefarious than a natural gift of the same magnitude (hearing). If, however, struggle can substitute for cure, at least to some extent – if struggle can at least partially do what a cure would – then there is a mode of change available to the individual that would be more genuine. And that, in turn, would take us a step toward consigning any such cure to the realm of the artificial, the realm of enhancement.

Arguably the struggles of therapy, introspection, and maturation substitute, at least to some extent, for a cure for mild depression – for a super-Prozac pill – which, in the eyes of those making such an argument, is precisely what brands the pill an enhancement. So, too, the struggle to exercise, train, and diet would seem to substitute, at least to some extent, for a cure for slow running, for supersteroids. And this is what, for critics, nudges such treatment toward the category of enhancement. It needn't matter that, in any given case, such struggle might substitute only partially, far from fully, for the cure, as long as it does to some extent. For a Kantian, any amount of struggle-born achievement, no matter how meager, is preferable to any amount of artificial achievement, however great. So the first question is: For each of the eight conditions, to what extent can struggle substitute for cure?

But there is a second, and reverse, question that also needs to be answered: For any given condition, would cure then substitute for whatever struggle had been going on? Conceivably, a cure could simply complement, without necessarily eliminating, the subject's struggle-born achievement. For example, a person taking super-Prozac, and cured of his neurotic depression, might in no way cease struggling to introspect, mature, or undergo therapy. He might simply rechannel his target from neurotic unhappiness toward a clear-eyed attempt to plumb the discontented depths of the human condition. But for another person, super-Prozac might indeed nicely substitute – whether to some extent or even entirely – for whatever struggle had been going on. Having freed her of the neurosis against which she had been struggling, super-Prozac might lead her to ease up, even to abandon as no longer necessary any continued efforts to introspect, explore psychic wounds, live life on levels other than the surface, mature, or undergo therapy. In which case, its unwelcome consequence would simply have been to take at least some magnitude of self-overcoming and self-control that had otherwise been genuinely achieved via struggle and transfer it to the realm of the artificial. If cure substitutes for struggle in this way, it is enhancement.

Similarly, imagine a runner who, having been brought to Donovan Bailey's socially ideal gifts via a cure, then continues to struggle as much as before: to diet, exercise, and train. He would not have ceded any ground from the subject; his cure-born gift would be no more troubling than Bailey's natural one. One who, in light of such a cure, did ease up – used the cure to replace at least a measure of his previous struggle – would have diminished his subject and the breadth of its genuine accomplishments, transforming the cure into an artificial mode of enhancement.

The twofold question, then, is whether (for any given condition) struggle can substitute at least somewhat for cure – a matter I'll consider in the first section following – and whether cure would at least to some extent supplant struggle, an issue I'll consider in the second section. If, for any given condition, the answer to either inquiry is no, then cure would not amount to subject-shrinking enhancement. But if it is yes to both, then cure would erode the subject and, hence, fall into the class of artificial enhancement.

In undertaking these inquiries, I will be making a couple of assumptions. First, I am going to assume that we are talking, here in Part 2, about only those group members who view their condition – physical slowness, deafness, obesity, mild depression, or any of the others – as a medical one and are seeking a cure. Prior to medicine's developing and distributing a cure, then, these are group members who would have been struggling against their condition, at least to some extent, since they want to get rid of it. If physically slow, they would have been exercising; if plain-featured, they would have been using cosmetics; if mildly depressed, they would have been trying therapy or at least some self-examination or self-control; if deaf, they would have been learning to speak or lip-read.

Of course, just because someone is struggling against her condition doesn't mean she's doing so with any meaningful effect. So, while I will be looking only at members of each group who are struggling against their condition, I still have to explore the sense in which, for each of the groups, such struggle does or does not substitute for cure; and this is the question I will address in the first section following. Such an inquiry would be irrelevant if we had no reason to assume that the group members we are examining were, in fact, struggling against their condition, at least to some degree, as would any who viewed it as a medical one. Since we are talking only about group members who seek to eradicate their condition, then, I am going to assume that we are speaking of people who – in the absence of a cure – would be struggling against their condition at least to some extent.

I will, however, make no assumption about whether each such person would be doing so to the maximum extent of his potential. To use the running example, I will make no assumption about the extent to which any given athlete is engaged in struggle – in training, exercise, or other exertions – beyond assuming that she is engaged in some such struggle. Nor, to use the mild-depressive example, will I make any assumption about the extent to which a neurotic person is engaged in struggle – in therapy, in self-examination – beyond assuming that he is engaged in some such struggle.

My avoidance of any assumption as to whether those with a particular condition are struggling against it to the maximum of their potential, as long as they are struggling to some extent, couches the question I will address in the second section following, the question of whether any given cure will supplant struggle. On the Kantian approach, a cure must not substitute for whatever quantum of struggle-born, that is genuine, accomplishment an individual is already registering against his phenotypic condition. But it certainly can substitute for whatever he *might have* accomplished had he struggled even harder, to the fullest of his potential. The Kantian doctor, in other words, cannot withhold a cure unless the runner or the mild depressive struggles more than he already is struggling. The Kantian doctor can withhold a cure only if it will cause the runner or the mild depressive to struggle less.

Every doctor swears to do no harm to the person. But the Kantian doctor additionally swears to do no harm to the subject. The Kantian physician pledges never to administer a cure if it will cause a retrenchment in the subject, a diminution in whatever magnitude of personal achievement is currently creditable to an individual's genuine subject, regardless of whether – at that particular moment – the subject is struggling to the maximum extent possible. The Kantian physician is not obligated to increase the bounds of the subject. She is obligated only not to shrink them; doing so would convert cure into enhancement.

The Kantian approach, then, takes its measure of struggle (and hence of the subject) from what is actually happening in real time. In determining whether struggle substitutes for cure, the Kantian approach excludes consideration of group members who merely *might* have been struggling against their condition; it focuses only on those who actually are struggling. And in determining whether cure substitutes for struggle, the Kantian approach excludes consideration of how much group members *might* have struggled against their condition; what matters is only how much they actually are struggling. The group members we are talking about, then, have neither foregone struggling at all nor (necessarily) are they struggling to the maximum of their potential. Apart from this, however much a person is struggling against her phenotype, the Kantian approach will apply. It is meant to be invariant to the degree of struggle going on.

Let me illustrate this invariance in a couple of ways, one having to do with Kantian egalitarianism and the other with the Kantian genuineness proviso. According to Kantian egalitarianism, it doesn't matter how much, or how little, a person might already be achieving in struggling against his phenotype – how much his struggle might already be substituting for a cure. As long as a cure would not diminish that struggle, then he is entitled to a full measure of such cure, one that will bring his gifts right up to the social ideal. Imagine a doctor who requires a runner under her care to maintain the full extent of his struggle – say, the runner's personal struggle to train brings his 100-meter time down from 12.0 to 10.5 seconds – and then prescribes only the partial increment of cure necessary to bring the runner the rest of the way to the populated social ideal of 9.8. That would still put the runner at a disadvantage by comparison with a Donovan Bailey, whose socially ideal gifts alone take him to 9.8 and who then can struggle to do better even than that. Kantian egalitarianism stipulates that if cure won't substitute in any way for struggle, then the runner is entitled to the full cure that would bring him to the social ideal – on top of which he will continue to struggle as much as before. Since he has not diminished any degree of his struggle, whatever he accomplishes with a cure is just as respectable as whatever anyone accomplishes with a natural gift outside of the subject.

The Kantian genuineness proviso, however, is also invariant to the amount of struggle going on. In particular, this means that no matter how little (or how much) a person might be achieving through struggle – in other words, even if his particular struggle minimally substitutes for cure – it's nevertheless better to achieve little genuinely than much through enhancement. If cure would then substitute for even some of that

struggle – if it would cause the person to let up even marginally in such
struggle – it would in effect have replaced some measure of genuine
achievement with a more artificial, an easier, attainment of the same
measure. Some quantum of accomplishment that had previously been
genuinely attained by this individual's subject through struggle would
now be artificially achieved by cure. Think, again, of a runner whose personal struggle to train brings his 100-meter time down from his natural gift
of 12.0 to 10.5 seconds. He then gets a cure, which gives him the socially
ideal gift for running a 9.8 100 meters. Let's say that the same measure of
struggle that took his previous natural gift of 12.0 to 10.5 seconds would,
if exerted on top of his new gift of 9.8 seconds, bring him down to 9.3.
In other words, a reduction of .5 second now represents the same measure of genuine accomplishment as a reduction of 1.5 seconds did previously, given that it becomes harder and harder to shave additional time
off as one approaches the limits of human speed. Suppose, however, that
the runner lets up; suppose that he exercises and trains a bit less than
before and shaves his time only to 9.5. Some measure of accomplishment
that had previously been creditable to the genuine subject would now
be carried by the cure. In which case that cure would become artificial
enhancement and hence fall outside the bounds of Kantian medicine to
supply.

Since I am trying to make arguments at the group level, what I say about
any given condition is meant to apply to all members of the group harboring it. More specifically, it is meant to apply regardless of the extent
to which any given individual might be struggling against her condition,
as long as she is struggling against it to some degree. I will look at what
the structure of a particular group's condition says, first about the extent
to which struggle can substitute for cure and, second, about the extent
to which cure, in turn, would necessarily substitute for such struggle.
Remaining at this group level, I will draw some conclusions, applicable
equally to each individual member of the group, as to whether whatever
he achieves with a cure should be deemed an authentic accomplishment
or an artificial one.

What if we don't remain at the group level in answering this question
about the individual? What if we allow individuals to answer it themselves?
Then, as Carl Elliott says, when it comes to using "the language of authenticity" to analyze "enhancement technologies," any given individual can
simply insist that "it was only when I got the face-lift, started on steroids,
got a sex-change operation, that I really felt like myself."[23] Any individual
can say, as did the bodybuilder Samuel Wilson Fussell in explaining his

decision to dope, that "[a]s long as the part I played was simply interior" – that is, imagined and hoped-for – "I felt like a fraud. No, I needed the juice in the worst way, to make myself whole. I needed to complete the new persona, to make myself into a body builder" in reality, on the outside as well as the inside.[24] The individual-level question – as to whether a treatment amounts to an aid that allows the individual to change in a genuine way or else a contrivance that leads him to change in an artificial, inauthentic way – cannot be answered at the individual level. It can be answered only by making general statements about his group's condition.

Finally, by way of introduction, I must acknowledge that the Kantian approach differs fundamentally from a perspective that has been most compellingly advanced by Michael Sandel. On that alternative view, which might be called "Aristotelian" in the same rough sense as the one I am suggesting is "Kantian," we "admire players like Joe DiMaggio, who display natural gifts with grace and effortlessness" more than "players like Pete Rose, who are not blessed with great natural gifts but who manage through striving, grit and determination to excel. . . ."[25] On this Aristotelian view, natural gifts are superior – more admirable – not only to struggle ("effort and striving") but also cure. Sandel equates cures, such as chemical performance boosters, with "wilfulness," the ability to choose or control one's abilities. And he equates natural "giftedness" with that which is given to us and is hence beyond our control. Giftedness, with its connotations of grace and blessing, does and should command greater reverence than wilfullness; hence natural gifts are more admirable than gifts resulting from cure.[26]

My discussion here takes place within a very different framework in which effort and striving are very much the point of sports. While on the Kantian approach giftedness is not disparaged by any means, it is not as admirable as struggle, and there is no moral difference between it and cure, between innate (or natural) and pharmaceutically induced gifts. Nor does the Kantian approach rely upon any equation of natural gifts with that which is nonchosen or of gifts born of cure with the wilfully chosen. To do so, I believe, would require us to enter the "morass of the free-will problem," as G. A. Cohen calls it.[27] It would require us to explore the murky question of whether runners really do have a choice to take steroids and whether, as Harry Frankfurt and others have argued, it's necessary for us in some sense to "choose" or embrace our innate traits before they can meaningfully be called our own.[28]

Here I can only acknowledge that I am writing within a very different set of basic presumptions than is Sandel, not that one set is superior to the other. But I would also call attention to what seems to me to be a tension in his position. The egalitarian aspect of the Kantian view, if not its notion of genuineness, exerts a pull on Sandel. At one point he writes that "the natural talents that enable the successful to flourish are not their own doing but, rather, their good fortune – a result of the genetic lottery. If our genetic endowments are gifts, rather than achievements for which we can claim credit, it is a mistake and a conceit to assume that we are entitled to the full measure of the bounty they reap in a market economy."[29] The "gifted quality of life," Sandel concludes, "conduces to a certain humility."[30]

Yet this egalitarianism sits in tension with Sandel's Aristotelian view, on which it is precisely the athlete's innate (or natural) gifts that command our admiration and merit rewards. We admire Joe DiMaggio, Sandel says, precisely because of his natural gifts and effortlessness; we accord less esteem to Pete Rose simply because his natural gifts are less abundant, and even though he exerts far more effort. "No one," Sandel continues in this Aristotelian vein, "believes that a mediocre basketball player who works and trains even harder than Michael Jordan deserves greater acclaim or a bigger contract."

But one wonders: How can Michael Jordan deservedly command (Aristotelian) "acclaim" for his gifts if at the same time the appropriate (egalitarian) response for him to take toward those gifts is "humility?" If, on egalitarian grounds, we recognize that "our genetic endowments are gifts, rather than achievements for which we can claim credit" – and that "it is a mistake and a conceit to assume that we are entitled to the full measure of the bounty they reap in a market economy" – then why isn't it a mistake or a conceit for Michael Jordan to assume that he is entitled to a big contract and great acclaim? It's not necessarily the case that Sandel's Aristotelianism and his egalitarian leanings, his tendency to find more to admire in natural gifts than in struggle or cure and his tendency not to do so, cannot be reconciled. It's just that a Kantian view, which finds more to admire in struggle than in both natural gifts and cure, avoids this particular problem.

When the rehabilitation therapist Chris Schombs writes that "the passion, perseverance, frustration and tenacity of the Special Olympics athletes are no different from that [sic] of any athlete who struggles to achieve, to be the best in his or her chosen event," she is crystallizing the Kantian view. The Special Olympics constitute a different league than the

Olympics – the level of natural gifts differs – but the genuine achievement is the same because the struggle need not be any different.[31] Likewise, some speculate that the prosthetics – the gifts born of cure – available to double-amputee Paralympic runners might soon enable them to score higher speeds than can Olympic runners.[32] For a Kantian, though, this is neither here nor there. An athlete should always compete against others whose total gifts – whether natural or cure-given or some combination of both – equal his own, making for different leagues such as the majors and the minors or the Olympics and the Paralympics. In this way, what would matter in determining the winner is, and should be, the magnitude of his struggle.[33]

Even if group members can legitimately deem their condition a medical one on the social-norm/social-ideal criteria that I set forth in Part 1, then they might still have to view cure as enhancement if it violates the Kantian criterion of individual genuineness that I examine here. Perhaps, on the criteria I suggest in Part 1, a person can ask to be brought to the socially ideal range of basketball skills achieved by National Basketball Association (NBA) players or the socially ideal range of musical skills attained by members of the New York Philharmonic. Even so, it remains to be seen whether his acquiring these traits via a medical procedure might not constitute artificial individual enhancement, instead of genuine individual improvement, on the arguments I set out here. For seven of the eight phenotypes under discussion, I ultimately conclude that cure wouldn't be enhancement. In one case, it could be under certain circumstances.

I'll also note that, in Part 1, I argued that all phenotypes under discussion, except for black racial features, can legitimately be eradicated by medical means. But I'll set aside that exception here and include in the discussion blacks who want to change their racial features. For them, too, I examine whether there are modes of struggling to become white that are somehow more genuine, more rooted in the real self, than a pill to eliminate black racial features would be, thus rendering artificial any degree of whiteness that the pill might furnish.

Does Struggle Substitute for Cure?

When it comes to the two conditions that critics of enhancement mention most frequently – physical slowness and mild depression – it is indeed possible for individual struggle to reduce or even surmount them through the ardors of diet, training, and exercise or therapy, introspection, and maturation. Speaking of slow runners as a group, struggle can substitute for cure. True, even assuming, as I am, that all slow runners who view their condition as a medical one will be struggling against it to some extent, not all will be totally successful. Some will be only partially so, and others still will barely make a dent in the phenotype. But for a Kantian, it needn't matter whether struggle's capacity to substitute for cure is complete or only partial. If it should be the case that cure would in turn supplant even a bit of such struggle (and this, of course, is the question to be discussed in the next section), then on the Kantian genuineness proviso, it would become artificial enhancement. Achievement might be greater with the cure, but *genuine* achievement wouldn't be; it would instead have been greater with the struggle.

The possibilities for struggle against mild depression resemble those for physical slowness. Consider Nicci Gerrard's Kantian-style comment, in her review of Andrew Solomon's memoir of depression *Noonday Demon*, that "each person's struggle" against his depression preserves (here she quotes Solomon) the " 'acreage and reach' of his soul."[34] Whatever is achieved via struggle – via therapy, introspection, or hard-won self-awareness – comes under the reach of the subject, the "soul," and hence is genuine, part of the self. Or as Peter D. Kramer puts it, "[a]ccording to psychoanalysis, to lose pain without quest or struggle is to lose self."[35] This suggests that whatever victories the self has managed to score over its psychic pain via struggle are more genuine, more part of the self, than would be similar victories wrought by a cure. For mild depression, in other words, struggle is available as a more genuine substitute for cure. If it should happen – and, again, I will examine this question in the next section – that super-Prozac, in turn, would supplant even a bit of this struggle, then such a cure would become a mode of artificial enhancement. It would allow the individual to accomplish more easily at least some measure of achievement that the subject had previously scored genuinely. It would shrink the subject.[36] It needn't matter, for a Kantian, that one person's struggle against neurosis allows her to barely make it through a cocktail party, while another's expunges the neurosis entirely. In either case, the subject has genuinely accomplished something. With a cure, the "something" might be greater, but the genuineness will be smaller.

What can be said about physical slowness and mild depression can be said about anorexia and obesity. Personal struggle of much the same type – diet, training, and exercise or therapy, introspection, and maturation – can at least to some extent substitute for cure by eroding, and in many cases even eradicating, these conditions at the phenotypic level.

An encomium-like usage of the word "struggle" pervades the writings and musings of anorexics seeking to overcome their condition. "I just fought [anorexia] all the time until it went," Morag MacSween quotes one anorexic girl as saying; "[i]t was a struggle, it was sort of like an internal struggle."[37] On both pro-anorexia and anorexia-recovery websites, one can find tales from those who are struggling against their condition, winning praise from others for stretching themselves. Her fight against anorexia is "such a gargantuan struggle," one woman writes;[38] another says that she is "struggling with this everyday, and trying not to be sucked in even deeper;"[39] another declares that "I have just won a little milestone in my struggle," and yet another states that "I really believe that this is a test that I will be able to overcome" through "constant internal struggle."[40]

Many researchers on anorexia believe that such struggle is not only praiseworthy on what are essentially Kantian lines, but necessary to a genuinely-achieved victory over the condition: one that should not be artificially short-circuited with drugs. Indeed, better a partial victory over anorexia that's genuinely achieved – better to grow as a subject, to have at least some measure of successful struggle under one's belt, even if one's anorexia does not entirely disappear – than a total victory that's artificially attained.[41] This is what I would call a Kantian view, and it's certainly a plausible one.

As for obesity, critics of pharmacological cures have, along Kantian lines, praised the struggle to diet and exercise for signifying a more genuine (even if often less than wholly successful) strike against fatness than anything that cure would bring. And that applies whether we have in mind the imperfect and impermanent cures now on the market or their perfect and permanent versions that I am imagining here.[42] The recent Eddie Murphy version of *The Nutty Professor* ends with the obese – and obviously Kantian – hero jettisoning a cure that he himself had invented. The professor prefers the struggle of diet and exercise, an alternative that he acknowledges will be less than entirely successful. But in doing so, he presumably touches a chord of approval in the audience. Whatever victory he gains over his obesity will be genuine, and that is exactly what would render cure an artificial enhancement. A person whose subject grows via exerting itself, taking genuine credit for whatever reduction in obesity he is able to achieve through diet and exercise – even if much obesity remains – may not be in a perfect situation. But for a Kantian, and plausibly so, he's in a better overall place as a person than is someone who merely swallows a pill and gets rid of his obesity entirely.[43]

We are, recall, talking about those subgroups of the physically slow, mildly depressed, anorexic, and obese who, on criteria set out in Part 1, see their condition as a medical one to be gotten rid of. The question here is: Can their group-typical struggle – diet, exercise, therapy, introspection – afford a more genuine alternative, a substitute, for cure? On Kantian criteria, there is little doubt that it can. True, while for some individuals such struggle will be wholly successful, for others – whether or not their capacities to diet or train or undergo therapy or introspect are maximally deployed – it will be only partly successful. And for still others its impact may be negligible, depending on the magnitude of the individual's condition and the degree to which she struggles.

But for a Kantian, all that is irrelevant. What matters is that all such individuals are struggling to overcome their conditions with some degree of success. And that, in turn, means that for the group – for the physically slow as a whole, say, or the mildly depressed as a whole – struggle can be said to substitute (whether entirely, partially, or negligibly depends on the individual case) for cure. Regardless of its magnitude, we can say of the group as a whole that whatever any given individual accomplishes with such struggle – even if an obese person delays dinner by an hour, or the mild depressive shuts out her neurotic fantasies during a social occasion, or the physically slow person shaves her time by 0.2 second – we can credit with being genuine.

If it turns out (see the next section) that cure wouldn't substitute for such struggle – if the person in question will continue her struggle in the same measure, if her subject will continue to be responsible for the same quantum of personal achievement – then a cure, no matter how substantial, will simply be like anyone else's natural gift, and she cannot be denied. But what if cure would substitute even a bit for that struggle? Then a Kantian can quite coherently say that the subject's struggle-born achievement, however meager, is at least the person's own. It will always be preferable to her scoring an artificial victory over her condition, however grand, via cure.

True, it's conceivable in outside cases that such struggle can make absolutely *no* dent in a phenotypic condition. Yet even so, on the Kantian approach, it would be superior to the artificial achievement a cure would bring, however great. Although what I'm about to say descends deeply to the level of the idiosyncratic, it may well be that a person could exert himself to his personal maximum in struggling against his mild depression or obesity, say, without eroding the condition even one whit. Perhaps his personal capacity to erode his neurosis or to exercise, however much he exerts it, is simply ineffectual; or perhaps his condition just has an incredibly strong grip on him. His struggle won't have brought even an iota of victory against the phenotype under the domain of the subject and, therefore, to his credit. Nevertheless, Kantians would praise the attempt. They would praise the struggle itself – the efforts at self-control or exercise – for being genuine. Although such an individual would not be wholly or even partially or even negligibly but "zeroly" successful, as I will say, nevertheless the struggle – the efforts at self-control or exercise, at introspection or diet – themselves represent genuine achievements, though they may register absolutely nothing against the condition. The way in which struggle might fail to substitute even a jot for cure in these occasional and idiosyncratic instances of mild depression and obesity, or in similar instances of physical slowness and anorexia, is, however, very different from the way in which struggle *as a general rule* doesn't substitute even a jot for cure in the case of the other four phenotypes, to which I now turn.

When it comes to blindness, deafness, plain facial features, and black racial features, struggle invariably fails to substitute for cure, even a jot, for the vast majority of group members. Struggle, understood as the most effective acts that the subject can take against a phenotype, will not erode these conditions even one whit, let alone partially, let alone completely. The most that struggle can do – the most effective action that one can take against these phenotypes – is to mask or hide them, not (what as a rule is impossible) erode or overcome them. And that is why, for these four conditions, and markedly unlike for the previous four, struggle against the phenotype gets tagged with the term "passing."

Consider what a blind child might do to "struggle" against her phenotypic condition "in a classroom geared to sighted students."[44] In her memoir of blindness, Georgina Kleege records that "I learned to read the blackboard from the motion of the teacher's hand while writing. If I suspected that I would have to read aloud in class, I'd memorize pages of text, predicting with reasonable accuracy which paragraph would fall to me. The routines of my teachers saved me. . . . Outside of school, if other kids said, 'Look at that!', I determined from the tone of voice whether they saw something ugly, strange or cute and would adjust my response accordingly. On the bus I counted streets to know my stop. In the elevator I counted buttons." Certainly all of these activities amount to struggle, and they amount to struggle against the phenotypic condition of blindness. Yet in undertaking them, Kleege says, she was "sham passing sight": hiding her phenotype but not eroding it.[45]

One might say that Kleege shouldn't have had to struggle; that she should have been accommodated with Braille texts, Braille elevator buttons, a bus driver who alerted her to her stop, and a classroom assistant who verbalized what the teacher was writing on the blackboard. Such suggestions would be relevant in cases where a person refuses our imagined cure because even though blindness is unequivocally a medical condition, as I argued in Part 1, she claims that it is also a culture worthy of such accommodation (about which, more in Part 3). Here we are addressing ourselves to those who seek to eradicate their blindness and asking whether struggle can offer any kind of more genuine alternative, whether it substitutes even a bit for cure. It would not seem so. What Kleege did, although it involved struggle, couldn't possibly have eroded her phenotypic blindness one whit, however strenuously she engaged in it. All that her struggle did was to mask her condition – sometimes partially, sometimes totally – which is why blind people who engage in such activity risk getting accused of (or, in Kleege's case, confront themselves for) trying to "pass."[46]

Likewise with those deaf people who regard their condition as a medical one. Any struggle that they might launch against their phenotype cannot even minimally erode it, let alone overcome it. Typically, struggle by the deaf against their condition assumes the form of "oralism": learning to speak or lip-read. In undertaking it, oralist deaf people engage – whether intentionally or unintentionally, successfully or unsuccessfully – in the endeavor to "pass as non-deaf. . . ."[47] Or, at least, they risk being so accused.

Why? Consider how oralism – lipreading, learning to speak – differs from manualism, the use of sign language. Both involve struggle. But unlike oralism, which is a form of struggle against phenotypic deafness, manualism is a form of struggle that relies on and even accentuates phenotypic deafness.[48] As Mary Ellen Maatman writes, "manual communication marks its users as deaf, whereas oral communication enables the deaf to pass as nondeaf." Of course, as Maatman goes on to say, such oralist passing "is more theoretical than real for most deaf persons . . . the reality is that most deaf speak differently from the non-deaf. . . ."[49] In other words, the struggle to *mask* a phenotype such as deafness or blindness – passing – can be partial as well as total in its success, just as the kind of struggle that can actually erode a phenotype – diet in the case of the obese, therapy for the mildly depressed – can be partial as well as total in its success. That, however, hasn't stopped oralism's partisans from praising it, and critiquing manualism, along Kantian lines. Although both oralism and manualism involve struggle, oralism struggles against the phenotype, while manualism does not, which is why, as Jack Gannon reports in his *Narrative History of Deaf America,* oralist deaf educators have "reject[ed] the use of sign language because it is 'the easy way out.' "[50]

But a Kantian, recognizing that oralist struggle cannot erode but only mask a deaf phenotype, could just as easily oppose it. After all, the Kantian's concern lies with preserving genuineness of achievement. And passing, even if successful, is at least from one perspective anything but genuine. In 2002, Sharon Duchesneau, with her partner Candy McCullough, chose a deaf sperm donor in the hope that she would have a deaf child. She did so, Duchesneau says, because she "recall[ed] struggles and humiliations as she attempted to master lip-reading and speech. . . . We feel whole as deaf people. . . ."[51] Here, "wholeness" comes when "struggle" – struggle that could never even minimally erode the phenotype and is inauthentic in trying to mask it – gets *abandoned.* In which case, for the deaf, it would be hard for a Kantian to deem struggle against the phenotype to be any more genuine than a cure would be.

Of course, for Duchesneau, who obviously isn't interested in becoming a hearing person, curing phenotypic deafness and struggling against it are to be equally rejected in favor of accepting deafness and weaving a life around it. That is why deaf (and blind) people who today – in the absence of a cure – choose not to struggle against their conditions get praised, by hearing and seeing people, for "accepting" their phenotypes. By abandoning the struggle against their conditions, what they are seen to be giving up is the inauthenticity of passing, not a genuinely achieved modicum of sight or hearing; better to accept than to struggle in vain. Thus, Beryl Lieff Benderly says, "[p]eople who belong [to the deaf community] 'accept their deafness,' as the saying goes. What this phrase – something between a cliché and a creed – exactly means is not easy to pin down. It has to do with assimilating the fact of deafness . . . into one's self-image, . . . seeing the whole of one's being and saying that it is good."[52] John Hull, in his memoir of blindness, talks of the fulfillment he feels, and the kudos he receives, for struggling to accept, not struggling against, his condition.[53] Unlike the blind and the deaf, however, those with conditions in which struggle can substitute at least to some extent for cure – mild depressives, anorexics, the obese, and the physically slow – rarely get praised, especially by anyone without those conditions, for accepting them. They are expected to struggle against them and get complimented when they do.

But now let's imagine cures for blindness and deafness to exist after society has successfully funded their development. For people who seek to overcome their deafness or blindness – for those, in other words, whom we are talking about here – such a cure would be no more threatening to genuineness than the struggle against those conditions already is. Struggle substitutes not a whit for cure, which means that there is no genuine accomplishment for the cure to supplant. For the Kantian, genuine struggle must have the capacity to erode or eradicate a phenotype – it must substitute to some degree for cure, whether completely, partially, negligibly, or even zeroly – if it is to embarrass cure by comparison, rendering it mere enhancement. But with blindness and deafness, there is no quantum of sight or hearing that struggle achieves. Taking a cure instead of struggling would in no way erode the subject, plucking some measure of achievement from the realm of the genuine self and delivering it to the artificial. Cure – sight or hearing afforded by medical intervention – would simply take its place outside the subject. It would be no more nefarious than a natural gift for sight or hearing. For blindness and deafness, then, cure wouldn't be enhancement even for a Kantian.

Put another way, where struggle risks being accused of the attempt to pass – as it does when the blind person pretends to read the blackboard or the deaf person mimics the capacity to hear through lipreading – then struggle itself raises serious questions about its own genuineness. Since genuineness is the key concern here, it's hard to see how, even on Kantian criteria, cure could be any less genuine. My statements here are not meant to be absolute. Possibly, there are individuals who, through struggle, can overcome certain degrees of blindness or deafness. But my discussion takes place here at the group level, and the possibility of such individuals remains on the plane of idiosyncracy. Speaking of the blind and the deaf as groups, we would say that struggle cannot substitute for cure; it cannot be deemed a more genuine alternative to cure because it is no alternative to cure whatsoever.[54]

In a similar manner, the struggles that individuals might wage against their phenotypic black racial features or phenotypic plain facial features – via the adroit use of cosmetics, clothing, or hair arrangements – almost always involve passing; such struggle cannot erode these phenotypes. Currently, cosmetic surgery is essentially incapable of altering black racial features. "[N]o amount of surgery will hide dark skin," Carl Elliott writes, and so "[h]istorically, the real debate for African Americans has not been about cosmetic surgery, but about cosmetics" – not changing the phenotype but masking it.[55] It's true that some skin-whitening creams might actually lighten black skin, but they do so only temporarily and marginally. Where "race is phenotypically obvious" to begin with, as Lawrence Blum writes, "the subject can do nothing about [skin color; it remains an] immutable characteristic. . . ."[56] Struggle substitutes for a Michael Jackson pill not a whit.

All that a person can do to struggle against his racial features, with greater or lesser success, is mask them and thereby risk getting accused of passing. In the "struggle to get into the white race,"[57] one woman whom Maurice Berger describes in his memoir *White Lies* "didn't look whiter – she looked like a person who was concealing something under layers of greasepaint."[58] This kind of struggle, however, can scarcely be deemed more genuine than a Michael Jackson pill would be; it can hardly make a pill look like artificial enhancement by comparison. Whatever a black person who seems lighter – or whiter – because of makeup and hair straightening may have done, it would certainly be no more genuine than what a black person who took a Michael Jackson pill would do. Indeed, the struggle to pass gets taxed regularly precisely for being "inauthentic."[59] A Michael Jackson pill, of course, would not be a legitimate medical offering on the grounds I set forth in Part 1. What the discussion here adds, though, is that for black racial features, struggle against the phenotype would scarcely be more genuine than a Michael Jackson pill would be. For the blind and deaf, by contrast, it is more apt to say that cure could not possibly be less genuine than struggle would be.

Likewise with plain facial features. Women who struggle against their plain noses, skin, or lips in the only ways currently available – via "costly cosmetics, hair treatments, and 'sexy' clothes"[60] – are, Wendy Chapkis writes, engaged in "the attempt to pass."[61] Their struggle is "tantamount to hiding" their phenotype, Rita Freedman says, not altering it.[62] Cosmetic *surgery*, of course, can actually alter plain phenotypic features. But I would classify current cosmetic surgery not as struggle but as cure, an imperfect and impermanent version of the cure we are imagining in this inquiry. And cosmetic surgery, whether imperfect or perfect, cannot be characterized as any more artificial than struggle, when that struggle comes in the form of using "[p]rops and paint," which, Freedman writes, "associat[e] femininity with phoniness, . . . with the false and trivial."[63] We needn't agree with Freedman's heated assessment to take the point that, by comparison with what people do to struggle against their plain-featured phenotype, one would be hard pressed to show how cure would be less genuine. Struggle doesn't substitute for cure one bit. It inauthentically hides but does not genuinely erode the phenotype, failing to meet the minimal Kantian requirement for a cure to be deemed enhancement.[64]

"We can compliment a writer or an architect by telling him or her how hard the work must have been to produce," Robin Tolmach Lakoff and Raquel L. Scherr write. But "we would never dream, short of really exemplary cattiness, of complimenting a woman by saying, 'It must have taken you *hours* to create that face!' "[65] For architects designing a building, struggle represents praiseworthy genuine accomplishment; a "creativity pill" would be enhancement. For women applying makeup, struggle represents nothing of the kind to put up against cure.[66]

It might seem to some readers that I have been too hard on the struggle of, say, the oralist deaf and the makeup-wearing plain-featured; that charges of phoniness or falseness or inauthenticity are over the top. People can disagree on the use of that language. But my point here is that the struggles that the blind and deaf – and those with black racial features and plain facial features – launch against their phenotypes attract this kind of criticism. By contrast, the struggles that the anorexic, the obese, the physically slow, and the mildly depressed unleash against their conditions do not. An oralist deaf person, in working hard to lip-read, is certainly accomplishing something. That something, however, is not the erosion of his phenotype, and although his struggle does bring a new trait or ability within the subject – he has genuinely learned to lip-read – the effect is to mask his phenotype without overcoming it. This is not the case with the anorexic or the obese, where the struggle to diet, say, either actually has some effect on eroding the phenotype or, where it doesn't dent the phenotype even one bit, at least doesn't mask that fact either.

It's true that obese people and anorexics also sometimes try to pass through the adroit use of clothing. Fat people will wear flattering shirts; anorexics will wear baggy pants. But if struggle is the *most effective* activity that the subject can undertake to attack a phenotypic condition, then for the obese and anorexics, it is diet, exercise, and therapy – not the adept use of clothing – that constitute struggle. Put another way, with the obese and the anorexic as groups, we can worry that taking a pill instead of struggling could erode genuine achievement. No such concern arises for those with plain facial features or black racial features.

Speaking of groups as a whole, then, for the blind, the deaf, the plain-featured, and for blacks, the subject – no matter how hard it might struggle – commands no possibility of eroding its particular phenotype even one whit. Instead, struggle becomes the effort to pass, to hide the phenotype. And if our criterion to begin with is genuineness – after all, that's the Kantian concern – then for these phenotypes, struggle's bona fides would be every bit as questionable as cure's (or a Michael Jackson pill's). Passers, after all, get accused of being inauthentic, false, and phony. It is hard to see how, even on Kantian grounds, cures for blindness, deafness, and plain facial features, or a Michael Jackson pill for black racial features, could offer an alternative to struggle that's even less genuine. Hence it's hard to see how, in the cases of deafness, blindness, and plain facial features, cure would be mere artificial enhancement. (Because a Michael Jackson pill would not be a legitimate cure on criteria set forth in Part 1, I say no more about it in this section.)

Those harboring blindness, deafness, or plain facial features thus cannot be asked to forego a cure on the grounds that struggle substitutes for it even to a modest extent – on the grounds that modest genuine achievement is superior to great artificial attainment. For those who are blind or deaf or plain-featured, "modest genuine achievement" in the struggle to erode phenotype doesn't exist. When it comes to these conditions, because struggle cannot substitute one whit for cure – because struggle does not offer a more genuine mode of pursuing the same ends – cure could not be enhancement. Sight, hearing, and beautiful facial features born of cure would simply resemble their innate, natural equivalents. They would be no more nefarious, on Kantian grounds, than the congenital capacities to see and hear, or the innate beautiful facial features, that countless people harbor outside their subjects. In no way would cures threaten a diminution in traits that would otherwise have been achieved by, and therefore located within, the genuine subject.

This is not the situation with the other four conditions: physical slowness, mild depression, anorexia, and obesity. Here, speaking of each group as a whole and ignoring idiosyncratic possibilities, there are Kantian grounds for deeming cure to be enhancement. More genuine alternatives to cure – alternatives such as training, exercising, dieting, therapy, introspection, and maturation – exist, and they engage the subject through personal struggle. True, not all the physically slow, mildly depressed, anorexic, or obese will be able to fully, or even partially, or perhaps even negligibly, overcome their condition no matter how they struggle. But I take it as testimony to the meaningfulness of that mere possibility that, for these four conditions, even an individual whose struggles are so ineffectual – or whose phenotypic condition is so severe – that she can only negligibly erode her slowness, depression, anorexia, or obesity, will still be credited for genuinely achieving whatever new speed, mental state, or body size she does manage to attain. In fact, even an individual whose dieting or therapy dents her phenotypic physical slowness, mild depression, anorexia, or obesity not one whit – zeroly – will still get praised for the genuine attempt, not accused of trying to pass. Because struggle against these four conditions substitutes for cure – whether completely, partially, negligibly or zeroly – it affords a more genuine alternative to cure, and that is what converts cure into enhancement on the Kantian criterion. Or, rather, struggle is more *genuine*. But whether it is an *alternative* to cure in these cases – or actually can coexist with it – remains to be seen.

Does Cure Substitute for Struggle?

Now let us reverse the arrow. Instead of asking to what extent struggle substitutes for cure, let us ask to what extent cure substitutes for struggle. To see how this matters, consider the physically slow runner. We have already observed that struggle – in the form of exercise, training, and diet – can zeroly, partially, or even completely substitute for a cure that would bring him to a socially ideal speed. Struggle can substitute for cure, in other words, in the sense that it can accomplish at least some of the same ends more genuinely. But now reverse the arrow. Would curing a runner's slowness necessarily substitute for his struggles, for his exercise, training, or diet? Would cure, in other words, substitute for struggle by supplanting, whether somewhat, partially, or completely, whatever struggle the runner had been waging, causing him to let up?

In one sense, there's no hard-and-fast answer. Certainly, one can imagine a runner taking a cure for his phenotypic slowness and then still continuing to exercise, train, diet, and otherwise struggle to the hilt as much as before in order to lift his performance even higher than cure by itself would allow. Even now, runners whose natural gifts place them at the social ideal struggle with diet and exercise to gain an even greater edge. There is no reason why the same would not be true of a runner whose socially ideal capacities came from a pill. As John M. Hoberman puts it, "in elected sport . . . drugs tend . . . to extend the agon rather than relieve the agony."[67] If indeed cure needn't substitute for that struggle – if, even when cured of his phenotypic slowness, the runner will still struggle every bit as much as before – then can the Kantian really have any objection?

Of course, the key word here is "needn't." While one can conceive of situations in which cure wouldn't substitute for a runner's struggle even one bit, one can certainly also imagine circumstances in which it would: partly, perhaps, or even completely. A runner might very well use the bump-up that comes from cure not to gain a better time but to ease up or even give up on the diet, the training, and the exercise necessary to gain his current time. Unlike those runners who continue to struggle fully even after having been cured, these runners would have allowed their Kantian subject to shrink. Not quite as much "acreage" would fall under the genuine subject's domain post-cure as it had pre-cure. Cure would be enhancement, because some quantum of achievement that had been creditable to the runner's subject would now, by comparison, be achieved artificially. Of the group of runners as a whole, it seems hard to know what to say about whether cure substitutes for struggle.

Think for the moment of the case where the physically slow runner, post-cure, does continue to struggle, via exercise, training, and diet, as much as he had previously: the situation in which cure doesn't substitute for struggle even one whit. His subject is contributing the same absolute measure of struggle to his success as before; hence cure has not eroded, or encroached upon, that acreage within the runner's total domain of accomplishments that can be credited to the genuine self.[68] In that light, cure wouldn't seem to be enhancement. But while the runner's quantum of genuine achievement won't have changed post-cure, his achievement, in total, certainly will have. After all, on top of a cure for physical slowness, his continuing the same level of struggle as before – the same level of diet, training, and exercise – will now take the formerly slow runner to an even greater speed than he could ever have attained without the cure. Doesn't that suggest that cure enhances his capacities, even if struggle continues unabated?

No, at least not on the Kantian criterion we have been assuming. On that criterion, cure doesn't render these new levels of achievement false or ungenuine as long as struggle remains undiminished. Kantians accept that the subject is always erecting its struggle-born accomplishments on platforms provided by traits that are external to it, whether muscle capacity or brain capacity. For the Kantian, the question of whether those external traits result from cure or, instead, are innate is a matter of indifference. The Kantian, in other words, knows that the subject – the range of the person's traits that come from struggle – is not all there is, and could not be all there is, to that person. What matters, for cure to elude classification as artificial enhancement, is simply that whatever ground within the person that his genuine subject covers, a cure not have the effect of retrenching it. What matters is that cure not cause a retraction in that acreage within the person that can be deemed genuine because creditable to the subject. And, in the case of the runner who struggles every bit as much as before to train, diet, and exercise, his subject would be providing the same measure of physical and mental boundary-pushing as it was previously. True, the domain of the struggle might shift, from taking a mediocre natural gift up a notch to taking a cure-induced, socially ideal gift up a notch. But assuming that the latter involves the same amount of struggle as before, the Kantian doctor, in offering a cure, would have done no harm to the subject before him.

Leon Kass has acknowledged as much. At one point during a July 2002 Bioethics Council meeting, Kass, on what I am calling Kantian grounds, noted that a runner's struggle – diet, exercise, training – can substitute for, offer a more genuine alternative to, cure in the form of what Kass calls "body engineering," presumably gene therapy. Later, though, Kass reversed the arrow and noted that such a cure need not substitute for diet, exercise, and other kinds of struggle. In doing so, Kass recognized that his own Kantian presumptions should lead him to accept a cure for slow running. In a series of thinking-out-loud rhetorical questions, Kass wondered:

> why wouldn't you want to say "Look, what really counts is what you make of your talents and you can't take credit for your talents because those are gifts"? Then why [not say] "look, what you really want to do to have real sport is to equalize talent and then what you really want to see is, what are each of us going to make, what is everybody going to make of the talents, on the basis of who you *really are*, which is not the gifts you were given, but your discipline, your effort, your aspiration?" Why wouldn't you then want to say, "look, body engineering is the possibility of really leveling the field in terms of gifts, so that we can find out who's who when it comes to what's in the salt?"[69]

In the case of physically slow runners, "who you really are" – the struggling subject – can, Kass here acknowledges, remain undiminished in the face of a cure that would give everyone who sought it a socially ideal gift for running. For Kass, at least in these particular comments, there seems to be no difference between natural gifts and cure-born gifts.[70] What counts is the amount of struggle that the subject launches on top of them. As long as it doesn't diminish the subject's struggle, cure-born speed takes its place outside the subject as nothing more objectionable than a natural gift for speed.

But, of course, Kass is conjuring up only one possible scenario. Post-cure runners can just as easily be imagined to let up on struggle, either in whole or in part. All possibilities would seem to exist. That is why, I believe, the best explanations for the acceptability of many proposed innovations in sports, including the introduction of drugs, rest not on whether the innovation is natural, or on whether it's external, or on whether it takes someone only up to, but not beyond, his personal peak. Rather, they hinge on whether the innovation can plausibly be thought to substitute for, or else conserve and complement, whatever struggle was previously being waged. Before returning to the case of running, let me show how this principle might work for a few other kinds of physical contest.

"If we use a twelve-pound shot put," Thomas Murray writes, "everyone will throw it farther than the sixteen pound one [and] the best at sixteen pounds will probably still be best at twelve pounds."[71] In other words, the shot put will be easier to throw, but the expected distance will grow commensurately longer, meaning that the measure of struggle expended, and hence the genuine accomplishment, will remain the same. Giving all shot putters "100 mg of Dianabol a day," Murray goes on to say, "will have a similar impact"; the shot will be easier to put, but the expectation is that one will have to hurl it farther, and so struggle will remain uneroded.

Just as a reminder, I am, unlike Murray, assuming that a cure wouldn't be available to *all* competitors, but only to those who (on the criteria I set forth in Part 1) can legitimately view their innate gifts as placing them below the populated socially ideal range. But Murray's broader point still stands for what follows. As long as the shot putter is competing against others whose innate plus steroid-induced gifts are also at the populated social ideal, he cannot simply ease up on the struggle he exacts of his new, more powerful muscles and throw the same distance as before. At least not if he expects to win. What is motivating Murray's conclusion is a view on which, if there is no reason to believe that a cure will erode struggle, then it can more aptly be viewed not as a subject-diminishing enhancement, but as something more akin to a trait that could just as easily have come to a person innately.

The aim of the shot putter is to put the shot as far a distance as possible. Hence, as Murray says, with Dianabol the shot will be easier to put but the athlete's expected distance will grow commensurately longer. Now, however, think of the baseball slugger who decides to take steroids. For him, at least insofar as winning a game or moving up in the record books is concerned, there's no meaning to his hitting a commensurately longer home run. With steroids sufficient to bring him to the populated social ideal of natural giftedness at batting, it becomes much easier than before for the slugger to hit the ball any given distance. But there is no requirement that he now hit it any farther than he had to, prior to taking steroids, in order to get a home run. And this will suggest to his critics that some measure of the struggle he needed to wage, and hence his genuine achievement, is likely to diminish, rendering steroids an artificial aid. Just such a notion seems to underlie sports commentator Doug Robinson's critique of Barry Bonds: "steroids gave Bonds a huge advantage," Robinson writes, "It's as if . . . they moved the fences 30 feet closer when he came to the plate. . . ."[72]

There are, however, those who defend steroid-taking by sluggers. In many instances, one can interpret their apologias as observations that the ballpark fences do not, in fact, set any limitations to the real distance, the most meaningful distance, that a hit ball can go. "I love 500-foot homes runs," a typical fan says.[73] Even though a 400-foot home run earns the same one point on the scoreboard and in the record books as a 500-foot one, batters will continue to struggle as much as before, even on steroids, if what they care about is the distance the ball goes beyond the fence. If the slugger aspires to hit the ball as far as possible, not simply as far as necessary, then there is reason to believe that he will perpetuate his struggle – his exertion while hitting the ball, his training and exercise – while on steroids. He will struggle every bit as much on steroids as off. Those who seem least perturbed by steroid use in baseball believe that the steroid-using batter won't let up, that cure won't substitute even one whit for struggle because what really counts, for him as for the shot putter, is how far he can propel the object.

Two things are key here. First, a Kantian approach underlies the arguments advanced by both critics and defenders of steroids in baseball (or, at least, those arguments that concern themselves not with safety or equality of access but with the matter of genuine accomplishment). Both sides agree at the most basic level. Steroids wouldn't be enhancement if they don't erode struggle, if no measure of the task is made easier. Where the two sides disagree is over whether that's what will happen. Accordingly, it would appear (and this is the second key thing) that nothing definitive can be said about the group of ballplayers as a whole as to whether steroids constitute enhancement. In fact, even those who believe, as does Doug Robinson, that what counts is the home run itself, not the distance the ball goes, have to allow for the possibility that in any given case a player on steroids might continue to struggle as much as before. Maybe a minor-league slugger who didn't need to struggle at all to hit home runs will, now cured and playing in the majors at the Barry Bonds social ideal, struggle even more than he did previously (certainly he won't struggle less). Whether struggle will persist in the same magnitude, that is, commensurately, post-cure as pre-cure, would seem to become a matter of case-by-case judgment and observation of each player on steroids and off.

Consider golf, where a related but instructively not identical debate has occured. When in the 1970s "manufacturers were quite successful in increasing the distance [that] balls would travel," the U. S. Golf Association (USGA) became concerned that such new technology "would become a substitute for the hours of practice and lessons necessary to develop a swing that would send a ball to the green."[74] The rationale for the USGA's concern is a Kantian one: Cure (the ball) would now substitute for struggle (practice and lessons). Since it would be easier to hit the ball farther, but the distance it would have to travel – the distance "to the green" – would not increase, commensurately, the USGA sought to restrict the use of such balls. They would have taken at least some measure of the achievement that had previously been attributable to genuine struggle – to the subject – and placed it outside, in the realm of gifts: the Kantian litmus test for an artificial performance enhancer.

Golf, however, tests not only strength, where the goal is to maximize a particular distance, to propel an object such as a golf ball as far as possible. It also tests accuracy, where the goal is to minimize a certain distance, the distance between an object and a target, as with the golf ball and the hole. And so, in a similar vein, the USGA once prohibited a golf ball that would have decreased the distance between the ball's actual trajectory and the trajectory needed to take it to the hole. This ball, the Polara, was "regularly more accurate," not simply in that it "held the line in which it was hit," but also in that it "returned to a center line despite being poorly hit." It didn't, in other words, slice or hook.[75] But a technology that threatened to decrease the distance between the ball as hit and the hole would, the USGA believed, have enabled some ease-up in the struggle to control one's aim properly. Since the hole would not have become commensurately more difficult to hit, the golfer would now be relying on the ball itself to accomplish for him artificially, at least to some extent, what he was no longer essaying genuinely. It would have constituted artificial enhancement.

Distance and accuracy, however, are not independent of one another. Those who defended the distance-increasing ball, accordingly, noted that while it indeed "increase[d] distance," it actually "decrease[d] accuracy."[76] The farther a ball goes, the less one can control where it lands (the reverse is also true: The accuracy ball didn't travel as far a distance as others). Such a defense relies, in effect, on a "struggle conservation" principle. Yes, the distance ball may well have reduced the yardage the golfer needed to move the ball through the struggle to develop and exert strength; the ball would now pick up some of that burden. But the ball also would have expanded by some increment the distance between where the ball would land and the hole, and so would have demanded a greater struggle to develop the control necessary to be accurate. Although the domain of accomplishment attributable to the genuine subject through struggle might have shifted, it would have remained the same size.

It is a belief in this kind of "struggle maintenance" that underlies other nods of approval given to innovations in sports. Corked bats in baseball – bats in which part of the wood has been replaced by lightweight cork – are easier to swing. Defenders argue, however, that such ease gets offset by the fact that a lighter bat doesn't have the same impact on a ball.[77] In these cases, it's not that an innovation is accompanied by commensurately higher expectations of achievement so that defenders are able to argue that struggle remains undiminished. Rather, those who have no trouble with distance-improving golf balls or corked bats rest their arguments, at bottom, on the claim that the innovation itself giveth and taketh away, so that overall struggle remains undiminished.

Again, I want to underscore two features of this kind of debate. First, both sides rely on what is essentially the Kantian criterion to determine whether the innovation is an illegitimate enhancement. Both agree that if the innovation diminishes overall struggle – the quantum of achievement attributable to the genuine subject – thereby rendering some measure of that quantum instead creditable to the innovation, then the innovation counts as an artificial enhancement. It's just – and here is the second point – that there's no general statement to be made concerning the group of golfers, as a whole, as to whether new golf balls such as the distance ball would have eroded struggle or not.

Indeed, the USGA might have been wrong even in thinking that the distance ball would necessarily have decreased the struggle necessary to develop strength for distance hitting, let alone whatever impact it might have had on increasing the struggle to hit accurately. True, the green would have remained the same distance away after as before the distance ball came into use. But – even with the ball – it would still have remained more than one stroke away. Any golfer who had wanted to score as far below par as possible wouldn't necessarily have eased up on her struggle to attain strength and hit as great a distance as she could. She might get to the green in two strokes with the same amount of struggle that had previously accompanied the three strokes she needed.

On the other hand, the defender of the distance ball was assuming that there would be an equality between the increased struggle to hit accurately that the distance ball required and the decreased struggle necessary to hit it a given distance. But that's a matter of looking at individual cases; it depends on the gifts for strength and accuracy that any given individual golfer already possesses. Nothing can be said on this matter about the group as a whole.[78] Any given Kantian contest manager or trainer would have to ascertain whether a particular golfer under his supervision would struggle just as much, or not, with the new ball as with the old, and allow it or bar it accordingly. And, of course, managers and trainers would have to ensure that each professional golfer would compete only against those whose gifts, whether natural or derived from the ball, equaled her own.

Turn from strength contests, like shot putting and batting, to endurance activities like a marathon or the Tour de France. Here the performance does not center on the length of the distance one can propel an object. Rather, (at least part of) the performance has to do with the length of time over which one can persist in executing the performance itself. And yet here, too, views about the propriety of a performance booster – say, erythropoietin (EPO), which by increasing blood oxygen levels makes endurance easier – depend on whether the critic in question believes that, with such a cure for subideal endurance capacity, an athlete will ease up on struggle.

One might reasonably conjecture that the long-distance runner who takes EPO is unlikely to increase commensurately the time during which he will now be running in the way that the shot putter who takes steroids might increase commensurately the distance he puts the shot. That would defeat the overall purpose of completing the race in the shortest possible time. Speaking of endurance events like "[c]ycling, cross-country or marathon running," sports scientist Clyde Williams invites us to assume that "a player's body is working through the match at 70 per cent of its maximum. With EPO in his bloodstream, he could perform all the same tasks at 60 per cent of his maximum, therefore he'd be less tired. . . ."[79] If the "task" – that is, the time over which he is to endure – indeed remains the "same," if that time doesn't grow longer with his taking the endurance booster, then EPO is plausibly deemed an artificial enhancement, eating into a measure of accomplishment that would otherwise have been attributable to the genuine subject. His struggle drops from 70 to 60 percent, and it is the EPO that now accomplishes that 10 percent.

Just as the golfer must pass the bar in both distance and accuracy, how-ever, the long- or middle-distance runner must meet the requirements of both endurance – where his goal is to maximize the time he can endure performing a particular activity – and speed, where the goal is to min-imize the time he needs to perform it. Consider again the case of the marathoner who takes EPO. On the one hand, he is very unlikely to want to increase the time he will need to endure commensurate with the greater ease of endurance that EPO provides; that defeats the purpose of the race, which is emphatically not to expand that time. Hence we might well think of EPO for endurance runners, in the way that Clyde Williams does, as a performance enhancer. On the other hand, by reducing some of the struggle necessary for endurance, EPO enables the runner to trans-fer that struggle to the realm of speed. If endurance boosters "reduce the energy needed to sustain a given level of performance, the reduced energy costs should allow an individual . . . to raise the level of effort that can be sustained" in other exertions, such as increasing his speediness.[80] If the struggle to endure eases, the struggle to speed increases, and the same magnitude of overall accomplishment remains creditable to the genuine subject.

Again, both those who oppose and those who defend EPO for endurance runners take a Kantian view, on which the conservation of struggle in the wake of using a performance booster is the key issue. If struggle remains at the same level, even if it shifts from the struggle to endure to the struggle to speed, then the magnitude of accomplishment attributable to the subject remains the same. The endurance capacity instilled by EPO takes its place outside the subject, as does any natural gift. If, however, overall struggle diminishes in the wake of EPO use, then some measure of achievement that had been genuinely scored by the sub-ject would now be achieved artificially due to enhancement. But there is no clear answer here – speaking of the group of mid- or long-distance run-ners as a whole – to the question of whether cure does substitute to some degree for overall struggle. It depends on whether, by how much, and in what ways the runner takes the struggle he used to wage to endure that extra 10 percent and rechannels it to the struggle to run more speedily.

Another way to look at endurance would be to pull back from the perspective of a single match and consider the matter of an entire sea-son. Think of a baseball player who will play more games if he takes amphetamines than he would if he didn't. Yes, he takes a cure for his subideal alertness and energy. But he then commensurately expands, by extending the time length of the seasonal performance he will now give, the amount of alertness and energy to be demanded of him. In doing so, he arguably requires of himself the same overall amount of struggle to remain alert and energetic as before. Players who defend amphetamine use point to this possibility. In doing so, they implicitly assume that as long as the quantum of struggle expected of them is preserved – amphetamines may make it easier to stay "up," but the player then incurs a countervailing increment of new difficulty by having to stay up longer – the drug won't have eaten into any terrain of genuine subjective accomplishment.

"We play 162 ballgames," major leaguer Gary Sheffield told the *Washington Post* in 2003; "[w]hen you do this 15, 16 years, sometimes you don't want to play a baseball game . . . guys just looking at me know whether I'm ready to play or not. If I'm not, if I'm not dressed [for the game], just sitting at my locker, they'll say, 'Hey, Gary, we need you in it tonight. Here's something to get you up.' All of a sudden, you're up for the game. . . ."[81] Alternatively, if one shortened the baseball season, then – to preserve struggle – some ballplayers would apparently do without amphetamines. "The fact is we're the only game that plays every night," an unidentified player told the *New York Daily News* in 2005; "if you want to get rid of 'greenies,' have us play four or five times a week and players can feel refreshed and well-rested. . . . I'm sure those players who take something would probably not feel the need to take it anymore. . . ."[82]

The arguments here seem quite definitively to be what I am calling Kantian. Performance can legitimately be enhanced as long as struggle is not diminished. Amphetamines instill capacities that simply take their place, as natural gifts for alertness and energy do, outside of the subject instead of eroding it. And again, others may disagree with that finding but not, in doing so, with the Kantian criterion. Of a National Football League (NFL) player who was disciplined for taking a diet pill, with no commensurate increase in the number of games he would be playing, Dr. John Lombardo, the NFL's chief adviser on performance-enhancing drugs, said that such pills can help "you perform better in a fatigued state."[83] When a player taking amphetamines fails to increase the measure of energy he will have to expend to offset the new boost he gets, the realm of genuine accomplishment attributable to the subject shrinks. Amphetamines, then, plausibly come to be seen as artificial enhancements. Neither Sheffield's nor Lombardo's judgments, of course, apply as a rule to the group of baseball players or football players as a whole; the best judgments can be made only on an individual, case-by-case basis.

Sheffield's argument resembles that advanced by athletes who need medicine if they are to be well enough to play a particular match. Yes, the argument goes, the medicine might relieve their struggle against pain, nausea, or breathlessness, but in doing so, it will enable them to engage in a new quantum of struggle by entering a contest that they otherwise would have foregone. Salbutamol for asthma is an example here. It is considered legitimate by those who believe, in any given case, that an athlete couldn't perform without it. And the notion of struggle – its conservance, its transfer from the struggle to breathe to the struggle to perform in the contest – is very much at play in the rationale for salbutamol use. Cyclist Mike Sanford's asthma "was a struggle" before he was treated, Sanford says, but now – freed of that particular struggle – he is able to "push . . . really hard" in his races.[84] "When inhaling and exhaling [was] a struggle," the sports journalist Greg Botelho writes, then "despite all his efforts," Richard Renzi often "couldn't get through an entire junior varsity [football] game." Salbutamol, by easing these "struggles," allowed Renzi to play longer and hence encounter a new struggle, the struggle to play for an entire game, not just part. Overall, Botelho suggests, struggle was conserved: Renzi's "efforts were a wash."[85] Where an observer denies that, overall, cure would substitute for any quantum of struggle – when he believes it will increase the time during which the struggle to play is to occur even if it eases the struggle to breathe – then he won't see it as eating away at the subject's quantum of genuine struggle-born achievement.

Yet when an athlete takes salbutamol, and the observer believes that no commensurate extension of the time being played will take place, then that observer is more likely to deem the drug an artificial enhancement. He will view it as relieving some element of struggle, allowing the athlete to endure the same amount of time he would have played anyway – the athlete not really suffering from asthma – with greater ease. According to Keun-youl Kim, a member of the International Olympic Committee Medical Commission, "[i]t is strongly suspected that athletes' team doctors abusively and improperly diagnose exercise-induced asthma in order to 'officially' justify the use of salbutamol, whereas their real purpose is to enhance athletes' performance during sports competition."[86] It makes it easier for them to breathe while exacting no new measure of struggle to play longer than they otherwise would have.

My intent, again, is not to argue that any new measure of struggle either is or is not commensurate with the old. That's a matter for individual cases. My point is simply that those who believe that the magnitude of struggle will get conserved, in light of a cure, will accept the cure as equivalent to a natural gift, equivalent to a nonasthmatic athlete's capacity to breathe, that in no way need diminish one's genuine achievement. Those who believe, by contrast, that cure will substitute for and hence diminish some amount of overall struggle will view it as an artificial enhancement eating into the subject, eroding its genuine accomplishments.

The same principle applies not just to the time involved in single contests or seasons themselves, but in the training necessary to prepare for them. And here is where much of the debate over steroids is to be found. Defenders, in their various ways, argue that runners can always take on more struggle or exertion – can always lengthen their training sessions – to make up for whatever measure of struggle, the struggle to ignore pain or exert tired muscles, that steroids happen to ease. In this way runners, while taking steroids, can preserve the quantum of genuine struggle-born achievement creditable to the subject. What steroids do is allow muscles to recuperate from training more quickly than otherwise – and in this respect they make training easier – but they, in turn, enable an athlete "to train harder, i.e., to exercise more vigorously and for longer periods of time," and thereby build bigger muscles.[87] The athlete is able to vary the time he struggles – to expand it to a "longer period of time" – to make up for whatever steroids bring by way of relief in struggle, the struggle he had been waging to train with a slowly recovering body and sore muscles.

At the age of twenty-six, Kelli White, a sprinter caught up in the Balco scandal, found herself "struggling with injuries."[88] With steroids, she believed she could set aside those struggles and, as she said, "run harder, longer. . . . If the workout was four 200s really, really fast, they wouldn't seem as hard as before. You could cut the rest down from five minutes to three. That's a big difference."[89] In one sense, steroids make struggle "harder," even if, in another, not "as hard." When steroids get defended, it is on these grounds. With overall struggle conserved – with the overall magnitude of accomplishment creditable to the subject maintained – whatever the steroids contribute to her performance simply comprise an addition to the athlete's natural gifts outside of the subject: the gift of fast recuperation. They in no way, or so White believed, supplant any magnitude of achievement scored by the subject.[90] Those, however, who believe that the magnitude of struggle that steroids eliminate (the struggle against fatigue, against burnout) is larger than the new magnitude they allow (to exercise harder, longer) – who believe overall that steroids make things easier for the athlete – will oppose them.[91]

This tour of other sports along with running is meant to establish two things. First, there is in the debate over cures such as steroids, EPO, and amphetamines a basic assumption that when struggle is conserved in spite of them – when the distances and times to be achieved vary commensurately with the cure – then the cure is not an artifical enhancement. The same quantum of achievement is attributable to the struggling of the subject as before; cure does not in any way substitute for it. Whatever new capacities the cure provides, they would, in Kantian-approved fashion, simply take up residence as gifts outside of the subject, no more nefarious than natural gifts. When, by contrast, commentators and critics believe that distances and times won't alter commensurately with the cure, they will oppose it. They will deem the cure to have necessarily diminished the amount of achievement being genuinely attained, which for them is what relegates such a cure to the class of artificial enhancement.

My first goal, then, has been to show how the arguments advanced by both defenders and opponents of steroids, EPO, amphetamines, and the like might be explained according to whether, in Kantian fashion, they believe that any such cure will preserve or else diminish struggle. I have, just as a reminder, set aside concerns with the dangerous side effects of such drugs and with the matter of fairness of access. The first vanishes in a world where medicine faces no technological limits; the second, in a world where it faces no resource constraints: our twofold governing assumption. Once they are set aside, the Kantian concern becomes prominent, even dominant, in debate, explaining why many participants take the positions they do.

However, and this is the second observation I would make, while there may be considerable agreement about the Kantian principles to be applied, there will not be consensus about the facts of any given case. We can draw – at least for the moment – no group-level general conclusion as to whether, for slow runners as a whole, steroids are enhancement. Nor as to whether, for the group of ball players as a whole, amphetamines are; nor again as to whether, for the group of cyclists as a whole, EPO is. The fact that we are looking at matters on a group and not an individual level doesn't mean that the group will *always* give us an indivisible answer to the question as to whether, for the group as a whole, a cure will make an individual member and his achievements authentic. We cannot, at least yet, conclude anything about runners as a whole at the group level. All we can say thus far is that where cure (steroids) wouldn't substitute for a runner's struggle even one bit, then on Kantian criteria it wouldn't be enhancement. But where a runner does allow cure to substitute for struggle – to push back the border of the genuine self, requiring it to cede at least some acreage to the artificial – cure would be enhancement. More needs to be said on the topic, and I will say more after looking at the other seven phenotypes.[92]

But first, Carl Elliott's discussion of apotemnophilia – the desire to have a limb amputated – raises an issue that I must deal with before I move on to those other phenotypes. Some apotemnophiliac websites, Elliott says, "show disabled men and women attempting nearly impossible feats – running marathons, climbing mountains, creating art with prostheses. It is as if the fantasy of being an amputee is inseparable from the idea of achievement." Elliott then quotes the apotemnophiliac John Money, who in a 1975 interview "sums it up this way . . . 'Look, Ma, no hands, no feet, and I can still do it.' "[93] And so a question: If it's the case that amputation can at the very least preserve the amount of struggle – the amount of genuine "achievement" – in which an athlete can engage, how could a doctor refuse to amputate the apotemnophiliac's limb on Kantian grounds? After all, amputation would not encroach on the subject. In fact, amputation might even increase the amount of struggle-born achievement creditable to the genuine self, not only in the realm of running but also in other avenues of life. Certainly, that would seem to be the case for John Money. Here the situation is not one in which an athlete takes a cure and then expands the difficulty of his task commensurately. Rather, he deprives himself of a natural gift but then does not reduce the magnitude of the task he faces commensurately.

To me, this observation points not to a flaw with the Kantian view but rather reminds us of why it's cabined. There is a prior question, one that we must entertain first before looking at whether an innovation would allow for genuine or artificial individual achievement, as we are doing here in Part 2. And that is whether the condition – in this case, having two legs – is a medical one on the criteria advanced in Part 1, where the matter at issue is whether a condition lies outside the bounds of social normality. And for it to be so deemed, two legs would have to fall outside a social norm of one leg and/or others would have to have reached a social ideal of one leg. This is so clearly not the case that the kind of amputation sought by apotemnophiliacs could never be a cure, regardless of whether or not it conserved (or increased) struggle.

Turn now to mild depression. Here, it would seem, the same set of observations applies as can be made of slow runners. As we saw in the previous section, a person's struggle – via therapy, introspection, or the hard work of maturation – can zeroly, partially, or even completely substitute for a cure. When we reverse the arrow, all possibilities would also seem to exist. On the one hand, cure needn't substitute one bit for struggle. Even if a person's mild depression is cured, it would make sense for her to continue the struggle – to continue the therapy, to introspect, to mature – in order to pursue an even higher level of mental awareness or control. Once a pill cures her neurotic unhappiness, she can transfer the struggle to Freud's ordinary, nonneurotic unhappiness. Writing of "Paul, the Renaissance historian who . . . off medication, could only imagine his feelings in childhood," Peter D. Kramer says that "on medication, he recaptures his past with all its richness of emotion, not least its pain. . . . For these people, . . . the drug seems to aid rather than inhibit the struggle to locate the self."[94] A cure for mild depression doesn't substitute for the struggle of maturation, introspection, and therapy in these cases, but rather allows that struggle – and the genuine subject who engages in it – to remain undiminished, perhaps even to expand.

Even those who criticize the use of Prozac for mild depression acknowledge that, in many cases, it simply gets rid of neurotically caused blockages or inhibitions, enabling the individual to continue a course of therapy, introspection, and maturation – to nonneurotically and clear-sightedly struggle with the real issues in her life – to far greater total effect. "[F]or purposes of the psychotherapeutic process," Elio Frattaroli writes, the main question is: "supposing that [Prozac] would take the edge off [of a patient's] moodiness, [would this] help or hinder her in getting in touch with whatever feelings might underlie [that] moodiness?"[95] Frattaroli acknowledges the possibility that Prozac might in fact help. But he also affirms the possibility that, on the other hand, it might not. All possibilities exist. Cure may well substitute not one whit for struggle; the patient might continue to pursue "getting in touch with her feelings" just as zealously if nonneurotically. But cure could as easily substitute for struggle, partially or wholly. With the edge taken off her moodiness, she might have no further interest in struggle.[96]

For neither the physically slow nor the mildly depressed, then, can anything be said thus far, and about the groups as a whole, as to whether cure substitutes for struggle. Certainly, cure can complement continued and utterly undiminished struggle, whether training, exertion, and exercise or therapy, introspection, and maturation. But cure, it would seem, can also substitute for struggle. In the first kind of case, where cure simply complements ongoing struggle, it would cause no retrenchment of the Kantian subject. Physical speed or a nonneurotic (or less neurotic) mentality would simply take its place as another gift outside the undiminished subject itself; but Kantians have no problem with such gifts as long as they don't erode the subject. And we will know that they haven't eroded the subject whenever struggle, the subject's mark, continues unabated. But in the second case – where the individual does allow cure to substitute partially or even wholly for her struggle – cure would have caused a retreat in the Kantian subject. The cure would have caused a diminution in genuine accomplishment and its replacement by something less than genuine, something artificial. In such cases, the Kantian would deem cure to be not a gift outside the subject but an enhancement encroaching on it. I will come back to the cases of physical slowness and mild depression, the most vexing ones for the question of whether cure abrogates individual genuineness, after first looking at cure's substitution for struggle in the other phenotypes.

Turn to the cases of blindness, deafness, and plain facial features. We saw in the previous section that struggle – the most effective actions that an individual can take against these phenotypes – does not as a rule substitute one whit for cure. Think of Georgina Kleege memorizing reading passages to veil her blindness, or oralism as an attack on deafness, or cosmetics and clothing to minimize plain facial features. Nor does struggle – using cosmetics to minimize one's black racial features – substitute one whit for a Michael Jackson pill (since Part 1 shows that "black racial features" are not a medical condition, the term "cure" could not be appropriate). It's more apt to say that the modes of struggle available to those harboring these conditions become ways of passing, and hence no more genuine than a cure/Michael Jackson pill would be.

Given this, how should we now approach the reverse-arrow question of whether, in the case of deafness, blindness, or plain facial features, a cure – and in the case of black racial features, a Michael Jackson pill – substitutes for struggle? If it does, even completely, it should be a matter of indifference from the perspective of Kantian genuineness. After all, a cure for plain facial features or blindness or deafness, or a Michael Jackson pill for black racial features, would simply be supplanting inauthentic struggle against the phenotype – passing, hiding, masking – and thereby putting it out of its misery. And, as it so happens, in each of these four cases, cures or the Michael Jackson pill would necessarily and entirely – not just possibly or partially, as with physically slow runners and mild depressives – substitute for whatever someone harboring the condition may have been doing to struggle against it.

There would be no continued need to struggle with lipreading if deafness were cured. There would be no continued point in struggling to memorize passages if one's blindness were cured. And there would be no continued purpose in struggling to use makeup or hair arrangements if one's plain facial features were cured or if one's black racial features were altered by a Michael Jackson pill. Of course, any given formerly black or plain-featured person might well continue using makeup or hair arrangements for other purposes: to be well-groomed, for example. But those purposes would be ones that she would have had all along, separate and apart from the (now superseded) purpose of also using makeup or hair arrangements to struggle against her black or plain features. These latter struggles are modes of passing, and so we should be indifferent between them, on the one hand, and plastic surgery or pills on the other.

Whichever way the arrow is pointing, then, we cannot – on Kantian grounds – classify cures for those with blindness, deafness, or plain facial features as enhancements. Nor, on Kantian grounds, can we categorize the Michael Jackson pill as an enhancement, although, of course, it is not a legitimate cure either. On the one hand, struggle never substitutes even one whit for a cure for blindness, deafness, or plain facial features, nor for a Michael Jackson pill. It simply becomes the endeavor to pass, mimic, or project without in any way achieving the traits of sight, hearing, beautiful facial features, or white racial features. And so the fact that, on the other hand, cure or the Michael Jackson pill will, as a rule, substitute entirely for such struggle means only that an inauthentic activity, not genuine accomplishment by the subject, has been precluded. From a Kantian perspective, there can be no objection to cures for blindness, deafness, or plain facial features, nor to the Michael Jackson pill for black racial features. None would constitute enhancement in the sense that it would render artificial something that could have been, let alone had been, achieved more genuinely by the subject. Instead, cured blindness, deafness, or plain facial features would be no more objectionable than innate sight, hearing, or beautiful facial features. And subjecting black racial features to a Michael Jackson pill would be no more objectionable, on genuineness grounds, than the struggle to pass.

Now consider anorexia and obesity. As we saw in the previous section, struggle in the form of diet, exercise, and therapy can substitute for a cure: sometimes only zeroly or negligibly, but oftimes partially and occasionally even entirely. In that way, anorexia and obesity resemble physical slowness and mild depression. But now, what happens when we reverse the arrow and ask whether cure substitutes for struggle? We will find a situation that differs from those of physical slowness and mild depression, where cure in some cases would substitute for struggle not at all, in others partly, and in still others entirely. For anorexics and the obese, speaking of them as groups and acknowledging the ever-present possibility of individual idiosyncracies, cure would necessarily substitute entirely for struggle. There would be no point to a person's continuing to diet, exercise, or get therapy, even one whit, once her anorexia or obesity is cured (permanently, as I am assuming) and she reaches the socially ideal weight. There would, however, be a point in a person's continuing to diet and exercise once her physical slowness had been cured and she reached a socially ideal running capacity. Likewise, there would be a point in a person's continuing to get therapy or self-explore once her mild depression had been cured and she reached a socially ideal mental state.

I want to be clear about what this means. I am not denying that an obese person cured of his phenotype might well continue to diet to fight cholesterol or ulcers. Similarly, an anorexic cured of her phenotypic anorexia might continue to need therapy for its underlying neuroses or anxieties.[97] But the obese person would have required that kind of diet even if he hadn't been obese and the anorexic that kind of therapy even if she hadn't manifested anorexia. In both of these cases – which in any event amount to individual idiosyncracies, not issues for the obese or anorexic as groups – cure would still inevitably terminate the rationale for some measure of struggle: that measure that had been involved in directly fighting the phenotypes of obesity or anorexia.

So whatever partial victory over her phenotypic anorexia or obesity an individual otherwise would have garnered genuinely by struggling – via diet, exercise, or therapy – a cure would, necessarily, rip it from the embrace of the subject. In its place would be complete victory over her anorexia or obesity but a more artificial one, one that had not been achieved by the subject. This, on a Kantian approach, would necessarily convert cures for anorexia and obesity into enhancements. Although it's likewise possible for cure to substitute completely for struggle in the case of the physically slow and the mildly depressed, it's also possible for them to be cured – brought to the socially ideal running capacity or mental state – without their giving up one jot of struggle. And in those cases, as we have seen, cures for physical slowness or mild depression would not, on Kantian criteria, be enhancement.

I take it that this set of outcomes violates our moral intuitions. We would, most of us, be more likely to view cures for physical slowness and mild depression than for anorexia and obesity as artificial enhancements. This is a situation in which "reflective equilibrium" suggests that we ought at least to modify, and if we can't modify then we should abandon, the Kantian approach. As it so happens, though, with a slight adjustment, the Kantian approach can generate a more acceptable conclusion.

Thus far, we have been assuming that any cure will be a full one. It will take a person from whatever state she would be in even if she hadn't lifted a finger to struggle against her condition – whether physical slowness, mild depression, anorexia, or obesity – and bring her to a populated social ideal. And I have argued that, in light of such a full cure, people with some conditions (physical slowness or mild depression) might still keep up the full measure of the struggle (diet and exercise or therapy and introspection) that they'd been waging against their phenotypic condition. But they might also do so only partially or they might do so not at all. Those with other conditions (anorexia, obesity), however, would – in light of a full cure – necessarily and entirely abandon the measure of struggle that they were waging against those phenotypes. In other words, we have been assuming that cure is full and that post-cure struggle can vary, depending on the condition, from as fully as before to zero.

But now, let's flip it around. Assume that cure needn't be full, that a doctor can apportion it in partial increments. She could still allot a full amount that would take the individual from his prior condition all the way to a populated social ideal. But she could also apportion an amount that would take him only partway in that direction. And assume that she would decide how much cure to give an individual by first looking at where struggle, if he were to continue exerting it as fully as before, would take him.

So, for example, a Kantian physician could say to an obese or anorexic patient, "I want you to keep up the full amount of struggle – exercise, diet, self-control – in which you're presently engaging, and then I'll offer you that measure of cure that will bring you the rest of the way to the socially ideal weight range." Assuming that they fully continue the level of struggle in which they are presently engaging, some fat people – those, say, whose struggles have brought them halfway toward the social ideal – will need less cure. Others – those whose struggles have brought them one-quarter of the way – will need more. But in neither case would the Kantian physician be violating her oath by prescribing a cure that shrinks the subject.[98]

This kind of approach might raise some eyebrows, but it would hardly be out of keeping with current medical practice. Doctors even now use the promise of medication or surgery as an incentive to induce struggle in their patients, including the obese and the anorexic.[99] More broadly, a physician might promise a patient gastric bypass surgery or a facelift only if she succeeds in her struggle to give up smoking.[100] Similarly, a Kantian psychiatrist could premise the prescription of a cure for neurotic depression on her patient's promising to continue the full amount of self-exploration, maturation, or "personal growth" – and, if needed, therapy – as before in order to struggle with ordinary unhappiness. Frattaroli, for example, essentially conditions the prescription of Prozac on a patient's agreeing to continue her sessions. Likewise, a sports doctor could premise the allocation of a cure for physical slowness on the runner's pledging to persist in diet, training, and exercise thereafter, to continue struggling as fully as before in order to achieve a speed even higher than cure alone could provide.

While a Kantian doctor could offer only a partial cure to obese or anorexic patients who continue to struggle against their conditions (a full cure would render struggle pointless), she could offer a full cure to physically slow or mildly depressed patients who continue their struggle, since full cure does not render their continued struggle pointless. In all of those cases, cure (in whatever full or partial increment) would take the obese, anorexic, mildly depressed, or physically slow person to the populated social ideal without falling afoul of the Kantian dictum that the subject continue its struggle as fully as before, that its acreage not be diminished.

But although this might be a step in the right direction, we are not done yet. Consider an obese person. Let us say that his struggle via diet and exercise has brought him from 350 to 250 pounds. The Kantian physician offers a partial cure that will take him from 250 to his socially ideal 150 – premised on the patient's continuing to struggle as fully as before – on the grounds that when cure supplants any part of struggle, it becomes enhancement. But what if the patient is also a Kantian and responds as follows: "Give me a full cure, so that I may cease struggling entirely against my obesity via exercise, diet, and therapy, and therefore embark on a new struggle, volunteering for Amnesty International"? He is asking the doctor to allow him not to shrink the acreage that his genuine self covers, only shift it. True, he would no longer be genuinely struggling to reduce his weight from 350 to 250. But for the first time, he would be genuinely struggling to achieve better conditions for political prisoners in Myanmar. "This is my prayer," says Eve Ensler in her play *The Good Body*: "to break free so that we may spend more time running the world than running away from it; so that we may be consumed by the sorrow of the world rather than consuming to avoid that sorrow and suffering."[101]

A Kantian anorexic could ask for a full cure on similar grounds. True, the personal territory under her subject's domain would shift post-cure. She would no longer be genuinely achieving whatever it was that therapy and diet were helping her to score against her condition. But her subject, her genuine self, would still encompass the same acreage, as long as she channeled the same amount of struggle in a new direction.[102] Cure would not make her life, as a whole, any easier and hence wouldn't constitute artificial enhancement.

Two things are key to the anorexic's or obese person's credibility in asking for a full cure while avoiding the Kantian concern that she will ease up on full (albeit rechanneled) struggle. First, a cure for anorexia or obesity is not prerequisite to any kind of further struggle in the realm of weight control. Once her anorexia or obesity is permanently cured, once she is brought to the populated social ideal of weight, there is no further point in a person's dieting or exercising for the particular purpose of gaining or losing weight. A Kantian doctor could not reasonably expect an obese or anorexic person to continue her struggles in that vein. Second, a cure for anorexia and obesity can be a prerequisite, for significant numbers of anorexic or obese people, to embarking on many other struggles in life, from intimate relationships to professional careers to campaigns for political office to working for Amnesty International. A Kantian doctor can reasonably assume – of anorexics as a group and of the obese as a group – that, once cured, they will take up struggle elsewhere. Of course, the Kantian doctor might not know the truth in any given individual case. But at the group level, she can assume that cures for the anorexic and the obese won't harm the subject.[103]

Neither of the two stipulations that apply to obesity and anorexia – that cure not be a prerequisite to any further struggle in the same realm, but that it be a prerequisite to struggle in many other realms – is true of physical slowness. First, as we have seen, a cure for physical slowness is indeed prerequisite to continued struggle in the realm of running: continued diet, training, and exercise. Once a runner is cured – once she is brought to the populated social ideal of running speed – there is indeed further point to her dieting, training, and exercising every bit as much as before for the purpose of increasing her speed beyond that which cure alone could provide. And hence the Kantian sports doctor can legitimately expect her newly cured runner to carry on not just the same extent but also the same kind of struggle as before.

Second, a cure for slow running is *not* prerequisite to struggle in other domains of life, save perhaps for some few that also fall into the athletic realm. The Kantian doctor can remain legitimately skeptical of a runner who says that she needs a cure for her physical slowness so that she can run for office. Imagine a runner who takes a full cure for her slowness. Now possessed of running gifts that equal Donovan Bailey's, she says that she doesn't want to be bothered to continue to struggle to diet, exercise, or train, to build on those gifts, because she now wants to devote her energies – her struggle – to campaigning for mayor. Or imagine a body builder who take a full cure, bringing his unimpressive body size, contours, and shape to the social ideal. He then foregoes any struggle to exercise, train, or exert himself further so as to score achievements beyond that ideal, saying instead that he wants to channel his struggles and energies into a gubernatorial race. In other words, imagine a slow runner or an unimpressive body builder who asked to be treated like an anorexic or an obese patient. She would tax credibility. Hence, it makes sense for the Kantian doctor to exact of runners, as a group, a continued commitment to struggle in exactly the same vein as before. It makes sense for the doctor to insist, of any member of the group, that he or she maintain as strict a diet, training, and exercise regimen as before, as a condition for a cure, in a way in which it wouldn't for anorexia or obesity.[104]

We could say the same thing about a musician who wanted to attain the social ideal, to play piano like Glenn Gould. She could legitimately be expected, now having been brought medically to the level of Glenn Gould's gift, to continue struggling unabated in the domain of music, just as Glenn Gould did. And if she did continue struggling, if she did continue to rehearse and practice every bit as much as before, then cure would not be enhancement for her. It would simply resemble Glenn Gould's natural gift. It would, however, be enhancement if the musician let up in such struggle, since being a socially ideal piano player is not obviously prerequisite to newly shouldered struggle in other domains of life. The subject's acreage would have shrunk. Some measure of the musician's struggle-born, genuine accomplishment would now be creditable to a medical intervention, hence artificial enhancement.

"I certainly can't take credit for any part of his golf game," said the physician who performed laser surgery on Tiger Woods. "I can only say that when you don't have to think about your vision any more, it gives you the ability to think about other things. . . . I believe this surgery gives you freedom to move on to something else."[105] If that "something else" is the struggle to read and calculate the ripples and furrows of the green now that the struggle to see it is surmounted – the golfer Dottie Pepper's caddy had to do that for her before she had laser surgery – then that's one thing. If that "freedom to move on to something else" is the ability to devote time and effort to starting a singing career, now that one can win golf matches without having to spend time and effort doing and recovering from eye exercises, that's another matter.[106]

Finally, what about mild depression? Imagine a patient who has been struggling against his neurotic depression – through therapy, introspection, self-exploration, and self-control – with whatever degree of success that his capacities, as he is exerting them, allow: His struggle substitutes, at least to some extent, for cure. His psychiatrist now has the ability to entirely eradicate that neurotic depression with a pill. Will such a cure substitute for struggle? Conceivably the patient, if cured of all of his neuroses, might believe that further struggle is no longer necessary for him (as Frattaroli worries) or, perhaps, that it is no longer possible. Yet the former reaction seems more characteristic of euphoria, and the latter of deep depression, than of a cure for neurosis that would send the patient on her way to confront, in a clear-eyed way, whatever unhappiness – and happiness – her life throws at her. Far from "robbing life of the edifying potential for tragedy," as Peter D. Kramer says, Prozac "catalyzes the precondition for tragedy, namely participation." Certainly, as a general statement about the group of mild depressives as a whole, it's plausible to think that super-Prozac would.[107]

Let me approach the question of whether a cure for mild depression will preserve struggle by comparing it with cures for slow running or amateur piano playing, on the one hand, and for anorexia or obesity on the other. On the one hand, as I argued, while being able to run like Donovan Bailey or play like Glenn Gould seems prerequisite to yet further struggle in the realms of running (further exercise and training) or piano (further practice and coaching), it does not seem prerequisite to struggle in any other domain. On the other hand, a cure for obesity or anorexia doesn't seem prerequisite to any further struggle in the realm of weight loss or gain, but it does for struggle in other domains, from the political to the athletic to the commercial to the romantic.

Now, what of a cure for mild depression? As it happens, such a cure shares characteristics with both a cure for slow running/amateur piano playing and a cure for obesity/anorexia. A cure for mild depression resembles a cure for slow running or amateur piano playing because it can, even for Frattaroli, be prerequisite to further struggle in the same domain, the domain of (now neurosis-free) personal exploration, self-understanding, introspection, and therapy. But a cure for mild depression also resembles a cure for obesity/anorexia, because it seems prerequisite to new struggles in any number of realms outside the domain of continued focus on self-exploration and self-analysis. For a therapist like Adam Phillips, the point of overcoming one's neuroses is definitely not to enable a person to struggle further to explore his own mind in an unclouded way. Rather, it is to allow the person to forget about himself for once and channel his struggle toward changing the world – to politics, the arts, social action.[108]

Even now psychiatrists (and psychoanalysts) cure patients of their neuroses via talk therapy, say goodbye to them, and then propel them out into the world with the expectation that they will continue to struggle and grow, except in a way no longer burdened by the neurosis cured. There's no reason why expectations shouldn't be identical with a super-Prozac that cured neurosis. So for mild depressives as a group – there are always individual idiosyncrasies – it is reasonable to acquit cure of the Kantian worry that it might be enhancement. With full cure, there is no structural reason to believe that struggle will abate. The genuine self, the subject, will remain whole, undiminished.

If we are "listening," to borrow Peter D. Kramer's term, very carefully to those who are neurotically depressed or anxious, or to physicians who write about them, we might hear a different concern about curing mild depression. Not all of the struggle to which a condition gives rise consists of attempts to erode or even mask it. Far from masking the condition, some such struggles reveal it. Think of a deaf person's struggle to learn and communicate in sign language or an autistic person's struggle to find and then execute the behaviors that for him will be adaptive in different environments, from flapping and bouncing to various degrees of withdrawal or refractoriness. Other struggles, far from eroding, in fact build on the condition, as when a deaf person, absent aural means of accessing the world, struggles to develop his other senses and attains for them an unusual degree of acuity, or when an autistic person, "[a]bsent . . . intuitive means to make sense of the world," struggles to develop and rely "heavily upon his analytical, logical abilities."[109]

Neurotic depression, too, gives rise to both kinds of struggle, the ones that reveal instead of masking and the ones that build on instead of eroding the condition. Consider, for example, the tendency for depressives to exhibit "diffidence": to assume the worst about any potential endeavor and to be pessimistic about their own abilities.[110] One could argue that such diffidence, though it hardly masks but (if anything) reveals their condition to the outside world, is actually adaptive for depressives. It "promot[es] escape and avoidance of situations" that could depress them further.[111] In the same way that flapping or withdrawal can create a level of social comfort for autistics, or signing can for the deaf, diffidence does for the mildly depressed/anxious person. It allows him to control the amplitude, to adjust the level of his engagement with the world in an optimal way.[112]

In addition to being diffident, however, neurotic depressives are also notably "artful."[113] They worry, and in worrying devise stratagems that can be extremely valuable, building upon and indeed capitalizing upon – just the opposite of eroding – their fretful condition. Foreseeing obstacles everywhere, "[d]efensive pessimists . . . those who set unrealistically low expectations," are continually anticipating and then figuring out how to surmount whatever barriers could possibly lie in their way.[114] In the same manner in which many deaf people channel their perceptual struggles into fostering highly developed senses of sight or touch, and many autistics route their cognitive struggles into the development of advanced analytical or scientific capacities, many depressives funnel their struggles with worry and anxiety into generating superior faculties of planning and strategizing. If we are listening to some neurotic depressives or to those who write about them, then, we might hear the following question posed: What would a cure for mild depression do to these struggles, struggles that do not mask or erode but rather reveal or utilize mild depression: the struggle to maintain an adaptive level and style of diffidence, and to develop and execute a functional measure of artfulness?

It doesn't matter that we might view diffidence or even artfulness as undesirable traits. What matters is that they represent genuine traits, traits for which the depressive subject struggles and makes its own. They are authentic characteristics, part of who the neurotic depressive is – part of the subject – and the Kantian doctor's goal is to ensure that cure would not erode that subject. The mild depressive who struggles to maintain an adaptive measure of diffidence, especially in today's environment of expected sunny extroversion, has clearly accomplished something, developing a trait that is part of who he genuinely is. It is on grounds of authenticity that Carl Elliott mourns the disappearance of the diffidence that goes with mild depression, lamenting what he sees as its replacement, thanks to Prozac, by an ersatz gregariousness in American social life.[115] One of Peter D. Kramer's Prozac-taking patients who claimed to experience a shrinkage of his genuine self, and an accretion of the artificial, did so because he felt the loss of his worry-born artfulness. He sensed an attenuation of the edgy looking-around-corners view of the world that he had built on the foundations of his neurotic depression. And he regretted its creeping replacement by what he took to be an ersatz what-me-worry cheeriness.[116]

The question, though, is not whether the mild depressive's personality traits of diffidence or artfulness would disappear with a cure for anxiety or mild depression. The question is whether there is any reason, speaking of mild depressives as a whole, to believe that those traits won't be replaced by others just as genuine. Here's one way to think about it. Recall, from Part 1, that neuroses generally distribute themselves on bell curves throughout the population from overly anxious to overly unperturbed, overly solemn to overly vivacious, overly sad to overly euphoric, and so forth. The kinds of neuroses that "mild depression" denotes fall on the anxious, solemn, or sad side – what Kramer calls the "dysthymic" side – of these respective curves. They usually involve a self-punishing person's seeing himself and his world as worse off than than they actually are; hence the traits of diffidence and artfulness.

But neurosis also embraces those ego-protecting individuals who, whether overly unperturbed, extroverted, or content – whether "fatuously optimistic" or "pleasantly grandiose" or imbued with "inflated . . . self worth"[117] – fall on the other side of these curves, what Kramer calls the "hyperthymic" end, tending to see themselves and their world as better off than they really are.[118] Just as the mild-depressive neurotic, who is unhappier with his lot than is appropriate, might develop a guarded diffidence with which to approach social reality, the self-inflated neurotic, who is happier with his lot than is appropriate, might nurture a self-satisfied complacency. He might develop the self-placating attitude that his life requires no further major reckonings or tweakings.[119] Also, just as a mild-depressive neurotic's fear of failure can inspire not only diffidence but great artfulness, a self-inflated neurotic's belief in his own inevitable success frequently induces not just complacency but surpassing boldness.[120]

Again, it doesn't matter, for our purposes here, that complacency or possibly even boldness might be considered undesirable traits. What matters is that they represent genuine traits, part of the self-inflated individual's subject, his authentic personality: part of who he is. We recognize such breezy complacency and brazen boldness, in other words, as double-barreled characteristics of an authentic personality type. A cure, we can imagine, would make those traits disappear. Would any replacements be as genuine? Or would the cure represent an artificial change in the self-inflated neurotic's personality?

Let's look at the two types of neurotic mentality, the mild-depressive and the self-inflated, in tandem. What a cure could well do is not so much eradicate their genuine personality traits as transform them into nonneurotic equivalents. So, for example, cure might well enable us to say good-bye to the mild depressive's diffidence, a trait that flows from his tendency to see himself and his world as worse off than they are, his tendency to see failure around every corner. But once he is cured of his neurosis, would we not then welcome his struggle to achieve humility as he now nonneurotically embraces his successes, his ordinary, appropriate happiness? And isn't humility but a preferable, indeed a nonneurotic, version of diffidence?

Cure, likewise, would allow us to bid adieu to the self-inflated individual's complacency, a trait that flows from his propensity to see himself and his world as better than they are and to view his life as one personal triumph after another. But once he is cured of his neurotic need to maintain that perspective, would we not then welcome his struggle to achieve acceptance as he now nonneurotically acknowledges his failures, his ordinary, appropriate unhappiness? And isn't acceptance but a preferable, indeed a nonneurotic, form of complacency?

Now what about the mildly depressed person's artfulness, which flows from his neurotic tendency to see the threat of failure everywhere? And what about the self-inflated person's boldness, which flows from his neurotic need to believe in his own inevitable success? Again, cure need not eradicate these traits so much as transform them. Boldness is not quite the same thing as courage, and courage is what the former self-inflated individual would have to struggle to attain, now that he must confront his failures in a nonneurotic way. Nor is artfulness quite the same thing as imagination. Yet imagination is what the former mild-depressive would have to struggle to cultivate, now having to embrace his successes in a nonneurotic way, knowing that once he has done so, he will then have to conceive of how to move beyond and transcend them.

With a cure for neurosis, whether of the mild-depressive or the self-inflated version, struggle as a rule needn't end. Nor need the authentic subject remain anything less than whole, although it certainly will change. There won't be as much mild-depressive neurotic expectation of failure, and there will certainly be less of the unquestionably authentic personal traits of diffidence or artfulness that it can foster. There will, though, be more call on the cured individual to develop, through personal struggle, the humility and the imagination that a nonneurotic embrace of one's successes can inspire. Likewise, there won't be as much of the self-inflated person's neurotic need to believe in his own inevitable success, and there will be less of the personality traits of complacency or boldness that it can precipitate. There will, however, be more call on the cured individual to authentically develop, through personal struggle, the capacities for acceptance and courage that a nonneurotic awareness of one's failures can inspire.

The concern that I have examined, here in Part 2, is that cure becomes enhancement when it shrinks the subject, replacing some measure of struggle-born and hence genuine achievement with easy, hence artificial, accomplishment. On the Kantian understanding that gives the most cogent meaning to this concern, cure escapes the charge of enhancement if it manages to allow the subject to continue the same amount of struggle as before. True, whatever an individual accomplishes with that cure might be greater in total than what he had been achieving without it. But it wouldn't be less genuine. Kantians, after all, acknowledge that the subject necessarily wages its struggle based on traits that lie outside of it, traits that it had no hand in creating. What counts, as far as achievement goes, is the magnitude of that struggle. As long as such magnitude remains undiminished, then any new trait born of cure – any new accomplishment – is, from a Kantian perspective, no more objectionable than an innate one. Like any innate one, it lies outside the subject. Cure becomes enhancement only when it encroaches on the subject by diminishing struggle. Here the new trait would be worse – less admirable, less genuine, more artificial – than the struggle-born trait it supplants.

I applied this approach to each of the eight phenotypes and, staying at the group level that allows us to fly above individual idiosyncracies, pursued the Kantian criterion wherever it would lead. At the end of the chase, and speaking of those harboring each condition as a group, it would appear that cure is not enhancement for seven out of the eight. For some of those groups – the blind, the deaf, the plain-featured – there is no genuine struggle, only modes of passing, for cure (or, in the instance of black racial features, a Michael Jackson pill) to supplant. For other conditions – anorexia, obesity, or mild depression – it would be reasonable to believe, of these groups as a whole (if not for each idiosyncratic individual anorexic or obese or mildly depressed person) that cure won't supplant genuine struggle, though it will shift that struggle.

Although the question that I posed in Part 2 concerns individuals, and especially individual authenticity and artificiality, I endeavored to answer it at the group level. I explored how far we could go by speaking at group levels of generality so as to avoid having to consult individuals' idiosyncratic views as to what medically induced traits would make them feel authentic and what false. But that does not mean that the group always gives an unequivocal response. It does for the seven phenotypes I have just mentioned but not for physical slowness. Here, where cure would bring the individual to a populated social ideal of world-championship running, or in similar cases in which it would bring an individual to (say) the populated social ideal of virtuoso cello playing, the claim that cure equals artificial enhancement has to be judged individual by individual.

What's key, though, is that it is not the individual himself, using his own subjective sense as to what he needs to be authentic, who gets the final say. Rather, in the wake of a group's not giving rise to a general rule, it is society itself, in the form of its representative, the Kantian doctor, who makes the decision on an individual-by-individual basis. In a way, this flips what happened in Part 1, where even though the question had to do with social normality, the matter of what's socially normal had to be settled from the group perspective, the perspective of the group harboring any given condition. And sometimes – as with mild depression or plain facial features – the group itself did not generate a definitive answer. In which case, however, it didn't fall back on society to say what's socially normal, but to each individual group member himself.

With physical slowness, cure is prerequisite to continued struggle in the sphere of running, but it is not prerequisite to struggle in any other domains of life. The Kantian doctor or trainer can quite legitimately require the cured runner not to ease up on her struggle in the realm of running – diet, exercise, and training – even one whit in the face of a cure. And the Kantian doctor would have no reason to believe, of any runner who did ease up, that the cure was somehow necessary to newly enable struggle in other spheres of her life. Speaking of physically slow runners as a group, any runner who, in the wake of a cure, did ease up on her running-related struggles would be allowing cure to erode what would otherwise have been some measure of genuine achievement. She would be permitting the cure to eat away at the acreage that falls within the compound of the genuine self. For such a runner, supersteroids would be artificial enhancement. The Kantian doctor should say no.[121]

3

Cultural Spouses, Cultural Siblings

Turn now from the question "when does cure become enhancement?" to "when does cure become cultural genocide?" Suppose that we eliminate deafness, plain facial features, or obesity. Would we not wipe out the cultural traditions associated with those conditions, from ASL, to "beauty is only skin deep" stories to the comedy of Dawn French? Of course, not all of those harboring any given condition will opt for a cure once one is available. Those worried about cultural genocide, however, acknowledge this. Their concern is that whatever damage a phenotypic cure does to a group's cultural tradition, it will begin far below the level at which every group member takes it. And it will simply grow more serious as more do take it. The question is: How exactly should we conceive that damage? What claim could group members who value their condition on cultural grounds lodge against medicine for developing a cure, and against society for funding and permitting it through the state?

Much of the debate concerning cultural genocide, and I'm of course speaking specifically of cultural genocide debate surrounding attempts to draw limits to medicine, pivots on groups' claims to have evolved a culture. But cultural status, especially for the particular groups in question, is a vexing thing to measure. So I suggested in the Introduction that in place of our conventional focus on the meaning of "cultural" in "cultural genocide," we concentrate instead on the meaning of "genocide." The conventional issue is something like this: "Assume that a cure that all took would destroy the particular life experiences associated with a given condition, along with the language, literature, music, dance, and theater interpreting and expressing those experiences. Now: do those experiences and art rise to the level of a genuine culture that deserves

141

protection?" A more pertinent question would be: "Assume that the experiences and art associated with obesity, deafness, mild depression, or any
such condition rise to the level of a genuine culture. Still, would a cure,
even one that all took, necessarily destroy that culture?"

As I have indicated, my own view is that no usable criterion exists for
answering the conventional question, for determining the extent to which
different groups, such as the deaf or the obese, have evolved genuine
cultures. But the fact of the matter is that members of these groups, in
equating cure with cultural genocide, try to do so by arguing that they
have evolved cultures of sufficient substance so as to place obligations on
the rest of society for their protection and nurturance. So before turning
to the matter of genocide, I first want to argue that even if a group's
claim to being a cultural one could be established in a way acceptable to
all parties, it wouldn't, in fact, have any bearing on whether and when cure
becomes cultural genocide. No matter how elaborate a group's culture
can be shown to be, and no matter how extensive its rights to recognition
and preservation are, none of that can defeat any given person's right
to exit the culture if he so desires. And all that cure does, assuming it
is justified on the grounds I outlined in Parts 1 and 2, is provide group
members – the deaf, the obese, anorexics, and others – with a means
of exit. Even if one can show incontestably that a group's culture is vast
and venerable, that in itself won't suffice to ground a cultural genocide
argument against members taking a cure. We have to look elsewhere.

Cultural Exit, Not Cultural Genocide

Let me show this by looking at some of the arguments groups make for
cultural recognition and support. I am not denying that arguments as to
how much and in what ways a group has evolved a genuine culture – a
language, a literature, a history of oppression – can be keenly relevant
to the question of how society, and the state in particular, should accommodate the various rights to recognition and assistance that the group
might assert. It's just that the question of how and in what ways the state
should accommodate a group's cultural rights, whatever they may be, is
irrelevant to the question of whether the state can in addition offer a
cure.

This is an important point to establish, since many group activists
believe that if the state has obligations to accommodate, to protect and
foster a group's culture, then it cannot in all consistency offer a cure
as well. After all, the very implication of a cure is that it would be best

for the group to disappear. Jan Branson and Don Miller write that "in Australia in 1991, the government's language policy recognized Auslan (Australian Sign Language) as the language of the Deaf community and yet, at the same time, poured copious funding into the development of the Australian Nucleus-22 [cochlear] implant."[1] In so saying, Branson and Miller seem to suggest that the government was contradicting itself, that whatever accommodation of the deaf community's cultural rights it furnished by recognizing Auslan was undercut by its support of the implant. But society's accommodating a condition's culture while at the same time providing a cure involves no contradiction.

To see this more fully, we must first take a brief tour of the kinds of accommodations that groups, on the basis of their claims to have evolved a genuine culture, typically demand. Accommodations come in two categories, "attitudinal" and "environmental"; begin with the attitudinal. Different groups might want society to adopt an attitude of respect toward them for different reasons. One group, for example, might want outsiders to respect it because of the ways in which the group values itself. This is a traditional multicultural demand that invites the rest of society to actually adopt, incorporate, or at least see things from the perspective of some of the group's own social or moral values so as to better appreciate the group on the group's own terms.[2] Alternatively, a group might insist simply that outsiders respect it in spite of the ways in which those outsiders may *disvalue* the group, given those outsiders' own moral or social values. This is a traditional *modus vivendi* demand that removes respect from the vagaries of mutual feeling or understanding, placing it on firmer footing than that allowed by a hit-or-miss attempt to bridge a gulf in social or moral values.[3]

Some groups, though – the obese, perhaps, or those with plain facial features – might ask for "aesthetic and carnal" attitudinal accommodations that "a traditional politics of equal rights," focused as it is on the accommodation of the group's social and moral values, "is not fully equipped to deal with."[4] We normally don't think that it's society's responsibility to concern itself with aesthetic or sexual attraction.[5] But, as Carl Elliot notes, "idiosyncratic preferences," such as the desire for a tall lover, can "almost always be redescribed as oppressive ideology." Such desires "might *seem* a likely candidate for the kind of idiosyncratic aesthetic preference" that we "can legitimately have," Elliott writes, "[y]et when growth hormone for short children was being debated in the mid-1980s, partisans were quick to point out that greater height for men is identified not only with . . . increased physical attractiveness [and] sexual desirability" but, both derivatively and independently, with greater "business success, and political electability."[6]

As long as the aesthetic and the sexual remain matters of personal taste, society has no obligation (or right) to try to alter them. If, however, groups can plausibly argue that those tastes translate into political or economic barriers, then society might have further responsibilities. At the very least, groups such as the obese or the plain-featured or the short might demand that the media – television, plays, fiction – show group members winning approval on nongroup members' "aesthetic or carnal" values. In other words, a group might reasonably ask that the media portray, as typical, a person outside the group being attracted to group members because of the ways in which that *outsider* values them, on her own aesthetic or sexual criteria. In Neil LaBute's play *Fat Pig*, "Tom is attracted to [the obese] Helen simply because he finds her lovely," which is precisely what is so gratifying to Helen.[7] Alternatively, a group might want the media to portray, as typical, someone outside the group who is attracted to group members despite the ways in which those members disvalue themselves aesthetically or sexually; despite the fact that group members, stricken with the low self-esteem that accompanies their conditions, do not meet their *own* criteria for aesthetic or sexual appeal.[8]

So groups can place a variety of demands for attitudinal accommodations on the rest of society: Respect us because of how we value ourselves on our own social-moral criteria or respect us despite how you disvalue us on your social-moral criteria. Appreciate us because of how you value us on your aesthetic-sexual criteria or appreciate us despite how we disvalue ourselves on our own aesthetic-sexual criteria.

Now consider a few examples of environmental accommodations that groups demand, accommodations having to do with the workplace, the classroom, or the public sphere. Many of the groups under discussion here – pointing to a record of historical oppression – seek some form of affirmative action, whether through the Americans with Disabilities Act or the civil rights laws. Beyond this, the types of environmental accommodations that groups pursue tend to implicate the structure of time and space. So, for example, the blind require accommodations, from Braille elevator buttons to guide dogs, that enable them to share access to spaces – offices, schools, auditoriums, and arenas – on the grounds that others already have such access. True, some blind activists continue to believe in separate schools and workplaces. But overwhelming numbers of "[f]ull inclusionists" among the blind, following the spirit of the Americans with Disabilities Act and the Individuals with Disabilities Education Act, now denounce separate schools and workplaces "as the moral equivalent of slavery and apartheid."[9] And while blind activists seek access to space because others have it, they also, when it comes to environmental accommodations, seek access to time precisely because others won't have it. Blind workers or students, for example, require extra time to complete professional or school tasks, despite the fact that nonblind workers or students don't have similar access. Indeed, if the nonblind shared such time, the purpose would be defeated.[10]

Other groups, such as some organizations representing American blacks, currently assert demands for temporal-spatial accommodation that take the reverse form: access to time *because* others will share it; access to space *in spite* of the fact that others wouldn't share it. Because black high school students get taught the histories of other groups, black leaders have argued that school time should be dedicated as well to black history, an exposure that they expect nonblack students to share.[11] Because blacks take work time off for holidays devoted to nonblack historical figures or (arguably) nonblack cultural traditions, black leaders have made the case that worktime should be devoted as well to marking black historical figures or cultural traditions, the observance of which many expect their nonblack colleagues to share. Martin Luther King Day is the obvious example, but Kwanzaa also qualifies; Kwanzaa, Anna Day Wilde writes, is meant to "involve . . . people of all races, despite the efforts of some exclusionists."[12] When it comes to space, though, in spite of the fact that white university students don't, and shouldn't, have their own exclusive spaces, some black student groups are seeking spaces – their own college dorms or even entire universities – that they pointedly do not expect others to share.[13] Notwithstanding the fight to racially integrate the public school system that has been going on for over a century, there have been times in the recent past when "[i]ncreasingly, all-black schools [have been] established by black-controlled school boards" and when "statistics [have] show[n] an increasing popularity of the roughly 100 historically black colleges and universities."[14]

So in brief, the kinds of environmental accommodations that groups demand embrace everything from shared space and nonshared time to shared time and nonshared space. And the kinds of attitudinal accommodations groups seek can include social-moral demands that others "respect us because of how we see ourselves" or "respect us despite how they see us." They can also include aesthetic-sexual demands that others learn to "love us because of how they see us" or "love us despite how we see ourselves."

Whether and to what extent society *should* accommodate any given group in these various ways will, to a large extent, depend precisely on whether and in what ways the group plausibly claims to have evolved a culture. It will depend on the group's claims to have a history of oppression, or a richness of way-of-life, or a music, art, and literature worthy of redress, recognition, or preservation. True, accommodating the blind, say, with extra work time and Braille elevator buttons currently serves, in part, as a substitute for a still nonexistent cure. But once a cure is available, the only justification for society's continuing to provide such accommodation would be a successful claim by blind activists that theirs is a group with a culture, a way of life along with the art expressing and interpreting it, that requires protection and nurturance.

Of course, what each group's culture requires by way of attitudinal or environmental accommodation will differ. A history of oppression implies affirmative action. A language implies interpreters. More broadly, suppose that the group has evolved a culture that it has a call on society to accommodate. Then nothing about the cultural character of its members – their wearing turbans, their observing holidays, their inability to see or hear, their weight – should place them at a disadvantage in society at large. It's possible, of course, that an individual outside any putative cultural group might also want to wear unusual apparel, or seek days off to go sailing, or feel more comfortable in a large airplane seat. But without any group-cultural significance, these aspirations would simply form aspects of a lifestyle that society would have no obligation to accommodate.

So the question of whether and in what ways a group's experiences, history, and art add up to a culture *is* very much relevant to the question of whether and how society should accommodate it. But now, I want to argue, the issue of whether and how society should accommodate a group's culture is irrelevant to the issue of whether society should offer cure. The claim that a group is a cultural one – and that society should accommodate it by any number of attitudinal or environmental means – cannot, in and of itself, defeat the simultaneous claim that it is a medical condition requiring a cure.

First and most fundamentally, however extensive a group's rights to cultural survival and flourishing may be, such group rights cannot ultimately trump an individual member's right to exit the group. A "well-ordered multiracial society," Randall Kennedy says in *Interracial Intimacies,* "ought to allow its members free entry and exit from racial categories . . . ."[15] Even the staunchest believers in group rights concede that whatever rights to accommodation blacks, aboriginals, or religious minorities might legitimately assert in aid of their cultural security and enrichment, they cannot include the right to stop people from leaving the group. "[A]t the very least," Joseph Shapiro writes, "cultural minority groups must leave their members an exit option."[16]

But once it's determined that a cure is legitimate from a medical point of view – that it doesn't constitute enhancement according to the criteria set out in Parts 1 and 2 – then, from a group-rights point of view, cure simply becomes a mode whereby an individual can exit. Yes, that mode would be given a boost by the state, through its funding the development and delivery of the cure. But if members have the right to exit a group, then why shouldn't the state be able to convert that right from a hollow wish into a reality? Group-rights theorists have always conceded that the state can do any number of things to assist members of (say) religious groups who wish to exit, such as providing income to women seeking to quit marriages in which, according to group customs, the husband controls all the property. From the perspective of any given cultural group, much that the state already does – funding public schools, educating about safe sex – eases, indeed induces, exit by group members. So why shouldn't the state finance a cure if on medical criteria a cure wouldn't be enhancement and on cultural criteria it's simply a means of exit?

Of course, the state's supplying a cure is a distinct method of aiding group exit, different from its supplying public schooling or secular divorce laws. But at the level that concerns us, this is a distinction that doesn't matter. It's simply an artifact of any given group's particular nature and circumstances. Members of different groups will always require different kinds of assistance – from cures to secular divorce laws to public schooling – to make the right to exit a reality. But that just mirrors the fact that they require different kinds of accommodations, from interpreters to holidays to extrawide airplane seats, to make real the legitimate cultural rights (whatever they can be argued to be) of those who want to remain in the group. Cure stigmatizes a group no more than does any other mode of assisting the right to exit, especially when, at the same time, the state is according that group whatever accommodation the group can justifiably seek. In any event, it is not the state's offering a cure that stamps the condition as a medical one. Rather, it's the capacity of those group members who want to exit – on criteria I set out in Parts 1 and 2 – to legitimately claim that it's a medical one that justifies a cure.[17]

It is not the case, then, that "mak[ing] the social world more accessible" to a group would mean "society's accommodating" a group's environmental needs "*rather than* using medical science to prevent or

correct [the condition]."[18] Nor need "the laudable fight to change negative attitudes toward" the obese, the deaf, the blind, or others be under-
mined if the state at the same time develops cures.[19] Society can quite
consistently offer a means of exit while combating social, political, aesthetic, or carnal discrimination as indicated against those who choose
to remain: fighting "sizeism" against the obese, "sightism" against the
blind, "audism" or "hearism" against the deaf, or "looksism" against the
plain-featured.

Indeed, there is no inconsistency in society offering a cure while at
the same time according a baseline respect to all individuals harboring a
given condition. And that applies even if those individuals are unable to
argue (or don't wish to argue) that they have spawned a culture and therefore possess group rights to accommodation. There is no inconsistency
between society's pursuing a cure for cancer, on the one hand, and treating individual cancer patients with basic human decency and respect, on
the other, even if cancer patients as a whole don't want to insist that they
possess a group culture. Nor should there be any contradiction between
society's finding and delivering a cure for deafness or obesity, say, and
according this basic human respect to deaf or obese individuals, regardless of whatever further accommodation they might demand as members
of a cultural group. Even Michael Fumento, one of the most outspoken
advocates of eradicating obesity – of encouraging fat people to exit the
group – takes care to emphasize that "this doesn't mean oppressing fat
people."[20]

Without in any way working at cross-purposes, then, society can quite
effectively assist those group members who seek to exercise their right to
exit by furnishing a cure while at the same time helping to realize whatever
group rights to cultural accommodation those who choose to remain can
legitimately demand. If we are looking for a cultural argument against
cure, we haven't yet found it.

Here's another candidate, a different version of the either/or argument
that we cannot both accommodate a group's legitimate cultural needs
and offer a cure: Even if *society* can quite consistently walk and chew gum
in this way, the psychology of *groups* is not so versatile. Once a cure is
found, it's naive to think that any group can long abide some members
viewing their condition as a medical one and seeking exit via cure, while
others regard it as culturally valuable enough to be accommodated. The
concern is this: If a cure is offered to those blind or deaf or obese people
who do view their condition as a medical one, then those who would have

preferred accommodation will begin to feel coerced into taking the cure as well. Suppose that group numbers start dwindling due to cure. More and more of those who might otherwise have chosen to remain blind or deaf or obese, growing increasingly isolated, will experience mounting pressure to abandon what they genuinely regarded as their own culture, their own traditions, their own way of life – and take the cure.

I believe that this concern is overstated. Suppose that those group members who would like to remain blind or deaf or obese successfully argue that their group has rights to be accommodated, that the group in some way rises to the level of a culture. Then, even as society offers cures, modes of exit, to those who want to leave, it would also have to accommodate, in the appropriate attitudinal and environmental ways, those who wish to remain. In doing so, society will tack against whatever pressure those group members who view their condition as a culture might feel – pressure to take the cure – from those who view it as a medical condition. In fact, such accommodations, whether attitudinal or environmental, might even attract as many people away from getting a cure as a cure will arm-twist those who would actually prefer accommodation.

In any event, coercion is a two-way street. Yes, those who prefer accommodation may well fear feeling coerced into taking a cure if one is offered. But won't those who would prefer a cure feel coerced – indeed, more than coerced – if a cure isn't offered? After all, they will be forced to continue in the group against their wishes. They will be compelled to remain afflicted with what (assuming they successfully meet the criteria set forth in Parts 1 and 2) they legitimately believe to be a medical condition. Many believers in the idea that deafness is a culture oppose oralism – learning lipreading and speech – because oralism enables a deaf person to participate in the hearing world. Oralism, in other words, equips the deaf individual in some sense to exit the group, possibly pressuring others to follow suit. Yet those very same activists, who believe that deafness is a culture and push for manualist training in ASL, are vulnerable to exactly the reverse charge. "[F]ull immersion in the ASL culture at an early age," David Ingram writes, "might well prevent exit from that culture in later life . . . ."[21]

In all eight groups – the blind, the deaf, the obese, the anorexic, blacks, mild depressives, cosmetic surgery seekers and even slow runners – one can find some members who want to leave, via a medical procedure, and others who prefer accommodation through attitudinal and environmental change. There are those who seek to exit and those who are devoted to the cultures that each group has spawned, from anorexia's quasi-religious intimations to angst-ridden comedy to minor league athletics.[22] And the fact that groups themselves are divided on the exit/cultural accommodation question allows us to dispose of one final concern that frequently comes up: the issues of false consciousness and bad faith.

If some group members think that their condition is something to be dealt with medically, so the worry goes, could we not ask whether they have fallen victim to false consciousness? Perhaps they desire a medical procedure only because they have adopted society's demeaning view of their deafness or obesity or plain facial features or physical slowness. In that case, in yet another variation of the either/or argument, a medical procedure wouldn't be the answer; accommodation – in which society altered its prejudiced attitudes and disabling environments – would be. But could we not turn the question around on those group members who believe that their condition should be accommodated? Couldn't we ask whether their thinking so isn't really a form of bad faith? Perhaps they are deluding themselves, out of a misguided need for self-esteem, into thinking that their condition is something intrinsically wonderful to be cherished, preserved, and accommodated when in fact it isn't. It's just a particular body weight or nose shape, or, in the case of blindness or deafness, an actual disability.

Where debate is so lively – where groups are divided and each side is available to keep the other honest – I think that we have to call such situations ones of disagreement on the merits, not false consciousness or bad faith. The hard-bittenness of those who have come to view their condition as one to be treated medically will tack against any bad faith, any misbegotten self-regard that might lurk in the view, held by others, that their condition is one that's preferrably accommodated. Conversely, the view that their condition is worthy of accommodation will challenge any false consciousness, any internalization of society's broader prejudices, that might operate on those who see their condition as a medical one necessitating a medical procedure. The fact that even, in the face of the other, each side holds fast to its views means that we have to credit both with being well-considered.

Indeed, not only need a group as a whole not adopt an either/or stance – either treat the condition medically or else accommodate it – but individual group members need not do so. In her book on cosmetic surgery, Kathy Davis writes of her friend who was "a feminist, and as a feminist she was very critical of the suffering women have to endure because their bodies do not meet the normative requirements of feminine beauty. She found such norms oppressive and believed that women in general should accept their bodies the way they are . . . yet she wanted cosmetic surgery. Was this false consciousness? . . . [N]o, she was just as critical as I of the beauty norms."[23] Even individual group members, it seems, can at one and the same time seek a cure *and* demand that society change its attitudes and environment to accommodate wrinkled skin or obesity or slow running. So why should the group – let alone society as a whole – have to take a stand exclusively one way or the other on that question?

I will now end what has been a bit of a detour. The point has been to show that group-rights claims for cultural accommodation cannot ultimately settle the question at hand here, which is whether the state should refrain from offering a cure for a particular condition on the grounds that, in doing so, it would be committing cultural genocide.[24] We have no more reason to conclude that those who seek a cure are burdened by false consciousness, by an internalization of social prejudices against their group's condition, than we do to conclude that those who seek cultural accommodation might be encumbered by bad faith, an unwarranted attachment to that condition. Those who seek a cure and begin to deplete group numbers are no more coercive of those who would like to remain in the group than those who oppose a cure, seeking cultural accommodation instead, are of those who would like to leave. Nor are those seeking a cure asking society to do anything inconsistent with its attitudinally or environmentally accommodating those who don't want a cure, in whatever way – depending on the group's claim to be a cultural one with its own history, art, and experiences – is indicated. Finally, and ultimately, cure is simply a means of exit that will always trump group rights to cultural accommodation, no matter how full-blown they are. But if group cultural rights do not ground an argument against cure, then on what grounds, if any, can we ever say that cure is cultural genocide?

Group Genocide or Cultural Genocide?

So far, in looking at cultural genocide, I have focused on the cultural part of the term. Even if one's culture is so extensive and elaborate as to justify a range of accommodations, those facts themselves can never establish that cure is anything more than legitimate cultural *exit*, not a form of illegitimate cultural *genocide* that somehow abrogates the culture's rights. Now, let me focus on the genocide part. And here, one further distinction needs to be made. We have to be careful not to confuse *cultural* genocide with *group* genocide.

Suppose the "worst-case" scenario occurs, in which every group member takes the cure. Certainly, the group itself would cease to exist: There would no longer be a group of people called the obese or the deaf or the blind. Nevertheless, the group's culture might still survive in society as a whole – in those who never harbored the condition but who came to value its culture – and in the individuals who formerly harbored the condition and who came to embody its culture. Assume that (some) members of the group legitimately regard theirs as a medical condition on the criteria I set forth in Parts 1 and 2. Then they are certainly entitled to know that the group's culture, and not just the group, will be threatened before we can ask them to give up cure on the grounds that it is cultural genocide.

So the double-barreled question is this: First, even if a cure eradicates the group, is there reason to believe that its culture can and will live on in society as a whole? Will it live on in those who never harbored the condition but who – in the Trudeauesque spirit of "embrac[ing] any style, cultural trope, or image of beauty that attracts [them] regardless of its origin" – can and might preserve many of the group's traditions?[25] And second, will the group's culture continue to live on, even if a cure eradicates the group, in the cured individuals who formerly harbored the condition? Is there reason to believe that it might live on in those individuals who, along the lines set out by Kymlicka, need to retain elements of the late group's culture to structure their identities? Every individual requires "cultural resources" to "navigate [his] way through life," Bhikhu Parekh writes, and, specifically, those particular cultural resources that played a role in shaping his identity to begin with. Without them, the individual courts "psychological and moral disorientation."[26]

By looking at each of the eight conditions, I will endeavor to show, we can make reasonable statements as to whether its culture is likely to survive the group's disappearance. We can say something about whether it will survive in society as a whole – in those who never were part of the group – and in the individuals who formerly comprised the group. And suppose that, upon investigation, we conclude that as a result of cure, the culture associated with a condition will probably disappear with it. Suppose that it is likely to become lost to the individuals who formerly comprised the group, so that they would now be bereft of the identity-structuring cultural continuity whose importance Kymlicka identified. And, likewise, suppose that the culture associated with the now-vanished condition is also likely to become lost to society as a whole – to those who were never part of the group but who, in Trudeauesque fashion, would have benefited from its continuing richness. Then we can begin to speak about cure as cultural genocide or, at the very least, about its inflicting cultural harm.[27]

In what follows, I assume that the experiences and art associated with each of the eight conditions rise to the level of a genuine culture. And I ask whether cure, assuming the "worst-case scenario" in which everyone took it, would necessarily destroy not just the group, but its culture. Would it obliterate that culture from society as a whole and from the individuals who no longer harbor the condition (and who, therefore, no longer make up that group)? Here I follow Lawrence Blum and equate the "culture" or "cultural tradition" associated with a condition with two things: first, the kinds of life experiences that that condition brings to a person harboring it, and, second, the art, literature, plays, music, and dance that express or interpret those experiences. Blum calls the latter "cultural products," and I will refer to the former as "cultural experiences" since, together, they form a "culture" or "cultural tradition."[28] By using the term culture or cultural tradition to capture the experiences and art associated with any given one of the conditions, I am totally bypassing the issue of whether group A's experiences and art rise to a certain threshold of cultural richness, while group B's do not. I will assume that the experiences and art associated with all of the eight conditions amount to cultures. And the question will be whether, by our curing the condition (or offering a Michael Jackson pill in the case of black racial features), its culture would cease to live.

I take it that a culture would not, on Blum's definition, be a living one if its art were simply preserved in libraries or museums. Nor would it be living simply if, at some point in the future, artists create works concerning it. Ancient Egyptian culture is dead notwithstanding the British Museum or Norman Mailer. A culture lives only if people – in the cases here, people who never had or no longer have a particular condition – nevertheless continue to have the kinds of experiences with which it is associated and, contemporaneously, create art expressing and interpreting them.

By the same token, a culture would not necessarily die if only some of the experiences with which it is associated, or the art expressing and interpreting them, peter out. "We can reject the idea," Brian Barry says, "that the elements in a way of life are so rigidly locked together that no part can change without causing the whole to disintegrate." Suppose that, for conservation reasons, the Canadian government prohibits the Musqueam Indians of British Columbia from fishing on the Fraser River, a traditional rite of the band. We would no more want to say that their culture has been eradicated, Barry says, than we would "define personal identity so that it was destroyed by a change in circumstances."[29] Cultures evolve, burying some of their characteristics – sometimes as a result of external interventions, sometimes as a consequence of internal eruptions – without themselves dying. Perhaps what a phenotypic cure will eliminate is only part of the culture associated with any given condition, in the manner of prohibiting the Musqueam from fishing on the Fraser. Cure would change that culture, certainly, but not wipe it out as a whole. Yet how can we tell whether whatever is lost culturally due to cure is merely part of a culture that continues to live or, catastrophically, the entire culture itself?

Assuming, as I am, that everyone harboring a phenotypic condition took the cure (or, in the case of black racial features, the Michael Jackson pill), let's identify in general terms what we would lose before we determine whether, for each specific condition, such a loss would rise to the level of cultural genocide or merely cultural change. We would lose the life experiences – and the art expressing and interpreting those experiences – that are directly attributable to the phenotype itself. Some of those experiences, and the correlative art, would be validating, light-hearted, or celebratory: anorexic chic, fat pride, the anticosmetics movement, dramatic works in the genre of *Children of a Lesser God*, memoirs such as John Hull's *Touching the Rock*, innumerable contemporary comic takes on neurosis, Black Is Beautiful, or "hare and tortoise" stories. And, over time, we would lose all that.

There is a sense, though, in which we cannot regret some of the cultural loss that cure or, in the case of black racial features, a Michael Jackson pill might occasion. Many of the life experiences associated with deafness or obesity or black racial features – as well as the art interpreting and expressing those experiences – come from the prejudice or oppression that these phenotypic conditions elicit. "[M]uch of . . . black culture," Lawrence Blum says, "is bound up with resistance to, or otherwise coming to terms with, racist oppression . . . [v]arious forms of black music – spirituals, blues, rap – are also deeply implicated in the experience of racist oppression."[30] Undeniably, if no one continued to possess black racial features, the black experience of racial oppression, along with the cultural products associated with it – the music, the memoirs, the fiction – would come to a terminus. But, of course, blacks and nonblacks alike fight against racist oppression, just as East European writers and activists fought against Communist oppression, while still acknowledging that the experiences of such oppression and the cultural products it inspired formed an invaluable cultural tradition.

To the extent that (say) a Michael Jackson pill for black racial features would eliminate racist oppression, it would bring no more – and no less – cultural genocide than would the fulfilled hopes of the most fervent groups-rights advocates of black cultural survival. Such advocates are obviously prepared to believe that the cultural tradition of American blacks will survive the end of the oppression they fight so hard against; it will be changed, certainly, but it will still live on.[31] So it would seem that our question, for each of the various conditions, must be this: Would whatever we might lose culturally due to cure – beyond the experiences and art elicited by oppression or prejudice against the obese, the deaf, the plain-featured, or the others on account of their phenotypes – amount to cultural death? Or would it simply constitute change in a culture that would continue to live in society as a whole and in the individuals who formerly harbored the condition? For seven of the eight conditions, I will argue, cure would bring cultural change. For one, it would spell a kind of cultural death.

Cultural Spouses

I want to begin by establishing, and then exploring the implications of, the following claim. The terms "blind," "deaf," "black," "depressed," and "slow" are used, even now, to describe people who are not phenotypically, literally blind, deaf, black, depressed, or slow. This is not the case with "anorexic," "obese," or "plain-featured."

Consider first blindness and deafness. "The fact that 'normal' people can get around, can see and hear, doesn't mean that they are seeing or hearing," Erving Goffman quotes a patient as saying; "they can be very blind to the things that spoil their happiness, very deaf to the pleasure of others."[32] Or as William Osler once remarked, "half of us are blind . . . and we are all deaf."[33] We cannot, of course, take Osler's and Goffman's usages of "blind" and "deaf" literally. But I do think we have to take them seriously. What they suggest is that two different phenotypes – the phenotype of being literally blind and the phenotype of being metaphorically blind – can, at one level, give rise to common life experiences, the experiences of being blind. With phenotypic literal blindness, that blindness takes a more directly perceptual form, as when a literally blind person is unable to see light or color. With phenotypic metaphorical blindness, it might assume a more cognitive meaning, as when a literally sighted person registers only a part of what he literally sees. Or it can assume the more psychological meanings that Goffman and Osler identify. And, of course, the same is true of deafness.[34]

Writing of "blindness both real and metaphoric," Naomi Schor declares that "the two are bound up with one another."[35] Though the phenotypic lenses (perceptual versus cognitive/psychological) through which they manifest may differ, there is a sense in which both blindnesses carry a large kernel of common experience, at least common enough that they share the same name: blindness. And because at one level they give rise to the same experiences, and indeed share the same name, I will describe the two phenotypes – literal and metaphorical blindness– as "cultural spouses." Of course, those experiences, in turn, give rise to cultural products: art dealing with the inability to see perceptually, cognitively, psychologically. Indeed, ofttimes that commonality of experience gets recognized in one and the same "cultural product." In Raymond Carver's story "Cathedral," a literally blind man helps a literally seeing man understand his psychological blindness. H. G. Wells's allegory "In the Land of the Blind" explores the similarities between the two phenotypes of blindness, literal and metaphorical. Again, all of this is true of deafness.

In a certain sense, there are more than two phenotypes of blindness here. Within metaphorical blindness, we could identify a range of cognitive and psychological blindnesses, from the blindness involved in missing your turnoff, to the blindness implicated in not seeing that your mate is cheating on you, to the blindness entailed by being unaware of the import of major political events. But, then again, there is certainly more than one phenotype of literal blindness, since literal blindness varies from the legal to the total. Whether literal and metaphorical are each one or many is irrelevant here; what matters is the existence of cultural experiences of blindness beyond the literal. With this caveat – one that will apply to my discussion of several other conditions – I will refer to the literal phenotype and the metaphorical phenotype while recognizing that there can be pluralities of each.

I think we have to credit this idea – that phenotypic literal blindness and phenotypic metaphorical blindness are cultural spouses (and likewise for the deaf) – for one reason in particular. Members of the phenotypically literally blind and phenotypically literally deaf communities themselves, as well as those who are close to and study them, forge such links. They make deep connections between, on the one hand, the experiences and art of literal blindness/deafness and, on the other hand, the experiences and art of the metaphorical blindness/deafness visited on those who can literally see and hear.

Even the "unimpaired human eye," Georgina Kleege writes in her memoir of blindness, *Sight Unseen*, "provides the brain with such a surfeit of visual information that only a certain amount consciously registers at any moment. In effect, your brain privileges certain aspects of the retina's images and disregards others . . . . "[36] Oliver Sacks quotes a blind woman, Arlene Gordon, offering a still more metaphorical reference: "Sighted people enjoy traveling with me . . . I ask them questions, then they look, and see things they wouldn't otherwise. Too often people with sight don't see anything!"[37] And, perhaps more metaphorically still, Naomi Schor speaks of the "psychical blindness . . . of the sighted."[38]

In a similar vein, Walker Percy, in his foreword to Henry Kisor's *What's That Pig Outdoors? A Memoir of Deafness,* describes the book as an "account from a novel perspective of the universal human experience . . . of the breakthrough into language. Or what should be a universal human experience. For in fact some of the beneficiaries of this book could well be not only the deaf . . . but so-called normal hearing people who have still not made a breakthrough into this kind of literacy." Literal deafness affords its own phenotypic lens; it gives Kisor his "novel perspective." But that perspective opens onto a far more "universal experience" of deafness: the fallibility of human communication and understanding. And Kisor's book is itself a cultural product expressing and interpreting that experience.[39]

Speaking of such cultural products in general, Trent Batson and Eugene Bergman, in their collection of fiction by and about the deaf, write that "deaf characters work well in the imagination of writers who are trying to transmit a sense of the modern condition as they see it . . . . It seems that a large segment of people today . . . feel they too are 'deaf' in the sense of being ignored, not heard, lost in a world which they cannot understand." Stories by and about the deaf, as Batson and Bergman say, are "allegor[ies] about communication (or lack thereof) between people . . . get[ting] to one of the key aspects of the deaf experience, the limitations of all forms of human communication."[40]

The phenotypically literally blind and the phenotypically literally deaf, then, often see their own experiences of blindness and deafness reflected in those of the phenotypically metaphorically blind and the phenotypically metaphorically deaf. They identify the experiences that their own phenotypes cause as part of a common body of experiences that those with different phenotypes, the phenotypes of metaphorical blindness and metaphorical deafness, also cause. It is as if literal blindness and metaphorical blindness were spouses and their common experiences – and the art expressing and interpreting those experiences– were their progeny. And the same, again, for deafness.

In making this spousal cultural connection between their phenotypes and those of others, literally blind and deaf writers depict their own particular experiences of blindness and deafness as parts of larger cultural traditions. Certainly, with a cure for literal blindness, the cultural tradition comprising experiences of blindness, and the art dealing with them, would be altered, just as the cultural tradition of the Musqueam would be altered if they could no longer fish the Fraser. But just as the cultural tradition of the Musqueam will live on, in a Brian Barry sense, postprohibition, so will the cultural tradition of blindness – the cultural experiences and art of blindness – live on in metaphorical phenotypes, following a cure for its literal variant: changed, but certainly living. And the same, again, for deafness.

It's true that if all blind and deaf people were to take the cure, the groups "deaf" and "blind" would disappear. But what concerns us here is that the group's culture live, which it can do even if the group itself disappears due to its members exercising their right to exit, their right to be cured of what they can legitimately deem to be a medical condition. And so our focus shifts from the group to the social and individual levels. On this kind of liberal valuation of culture, only two things matter. First, even if the group disappears due to cure, will its cultural tradition continue to live on in society as a whole? And, second, will the individuals who formerly harbored the condition – who formerly comprised the group – discover enough cultural commonality between their pre-cure and post-cure selves that they won't find their previous experiences totally "erased," as Kymlicka says – that they won't suffer cultural shock in the new world? If the answer to both questions were no, then we could begin to talk about cultural genocide.

But, for the blind and the deaf, the answer to both questions inclines far more toward the affirmative. Post-cure society will retain the cultural traditions that comprise experiences of blindness and deafness, as well as the art that expresses and interprets those experiences. Those traditions will be changed, but they will live. And individuals who were formerly blind and deaf will find in their post-cure situation a world that doesn't wholly, and therefore jarringly, differ from their pre-cure one. What will remain as a continuing thread, as Walker Percy says, are the challenges thrown up by partial apprehensions – now more cognitive or psychological than perceptual – along with the fulfillment that comes when fuller understanding is achieved; and, as well, the art that expresses and interprets such experiences. Blind and deaf writers, who weave their own expressions of phenotype into broader expressions of metaphorical blindness and deafness, attest to this.

One loose end concerning blindness and deafness. Suppose that we compared the blind and the deaf according to the traditional approach to cultural genocide, the one that assumes cure would extinguish a group's experiences and art, and then tries to assess whether those experiences and art rise to the level of a culture. We might conclude that the deaf have a greater claim than the blind to cultural protection. ASL displays more of the characteristics of a language, including its own grammar, than does Braille. And, in fact, deaf activists have been considerably more vocal on the cultural genocide front than their blind counterparts. But on the analysis I have offered here we should, in making the cure/genocide cut, move away from group-on-group comparisons of linguistic or artistic development. Instead, we should assume that each group's experiences and art rise to the level of a culture. And we should then ask whether those experiences and that art would live on post-cure, changed perhaps but far from terminated, in society as a whole and in the individuals who formerly harbored the condition. Our reasoning would then be more or less the same for the blind and the deaf. Both have cultural spouses.

If ASL were to cease being a living language due to a cure for deafness, that would obviously be a poignant loss. But cultures can survive – and have survived in a Brian Barry sense – though their languages may no longer be living ones; and, of course, vice versa. In their introduction to *Deaf in America: Voices from a Culture*, Carol Padden and Tom Humphries state that "in contrast to the long history of writings that treat [the deaf] as people with 'disabilities,' who 'compensate' for their deafness by using sign language, we want to portray the lives they live, their art and performances, their everyday talk, their shared myths, and the lessons they teach one another."[41] Padden and Humphries's understanding of culture, centered as it is around the experiences associated with deafness and the art interpreting them, comports with the one I am using. Many of those experiences and artistic works, as Padden and Humphries document them, have to do with failures and successes in the broad domain of human communication, including lampooning the extent to which hearing people fail to hear one another. Experiences and art of this sort would survive the disappearance of deafness and even of ASL: changed, in a Brian Barry sense, but very much alive.[42] None of this, of course, means that ASL cannot or should not be accommodated with various linguistic protections, assuming that the deaf community can claim group cultural rights. It is only to say that since no such group rights can preclude a deaf person's right to exit due to cure, there wouldn't be a genocide argument against cure either.

I previously argued that a Michael Jackson pill enabling blacks to acquire white racial features would not be a legitimate medical procedure. Medical science should not develop, or doctors prescribe, such an item. But I nevertheless want to give some thought to the cultural consequences of a Michael Jackson pill. I do so to emphasize that the principal grounds for opposing the pill are precisely that it falls outside the bounds of legitimate medical cure, and not – with an important qualification to come later – that it would spell cultural genocide.

Here, it's significant that black writers often use the term "black" metaphorically to describe the life experiences of people who are not phenotypically literally black, along with the art that those experiences inspire. Toni Morrison famously called Bill Clinton "the first black president," meaning that he "displays every trope of blackness: single-parent household, born poor, working class, saxophone-playing, McDonald's and junk-food loving boy from Arkansas."[43] I call metaphorical blackness a phenotype simply because, following Fukuyama's definition of phenotype, it is identifiable as a set of "conditions and behaviors." Among them are the "tropes" that Morrison lists: single-parent household, born poor, working class. And this phenotypic metaphorical blackness, according to Morrison, leads to a set of life experiences in common with those to which phenotypic literal blackness leads. In Morrison's truncated list, these experiences would apparently involve cooking and eating certain foods, but they would also include a long list of encounters with obstacles set in place by the economic, social, and legal systems.

Certainly, literal black phenotypes have elicited a purely racial oppression that metaphorical black phenotypes will never know. But, as I have argued, anyone who cares about the preservation of black American culture would prefer to lose whatever part of it comes from those experiences of oppression than to continue that oppression for the sake of the culture it provides. To borrow from Maurice Berger, "Are we [saying] that black people don't matter unless they're oppressed?"[44]

But, of course, "we" are not. Phenotypic literal blackness also gives rise to any number of non-oppressive experiences, and artistic expressions and interpretations of those experiences, that do exclusively concern a literal black phenotype. Those experiences and art would survive the end of racism but not a Michael Jackson pill for black racial features, assuming that everyone took it. Such experiences – "experiences peculiar to being black in this society," as James M. Jones writes – "represent aspects of black culture that do not include features common to others."[45] Consider, as an obvious example, any cultural trope that falls even remotely under the rubric Black Is Beautiful.

And yet, Toni Morrison's comments imply, of the cultural experiences to which phenotypic literal blackness gives rise, only part are those to which phenotypic literal blackness *exclusively* gives rise; many, as Jones himself says, are "common" experiences.[46] Many, in other words, are also caused by metaphorical blackness. "[D]epression, bad faith, poor nutrition, poverty and self-doubt. The young black kid growing up in Bed-Stuy," Stephen Talty writes, "has far more in common with . . . the white Appalachian teen than he does with the black middle-class homeowner anywhere in this country."[47]

A point of clarification. Any particular person who is literally black might also, at the same time, be metaphorically black: in Morrison's terms, born to a single parent, poor, and working class. For such a person, both her literal and her metaphorical blackness can and often will elicit life experiences of hardship, estrangement, or invisibility and, if she is so inclined, art expressing and interpreting them. My point is not that phenotypic literal blackness and phenotypic metaphorical blackness sort themselves into exclusively different individuals. Rather, it's that they each – independent of the other – give rise, in America historically and today, to a set of common cultural experiences, experiences of striving against the odds, sometimes succeeding and sometimes failing; and, derivatively, to a common tradition of art.

Readers who for whatever reason don't like the term "phenotypically metaphorically black" to go with "phenotypically literally black" can simply recast my point in different language. Specifically, we could just as easily say that phenotypic literal blackness and phenotypic literal whiteness are married in a particular family of cultural experiences and products of the sort that Toni Morrison, Stephen Talty, and others sketch. We would then simply have to bear in mind that while by no means do all of the experiences and art of the phenotypically literally white have to do with the sense in which they are "black," neither do all of the experiences and art of the phenotypically literally black.

The tendency for black writers to find a common black experience and culture in metaphorical black America has itself become something of a cultural trope. So has the same tendency for those nonblack commentators who study black experience and culture. "Blackness becomes a cultural style," Onyekachi Wambu says, "a signifier that has floated free of its moorings in pigmentation."[48] "[A]bandoning race might feel like giving up black culture," Lawrence Blum writes, "[b]ut I think this is not so. . . . Abandoning race would perhaps affect the way some black Americans think about their relation to their cultures. It might, for example, weaken a sense of *exclusive possession* of them. . . . Whites, Latinos and Asians can learn to sing gospel, and perform and develop jazz and hip hop. This is all to the good. . . . "[49] "Black culture," Stephen Talty writes, "has been one of [white Americans'] chief resources. The rap music that so many white teenagers grow up with is only the latest chapter in an old story."[50]

David R. Roediger has pioneered the study of "wiggers" – "wigger" being a term that some (although by no means all) observers believe "originated among African Americans to denote whites who seriously embrace . . . African American cultural forms and values." In his book *Colored White*, Roediger notes that the criminologist Zaid Ansari, "moved by white young people's enthusiasm for a music that honored Malcolm X . . . raised the possibility of significant numbers of whites 'becoming X.' "[51] In explaining "how white southerners came to have the right sensitivity for cutting R&B hits for black audiences," Vron Ware and Les Back quote the white rhythm and blues musician Rick Hall from a 1977 interview: "I think that black people and white people in the South – and I consider myself poor white trash – the black people and the poor white trash have a lot in common that they don't even know they have. Their skins are [a] different color, but they had the same hardships. I picked cotton, hoed corn, went barefooted. My daddy cut my hair under the shade tree with a pair of scissors. I shared the same depression, the same thoughts that the black boy did who was poor also, and picked cotton and did all those things. . . . *The same culture, right. At the same time, a different color.* . . . "[52]

In his famous 1970 essay "What Would America Be Like without Blacks?," Ralph Ellison takes a position far removed from any claim that the disappearance of black racial features would be a form of cultural genocide. The "values and lifestyle [of] most American whites are culturally part Negro American without [their] even realizing it," Ellison declares. Walt Whitman, Ellison continues, "view[ed] the spoken idiom of Negro Americans as a source for a native grand opera"; that idiom was "absorbed by [other] creators of our great nineteenth-century

literature. . . . Mark Twain celebrated it in the prose of Huckleberry Finn."
Indeed, he may even have celebrated it in the speech of Huck himself,
as Shelley Fisher Fishkin has argued.[53] On the subject of black music,
Ellison describes soul as an "expression of American diversity within
unity, of blackness with whiteness."[54] Ellison's purpose, which he achieves
magnificently, is to establish the irreplaceable value of black culture, not
just to blacks but to whites in America. But for my purposes, the value
of a culture, its richness and texture, are not at issue. What is at issue is
American black culture's capacity to survive a Michael Jackson pill for
phenotypic black racial features. Precisely because of its vibrancy, Ellison
provides ample reason to believe it would survive, though it would change
as cultures always do.[55]

Much of the cultural experience and art to which a literal black phenotype gives rise is also caused, and therefore shared by, a metaphorical
black phenotype, by whites and other nonblacks who, in various ways, are
metaphorically black.[56] Those experiences, and the cultural products
they inspire, would survive the disappearance of black racial features
with sufficient robustness that the same term – "black" – can evidently
apply. The phenotypes literally black and metaphorically black, then, are
cultural spouses. They are married in a particular family of cultural experiences and products, one that would live on in society as a whole even as
it would undeniably change, in a Brian Barry sense, due to the loss of one
of its parts: the literally black phenotype part. "The same culture," as Rick
Hall says, would live on, even if one of the "different color[ed]" lenses
through which that culture is experienced would no longer exist. That
cultural tradition would also remain available – everything from gospel
to rap to life experiences of struggle and dignity – for formerly literal-
phenotypic black individuals who find meaning and beauty in them, many
of whom are also themselves metaphorically black.

I am not claiming that the disappearance of black racial features would
be a matter of indifference; far from it. I'm claiming only that – precisely
since such a disappearance would signify a change, not an end, to black
culture in America – it cannot rise to the level of a cultural genocide
objection against a black person exercising her fundamental right of
group exit, whether by taking a Michael Jackson pill or through some
other means. In a world in which there are reasons not only to accept
but encourage interracial intimacy, and in which the very notion of phenotypic racial features is a troubled one, it is a very good thing that the
survival of black culture needn't rely on preserving a literal black racial
phenotype on any understanding of that concept.

I earlier quoted Randall Kennedy, who in his book *Interracial Intimacies* says that a "well-ordered multiracial society . . . ought to allow its members free entry and exit from racial categories. . . ."[57] As the previous discussion argues, there is abundant reason to believe that black culture would survive group exit due to interracial marriage, or via the breaking through or remaking of what are already fungible and fragile racial categories, and so there can be no cultural genocide argument against these enterprises. True, as I argued in Part 1, there is one mode of exit that should not be available to black Americans, namely, a medical procedure, and that stands. It would seem, though, that even if that mode of exit were legitimate too, there would be no cultural genocide argument against it.

And yet, this is not quite true. There is a sense in which a Michael Jackson pill would amount to cultural genocide, whereas other modes of exit from black racial categories would not. Before exploring it, however, I must discuss the remaining conditions.

What of mild depression? The term "mildly depressed" is not applied only to those who are, in fact, phenotypically mildly – that is, neurotically – depressed: those whose unhappiness is neurotically disproportionate to their experiences and that a super-Prozac would be meant to cure.[58] It is also used to describe those who are phenotypically *non*neurotically depressed: those who are ordinarily unhappy in the Freudian sense, those whose unhappiness is proportionate to their experiences. What Peter Whybrow says of major clinical depression – it bleeds into "despair and human misery, conditions people consider to be part of the slings and arrows of life" and "not a human illness"[59] – can be said of phenotypic mild, neurotic depression. It bleeds into the phenotype of ordinary unhappiness, meaning that the range of life experiences to which each of these two phenotypes give rise – discontent, unfulfillment, self-absorption, angst – are of a type, as are the cultural products whose creation they provoke.

Even now, it is often impossible to differentiate the experiences of neurotic mild depression from nonneurotic ordinary unhappiness, to say nothing of the art that each motivates.[60] If the two phenotypes are spouses sharing such a close cultural marriage and producing the same kinds of progeny (even if some offspring look more like the neurotic parent and others more like the nonneurotic one), would not the cultural tradition of neurotic mild depression live on, post-cure, in the cultural tradition of nonneurotic ordinary unhappiness? After all, are they not the same tradition?[61]

Certainly, there would be a loss of the experiences and artworks that are informed substantially or exclusively by the phenotype of neurotic depression. We would have less of the neurotically depressed Woody Allen and more of the nonneurotically depressed Ingmar Bergman, whom, in any case, Woody Allen even now seeks to emulate. We would have less early Philip Roth and more later Philip Roth. But, as Brian Barry says, cultures are always changing in the face of new external and internal developments. A cure for phenotypic neurotic depression, even assuming that every neurotic depressive took it, would not amount to cultural genocide (unless, perhaps, the cure was a euphoric that wiped out ordinary unhappiness too, but that is not at issue here).

True, the group "neurotic depressives" would disappear. But our concern lies with whether a cultural tradition of which it is a part could survive in society as a whole, post-cure, as well as in those individuals who formerly harbored the condition. Whatever cultural riches come from the experience of neurotic depression, and from the art dealing with it, they will not entirely be lost to society as a whole: The neurotic might disappear, but not the depression. Nor – if Woody Allen's identification with Ingmar Bergman is any indication – would individual former neurotics find themselves adrift in a world bereft of the cultural significance they attach to the unhappy state of the human condition.[62]

Finally, I would say the same for slowness. The term applies to both the phenotypically physically slow and the phenotypically nonphysically slow: being slow at work, being slow at school. And since "physical slowness," as I am using the term, can mean being slower not just than the many but the few, not just than the norm but the populated ideal, so does "nonphysical slowness."

The two phenotypes, physical slowness and nonphysical slowness, are cultural spouses. They give rise to a common set of experiences of challenge, frustration, trial, and elation. And, in turn, those experiences give rise to a certain set of interpretive and expressive cultural products, on the theme of the hare and the tortoise, for example, or on how it isn't whether you win or lose. That art, certainly, is colored by the different phenotypic lenses of the physical and nonphysical variants. But at one level, it deals with a common experience of slowness. And at that level – and in a Brian Barry sense – the pertinent cultural tradition would survive a cure for phenotypic physical slowness. Whatever cultural riches the experience and art of slowness give to society as a whole would outlive a cure for the physical variant, the slow runner. And, given that few of us are good at a great many things, so would whatever cultural context the challenges betokened by slowness provide to individual runners who were formerly physically slow.

In describing competitive bicycling as a "metaphor for life . . . exalting and heartbreaking and potentially tragic, [full of] setbacks, and . . . hand-to-hand battle[s] with failure," Lance Armstrong signals that, in crucial ways, the experience of being slow would live on even if all cyclists, and by implication all runners, were fast.[63] Indeed, just as Peter D. Kramer speaks of the "valorization" of sadness, of cultural efforts to preserve and value a depressive state, there are movements afoot for the valorization of slowness, cultural efforts to nurture slowness – even with its entailed consequences of not coming in first – in "spheres of life" outside the athletic.[64]

When it comes to the blind, the deaf, blacks, (mild) depressives, and the (physically) slow, the fact that these terms extend themselves to cover nonliteral phenotypes argues that, at one level, the cultural traditions of which they are a part can live on after them. Yes, those traditions would undergo change. Whatever the experiences are that have most specifically to do with the literal phenotypes themselves – walking with a white cane, using an ASL interpreter, Black Is Beautiful, neurotic sensations of insignificance, feeling less gifted than Carl Lewis – they will disappear, along with the art that expresses and interprets them. But the experiences to which such literal phenotypes give rise are not all so tightly bound to them that, at one level, other phenotypes cannot also cause the same kinds of experiences: the experience of driving the same road for ten years but never seeing the landscape around it, of listening to what your spouse says but not hearing it, of encountering social hurdles and overcoming hardship, of the existential confrontation with death, or of finishing in the 30th or 50th or 80th percentile in the Law Scholastic Aptitude Test (LSAT). Those experiences, and whatever art they provoke, will survive the cures we are contemplating.

It's true that many of these surviving cultural experiences would center on obstacles and limitations. Think of the barriers to communication that metaphorical deafness causes or the deck-stacked-against-you that metaphorical blackness elicits. Consider the existential discontents that nonneurotic ordinary unhappiness initiates or the frustration that nonphysical slowness provokes. In noting that such experiences would live on after the disappearance of phenotypic literal deafness, black racial features, neurotic depression, or physical slowness, I'm not saying that these experiences are all necessarily good ones. But black culture (for example) will very much continue to comprise the story of struggle against stacked decks, even absent a Michael Jackson pill. And not only are such obstacles the stuff of black cultural experience and art, so is each triumph over an obstacle. As each is overcome, black culture will evolve in new directions, and assimilate new grist for the mill, unknowable today. Black culture can and will change over time, even absent a Michael Jackson pill.

In arguing that these various cultures can survive the disappearance of their underlying phenotypic conditions, I am making no claim about whether each will survive *as is* into the indefinite future. My only claim is that each will survive, in a Brian Barry sense, into the immediate future. I am assuming only, as Kymlicka says, that people "are initially bound, in an important way, to their own culture." As long as "initially" that culture survives post-cure, the identities of those individuals taking the cure will not suffer the break that Kymlicka fears: even if, over time, the culture changes, as that culture surely would even if the condition did not disappear.[65] Likewise, if its culture will inevitably change over time even if a condition continues to exist, then we cannot expect any less fluidity if the condition disappears and its culture has to rely for its survival on its continuing to live on in society as a whole: in those who, never having harbored the condition, nevertheless, in cosmopolitan fashion, value and perpetuate the experiences and art of its culture.

My assertions about the survivability of blind, deaf, black, mild-depressive, and physically slow culture amount to informed speculation, not conclusive proof. Yet total certainty is not what we require, since there is an implicit burden of proof here. I have argued that a Michael Jackson pill for black racial features would be illegitimate on grounds set out in Part 1, namely, that black racial features cannot legitimately be seen as a medical condition. But for a cultural genocide argument against a Michael Jackson pill, or against any other form of exit from a group, to be successful, those seeking to exit are entitled to know that if everyone acted on that right, the group's culture would die. Not just change but end, vanishing from society as a whole and the individuals who formerly harbored it. Those who want to exercise their right to exit are entitled to know, on the preponderance of the evidence if not beyond a reasonable doubt, that the consequences of their doing so, on the worst-case

scenario on which no one continued to harbor the literal phenotype anymore, would be cultural genocide. For cure or a Michael Jackson pill to be
legitimate on cultural genocide grounds, it is enough to cast reasonable
doubt on the proposition that the group's culture would consequently
end, not prove it absolutely wrong. And that is what I have attempted to
do here.

Now turn to the remaining three phenotypic conditions: obesity, plain
facial features, and anorexia. These terms do not extend themselves in the
same metaphorical way to embrace cultural spouses. True, we sometimes
speak not just of a literally phenotypically fat person but of a wealthy
person, metaphorically, as "fat." And we occasionally speak not just of
a phenotypically plain person but of a simple, unvarnished person as a
"plain fellow." Yet we are not talking of cultural spouses here.

Why not? Let me begin with an observation meant merely to be suggestive; it may well admit of quibbles, but I think it hints at something
important that I will then explore further. Consider that even when we
use the term "fat" to describe the wealthy, we usually conjure up the physically corpulent Diamond Jim Brady, not the physically lean (and hungry)
Ivan Boesky. And even when we use the term "plain" to describe someone
unvarnished, we generally do so concerning a person who is also physically plain: plain-spoken, plain-featured Abe Lincoln. If we wouldn't use
the terms fat or plain metaphorically unless the individuals concerned
were also fat or plain literally, then are wealth and unsophistication really
cultural spouses to phenotypic fatness or plainness?

If a wealthy person were not literally fat, then we wouldn't see him
as metaphorically fat. And that suggests that there is no common culture of fatness to which wealth independently – in the absence of literal
fatness – contributes. If an unsophisticated person were not also physically plain – if she instead were physically beautiful – then we wouldn't
see her as metaphorically plain. The beautiful Queen Esther appeared
before the king of Persia in plain garments and was herself unsophisticated and unvarnished. But her physical beauty made her garb beautifully
simple, not plain, and it rendered her unsophistication and lack of polish
beautifully wholesome, not plain. All of which suggests that there is no
common culture of plainness to which unsophistication – in the absence
of physical plainness – independently contributes. By contrast, as we have
seen, there is a common culture of blackness to which poverty and single
parenthood – even in the absence of literal blackness – independently
contributes.[66]

Obesity and plain facial features, then, do not really extend themselves metaphorically. Rather, their literal presence in some people projects itself onto other traits those people possess: their wealth, their unsophistication. Without that literal presence, however, wealthy or unsophisticated people do not generally get described as metaphorically fat or plain. As for the term "anorexic," possibly some very physically thin people who are not phenotypically anorexic get called anorexic. But that's because they come so close to the literal phenotype, not because they are independently anorexic in some nonliteral sense.

These are but suggestive glimmers of a distinction between obesity, plain facial features, and anorexia, on the one side, and the other five conditions on the other. And perhaps, when it comes to plain facial features, I might be stacking the deck by using the term "plain-featured." "Unattractive" or even "ugly," by contrast, clearly are used metaphorically. Yet when it comes to their literal usage, these terms may indicate more a need for reconstructive than cosmetic surgery, of a sort that is relatively uncontroversially thought to justify a cure.[67] In any case, I think there is something more palpable here that applies – that explains why the plain-featured, obese, and anorexic have no cultural spouses – regardless of what terms we use to describe them.

Recall my discussion of blindness. The cultural experiences and art to which a person's literal blindness can lead him will, in part, be ones that only literal blindness can cause. But his literal blindness will also lead him to experiences and art of a sort to which others' nonliteral blindness will lead them. Phenotypic literal blindness, in other words, gives rise to experiences and art that are due exclusively to that phenotype, but also to experiences and art that are common to phenotypic metaphorical blindness. Phenotypic literal blackness, too, leads to experiences and art that only such a phenotype could cause; but, as well, to experiences and art that are common to phenotypic metaphorical blackness. By contrast, literal obesity, plain facial features, and anorexia – far more disproportionately – provoke cultural experiences and art that only those phenotypes could bring on.

Why? Because in our culture, plain facial features, obesity, and anorexia are markers of physical attractiveness or unattractiveness. Among the eight conditions, these three provoke cultural experiences that most uniquely and deeply have to do precisely with the valuation that contemporary cultural standards place on the literal phenotype itself. It's hard to imagine a person with beautiful facial features undergoing the same kinds of cultural experiences that a person's plain features would elicit, in the same way that we can imagine a seeing person undergoing the same kinds of cultural experiences that literal blindness would elicit. To even conceive of a beautiful person encountering the same kinds of cultural experiences as a plain person, we would also have to imagine our totally inverting the culture. We would then have entered the world of that *Twilight Zone* episode in which a species of grotesque posthumans, failing in their attempt to alter the features of a woman whom we would consider beautiful, banish her. Nor can one conceive of a svelte person undergoing the same kinds of cultural experiences that obesity or anorexia elicit – in the way in which a metaphorically black white person might share the experiences elicited by literally black racial features.

Let me press this a bit. Phenotypic plain facial features often give rise to experiences – and the attendant art – having to do with romantic failure. But the plain-featured are certainly not the only people who suffer romantic rejection because of their phenotypes and then write about it. True, many of these others may be obese or anorexic, so we have to set that aside. But almost any phenotype – dullness, intelligence, sensitivity, insensitivity, even being too good-looking – can lead to romantic rejection, depending on the circumstances. The experience of such rejection, and the art it provokes, will surely survive the death of plain facial features. So wouldn't that mean that "plain facial features" does, after all, have a cultural spouse – in all those non-plain-featured individuals whose particular phenotypes have led to romantic rejection and then expressed or interpreted that experience artistically? Doesn't the fact that any phenotype can elicit romantic rejection mean that plain facial features has itself found (many) a spouse?

No. The key here is that *any* phenotype can give rise to the experience of romantic failure. Remember, a phenotype has a cultural spouse if it is not the exclusive cause of (at least a good part of) the kinds of cultural experiences and art to which it gives rise. There is a tension in this definition. On the one hand, the cultural experiences and products in question can't be so tightly bound to the phenotype that it becomes their exclusive cause. Otherwise, there can be no surviving spouse. On the other hand, the cultural experiences and products must be bound tightly enough to the phenotype that they are ones to which the phenotype can be said to give rise. Otherwise it would be hard to say that anything of *it* survives in them. If *any* phenotype can lead to romantic rejection, though, then romantic rejection is not a cultural experience that belongs to plain facial features any more than it belongs to any number of other phenotypes. We can't say that with the death of plain facial features, something of them *in particular* would survive in the experiences and tales of romantic rejection that any phenotype can elicit. The romantic rejection experienced by the plain-featured "average Joes" on *Average Joe* does not live on in the romantic rejection experienced by, say, the handsome Robert from Harold Pinter's *Betrayal*, except in the most universal sense: abstracted from anything having to do with plain facial features.[68] By contrast, while it is not only phenotypic literal blackness, it is not just any phenotype either, that gives rise to the experiences and art of being black. The rhythm and blues of the black musician Big Joe Turner live on in the music of the white "Tutti" Grayzell.[69] The black rapper Dr. Dre and the white rapper Eminem contribute to a much-discussed common cultural tradition.[70]

The lack of a metaphorical usage of the terms obesity, plain facial features, and anorexia, then, does signify something. As a general rule, the literally obese, plain-featured, and anorexic do not, in looking around themselves at the social level – at society at large – see any other phenotype eliciting cultural experiences, or consequent cultural products, sufficiently contiguous that they could be deemed spouses.[71] That's because the cultural experiences that only a plain-featured phenotype elicits, or only an anorexic or only an obese phenotype elicits, virtually exhaust the cultural experiences to which each of these phenotypes gives rise. And at the individual level, post-cure, the formerly obese, plain-featured, or anorexic individual will be vulnerable to a kind of culture shock. Perhaps that is why even now, among all the conditions under discussion, only individuals who get treated successfully for their plain facial features, obesity, or anorexia routinely seek psychotherapy to help them come to terms with their post-cure selves. They need assistance in coming to terms with the profoundly new way in which the culture values them and others treat them. Disoriented, they feel a rupture in their identity of the sort that Kymlicka attributes to the loss of cultural context.[72]

Yes, it's true that those cured of mild depression sometmes ask their psychotherapists to return them to their former condition. But that is generally because antidepressants, at their current imperfect state of development, have overshot ordinary unhappiness, bringing patients to a state of unwarranted and unwanted tranquility or mellowness. Records of the rare cases in which severe congenital blindness gets cured sometimes do include reference to the patient's consequent disorientation and depression. But that's because, once cured, he finds himself struggling with Georgina Kleege's "surfeit of visual information." What he faces, in other words, is continued, if changed, blindness: the blindness associated with having to make sense of a world of visual shapes and colors instead of a world of haptic shapes and textures. The cured blind require therapy precisely because the cultural experiences of blindness persist – live on – when, by seeking a cure, they expected a break.[73] It's likewise true that those light-skinned blacks who can now pass as white with surgical assistance sometimes seek therapy. But that's not generally because they have altered their phenotypes. It's because they have had to cut ties with relatives, friends, and members of the black community in order to protect their new identity.[74]

It's only for the plain-featured, anorexic, and obese that psychotherapy is sometimes sought to help them find themselves again, once they have severed the cultural threads in their identities that came with their phenotypes. With a cure for plain facial features, anorexia, or obesity, the cultural experiences and products to which each gives rise – tightly bound as they are to the literal physical phenotype – will not live on in society as a whole, in the experiences and art of those who aren't literally plain-featured, anorexic, or obese. Nor will those cultural traditions live on, post-cure, to provide a continuing thread of identity to those individuals who were formerly plain-featured, anorexic, or obese.

Let me take a break to recall where we are heading. Under the "worst-case scenario" in which everyone took a cure for a particular condition – or, if not everyone did, then in proportion to the number who did – cure would inflict cultural loss. That loss, of the experiences and art to which only the literal phenotype gives rise, would be real and exists in all eight cases. But with three of those conditions – plain facial features, anorexia, and obesity – the experiences and art are overwhelmingly of a sort that only the literal phenotype itself could elicit. We thus have reason to worry about the cultural consequences of a cure for these three phenotypic conditions, since they have no spouses. But with blindness, deafness, black racial features, mild depression, and physical slowness, the experiences and art they provoke are also of a sort that other phenotypes can elicit: being blind to certain realities, deaf to certain problems, poor and working class, ordinarily unhappy, challenged at math. We then have less cause for worry. These phenotypes do have cultural spouses. In which case, even if the groups "the blind," "the deaf," "blacks," "the mildly depressed," or "the physically slow" were no longer to exist, their cultural traditions would still live on – changed, certainly, in a Brian Barry sense – in society as a whole. And individuals, once cured (or having taken a

Michael Jackson pill), would still find a world of familiar cultural touch-stones with which to orient themselves.[75]

Cultural Siblings

There is, however, another (and cross-cutting) way to look at the issue of cultural survival. As we have seen, different phenotypes can give rise to a recognizably common tradition of cultural experience and art that, while reflecting the differences in phenotype, nevertheless also embodies what's common to them. In this way, the two phenotypes become cultural spouses, and those common aspects of their experiences and art represent a kind of marriage.

But now, reverse the causal arrow. It's possible not just for different phenotypes to give rise to common cultural experiences, but for common cultural experiences to give rise to different phenotypes. In this way, the common cultural experiences form a parentage, while the two phenotypes become cultural siblings. Yes, those experiences – and the art to which they give rise – get colored by the different phenotypes; siblings aren't necessarily twins. Yet their common experiential parentage is very much in evidence in the two phenotypes, and in the associated art as well.

Consider anorexia. When scholars or memoirists describe anorexia as a "crystallization of the psychopathology of contemporary culture"[76] or as "a symptom . . . of cultural conflicts,"[77] or when they urge that anorexia is "a cultural artifact"[78] or the "product of . . . a confluence of cultural forces,"[79] they are saying something that would not be said of (for instance) phenotypic blindness or deafness: namely, that phenotypic anorexia can itself be *caused by* cultural experiences. What they have in mind are claims such as Morag MacSween's that "anorexia is an attempt to resolve at the level of the individual body the irreconcilability of individuality and femininity in a bourgeois patriarchal culture"[80] or Mara Selvini Palazzoli's argument that "underlying . . . anorexia [are] a host of cultural conflicts, having to do with the admission of women into traditional male preserves" while at the same time "women must . . . be romantic and wife."[81]

Of course, the experience of these cultural conflicts is not anorexia's only cause. Family dynamics, hormones, and genes also contribute.[82] Nevertheless, as Bryan S. Turner writes, "[w]hile it would be futile to deny that anorexia has . . . physiological features, it also has a complex sociological aetiology and is deeply expressive of . . . the culture of narcissism, consumerism and the patristic forms of slender femininity."[83] Obviously, the people I have here quoted hope that the "individuality" side of the cultural conflict between "individuality" and "femininity" dominates. Others may be partisans of the opposite side. But the very presence of both sides buttresses the point I want to make. There exists a cultural conflict or tension over female roles, the experiences of which substantially, if by no means exclusively, cause anorexia.

What's of further interest here, though, is that many "non-anorexic women embody the [same] cultural tension . . . between femininity and living independent lives,"[84] and express and interpret that tension artistically. Precisely the same cultural experiences – the "irreconcilability of individuality and femininity in a bourgeois patriarchal culture," as MacSween puts it – give rise to, or parent, two different phenotypes. There is the anorexic one and there is a sibling nonanorexic one, characterized not by an eating disorder but certainly by a range of feelings and emotions, such as confusion, low self-esteem, and anger. Of course, any given individual with the phenotype of physical anorexia may display symptoms of the sibling phenotype, such as anger and low self-esteem. The point is that both phenotypes, literal anorexia and anger/low self esteem, are caused by the same cultural experiences. It's the two phenotypes – Leslie Heywood calls them "physical anorexia" and "mental anorexia" – that are cultural siblings.[85]

The "central psychological problems experienced by patients with eating disorders, which center on issues of self-esteem, autonomy and achievement," Richard A. Gordon writes, "are a magnified reflection of much more pervasive conflicts in the wider culture about the female role."[86] In so saying, Gordon is pointing to the existence of an underlying cultural parent – the "wider culture" – and the existence of two siblings: the phenotype of "eating disorders" and the phenotype of self-loathing, resentment, and rage. Both stem from experiencing the culture's demands that women, as Gordon puts it, be "competent, achieving and ambitious, and feminine, sexual and nurturing."

So conceived, anorexia could be cured as a phenotypic condition while leaving these underlying cultural experiences – the experiences that preoccupy much of the thought and activism, the memoirs, stories, and humor associated with anorexia – quite intact. No, we would not retain the specific coloration that the anorexic phenotype lends to those common cultural experiences or the art to which they give rise. But we would retain those experiences themselves, as well as their artistic expression, manifest through a slightly different set of lenses – the lenses of a sibling embodying a different phenotype but the same cultural parentage.

On the television show *Frasier*, some of the jokes that the character Niles Crane makes about his (never seen) anorexic wife Maris would disappear with a cure, those directly related to her dieting and physical appearance. Maris, Niles says, is "ounces of fun" or "100 percent fat free." But many of Niles's jokes – about the high-strung obsessiveness and perfectionism that stem from the same cultural experiences as does Maris's anorexia – would survive. His jests about Maris sleeping with a pistol under her pillow, her ownership of a sensory deprivation tank, her losing all coordination when she passes a shoe shop – I'm not saying that any of these are gems – could all be made about a woman who experiences and crystallizes the same cultural tensions as does Maris, but who happens not to have expressed them through phenotypic anorexia.

"Erica Jong," Rita Freedman writes, "warns that women artists will continue to feel a deep sense of conflict about their femaleness as long as femininity is associated with ruffles and flourishes and a lack of directness and honesty."[87] In taking this view, as she always has, Erica Jong identifies herself as a nonanorexic cultural sibling to the putatively anorexic television character Ally McBeal, a woman trying to negotiate "the pull between patriarchy and the reverberations of radical feminism."[88] Their common mother – whose characteristics they both display despite their different phenotypes – is the cultural experience of those women whose lives place upon them conflicting and unrealistic demands.

No, as I have suggested, anorexia does not have a cultural spouse. The experiences to which the phenotype of anorexia gives rise – as opposed to those that give rise to the phenotype – are unlikely to live on in a broader cultural tradition. That's because the kinds of cultural experiences to which anorexia gives rise are, by and large, so entirely bound up with the physical phenotype that they are ones that only phenotypic anorexia, not a normal weight, could elicit or provoke. But the kinds of cultural experiences that provoke phenotypic anorexia are not experiences that give rise to only an anorexic phenotype; they provoke others. Phenotypic anorexia may not have a cultural spouse, but it does have a cultural sibling.

The phenotype of anorexia, and its experiences and art, are thus very much part of a broader cultural tradition of experiences that embody, and art that wrestles with, contemporary conflicts between individuality and femininity, ambition and nurturance. This broader cultural tradition will survive a cure for anorexia, just as the Musqueam cultural tradition of barter and feasting, naturalism and subsistence, will survive a prohibition on fishing the Fraser. The group "anorexics" may disappear. But our concern is with whether its culture can continue to live on in society as a whole – in those who never were anorexic but who may embody aspects of its culture – and in the individuals who formerly harbored the condition and who require cultural continuity. And, as much as anyone can expect of any culture, given that living cultures are always changing, the cultural tradition of anorexia will survive a cure. Society as a whole will continue to stage the conflict between various female roles that so substantially gave rise to anorexia, and to sustain the experiences and art that that conflict provokes. And personal engagements with those conflicts – accompanied by hard-won insights into and victories over the culture's competing and violent tugs – will remain every bit as central, every bit as available as cultural touchstones, for those individual women who formerly were anorexic.

Likewise with obesity. While obesity exhibits genetic origins, it also very much displays cultural roots. One of the phenotype's major causes is a set of cultural experiences – much the same set of experiences that give rise to anorexia[89] – that would survive phenotypic obesity's disappearance due to cure. An obese woman, as Susie Orbach says, must "allow . . . herself the possibility that she could be thin and have conflicts, that whatever conflicts she had . . . with her own sexuality, with her rage or whatever, they could all exist as part of her when thin."[90] Of course, not all obesity is a feminist issue. "Does the [cured fat] boy without his gut have a different character?," Sander L. Gilman asks, or "is he merely an unhappy fat boy in disguise? Has the surgeon merely stripped away the fat, leaving an obese personality behind?"[91] If the latter, then it would seem that the cured fat boy would still harbor his cultural identity; the no longer literally fat boy would remain metaphorically obese. Many obese people, Hilde Bruch writes, "succeed in becoming and staying thin, but [their] conflicts are far from solved by having lost weight . . . they still resemble fat people with all their unsolved problems, conflicts and exaggerated expectations. . . . It is to this group that I wish to apply the term *Thin Fat People*."[92]

Thin Fat People, it would seem, are cultural siblings to Fat Fat People. The term "Thin" in "Thin Fat People" and the first "Fat" in the correlative "Fat Fat People" betoken their differing phenotypes. The final "Fat" term in each describes their common cultural parentage in the "conflicts and exaggerated expectations" that cause the two phenotypes. The thin phenotypic sibling is characterized by feelings of unfulfillment, failed expectations, and role conflict. The fat phenotypic sibling is characterized, obviously, by physical obesity. Any one person can embody both. But the point is that both are substantially caused by the same cultural experiences. Even if the fat fat phenotype is cured, the thin fat phenotype will live on.

Certainly, with a cure for obesity, there may be no more fat jokes. There will no longer be art that expresses and interprets those broadly shared cultural experiences – of role conflict and impossible expectations – through the specific lens of phenotypic obesity. But many of the jokes that overweight comedians make, though tinted through the lenses provided by their particular phenotype, are really about the absurd and contradictory demands they experience in the culture and that are equally manifest in other (thin fat) phenotypes.

Roseanne Barr recently quipped, "I just want to go around examining things that make me mad, and eating."[93] If eating (or at least the consequences of eating) weren't a part of it, her routine, certainly, would change. In fact, this particular quip would itself not be possible in its current form. But the things that make Roseanne Barr mad, and that also make her eat and get fat, would certainly persist following a cure for obesity, and so would the humor they provoke. The experience of such things, along with the phenotypic anger and the art (humor) to which they give rise, would continue to live on in the absence of the phenotypic obesity that they also currently cause. This gives us reason to believe that, even with a cure for obesity, its cultural tradition will continue. Changed, certainly, in the Brian Barry sense by the eradication of obesity, but not killed. The cultural tradition of phenotypically literally fat people will live on through their cultural siblings in the cultural tradition of Thin Fat People. Roseanne Barr is a cultural sibling to Sandra Bernhard.[94]

True, obesity, like anorexia, has no cultural spouse. That's because the phenotype of obesity itself plays such an exclusive role in the cultural experiences to which it gives rise; no other phenotype causes the same. Yet obesity, like anorexia, has a cultural sibling. That's because cultural experiences (role conflict, impossible expectations) play such a dominant role in giving rise to the phenotype of obesity, and those same experiences cause other phenotypes. Because obesity has a cultural sibling – because many cured Fat Fat People will turn into Thin Fat People – phenotypic fat individuals will not experience a cutting away of their cultural context with a cure. Nor will society lose the rich vein of art associated with those nonobese phenotypes that are rooted in the same cultural experiences.

Now consider mild (aka neurotic) depression. It's certainly the case that, as with anorexia or obesity, this phenotype gets caused by cultural experiences. In *Listening to Prozac*, Peter D. Kramer says that the substantial majority of cases of mild (neurotic) depression that he treats are (unlike major, clinical, or bipolar depression) the result of the psyche's "wrestling with cultural causes."[95] Neuroses more generally, Lionel Trilling observed in his essay "Art and Neurosis," must "be understood as exemplifying cultural forces of great moment."[96] Yet the very same cultural experiences or "forces" to which Kramer and Trilling refer – emotional isolation, organizational torpor, existential meaninglessness – give rise, depending on the individual, not only to phenotypic neurotic depression but ordinary, nonneurotic unhappiness: moods that are appropriate and proportionate, not inappropriate and disproportionate, responses to those experiences. In this way, phenotypic mild depression and phenotypic ordinary unhappiness are cultural siblings.

But haven't we already seen that phenotypic mild depression and phenotypic ordinary unhappiness are also cultural spouses? Don't the two phenotypes also *give rise* to many of the same cultural experiences – experiences of futility, sadness, bittersweetness, angst, and hard-won insight – tinted, of course, by the differences between neurotic and nonneurotic lenses? To say that phenotypic neurotic depression and phenotypic ordinary unhappiness are cultural *siblings* is to say that common cultural experiences (anomic failures at intimacy, bureaucratic impersonality, the awareness of mortality) give rise to, cause, or manifest in the two phenotypes. To say that phenotypic neurotic depression and phenotypic ordinary unhappiness are cultural *spouses* is to say that the two phenotypes give rise to, cause, or manifest in common cultural experiences (world-weariness, discontent, regret, irony, consolation, insight). Both the cultural experiences that provoke phenotypic neurotic depression and the cultural experiences that it provokes will survive a cure. And likewise with the correlative art.[97]

Of course, the same cultural experiences could fall into both categories. When *Prozac Nation* author Elizabeth Wurtzel writes of feeling "deracinated, unstable, and alienated," those experiences could both cause her phenotypic neurotic depression and be caused by it.[98] In either case, what matters is that those experiences – as Wurtzel recognizes – will survive a cure for her mild, neurotic depression, albeit in a form in which they cause or are caused by ordinary, nonneurotic unhappiness. And so we should, of all the conditions under consideration here, be least worried about the cultural consequences of a cure for mild; that is, neurotic depression. Mild, neurotic depression has the same partner – nonneurotic ordinary unhappiness – as both sibling and spouse: an incestuous situation appropriate in its way for a syndrome originally diagnosed by Freud.

By the same token, the cultural consequences of a cure for phenotypic mild depression would seem to differ from the cultural consequences of a cure for phenotypic major (especially bipolar) depression. Phenotypic major depression, comparatively rooted as it is in brain chemistry, is less caused by cultural experiences than is mild neurotic depression; it has no analogous cultural sibling. And, by comparison with mild or neurotic depression, phenotypic major depression is proportionately far more often the exclusive cause of the kinds of cultural experiences – and the uniquely extraordinarily febrile artistic creativity from Robert Schumann to Robert Lowell – to which it frequently gives rise; it has no analogous cultural spouse. Kay Redfield Jamison, most notably, has argued for a unique link between bipolar disorder (in both its manic and its depressive states) and certain kinds of artistic or scientific genius. While the exclusivity of that link has been contested by others, no one seems to dispute that it is much more singular than are the links between mild neurotic depression and the kind of art it provokes.[99] As a relative if not absolute statement – compared, that is, with mild depression – major depression, especially in bipolar disorder, thus has neither cultural siblings nor cultural spouses. That is why the question of curing it can become so culturally poignant.[100]

Unlike anorexia, obesity, and mild depression, the other five conditions – phenotypic blindness, deafness, plain facial features, black racial features, and physical slowness – are not caused by cultural experiences. This isn't to deny that these phenotypic conditions are cultural constructions. But those constructions rely on the prior existence of phenotypic characteristics – corneas, eardrums, pigmentation, noses, muscle mass – that the culture picks out as blind, deaf, black, plain, or slow. It's true that the three conditions that I've just discussed – anorexia, obesity, and mild depression – are also culturally constructed in this sense. Particular phenotypic characteristics, particular weights, body shapes, and moods, get picked out by the culture as anorexic, obese, and mildly depressive. But in their case those phenotypic characteristics themselves – the weights, the body shapes, the moods – are also, comparatively speaking, far more substantially caused by the culture. They far more frequently come into existence in the first place as a result of cultural experiences: experiences, as we are told, of role conflict, impossible expectations, failures to connect intimately, social alienation, existential meaninglessness, and more. Anorexia, obesity, and mild depression can thus be called "cultural artifacts" in a way that would be inapt for blindness, deafness, black racial features, plain facial features, and physical slowness.

Of course, *metaphorical* blindness and deafness – shortfalls, for example, in broader kinds of apprehension – or metaphorical blackness, such as poverty and social disadvantage, or metaphorical slowness, such as difficulties in the form of intellectual achievement, may be cultural artifacts, culturally caused. But that only makes the point more trenchantly, since *literal* blindness, deafness, blackness, or physical slowness aren't culturally caused. The metaphorical and the literal in each pair, then, could not be cultural siblings, since only one member in each, the metaphorical one, is caused by cultural experiences to begin with. The metaphorical and the literal in each pair can only be spouses, causing at one level the same cultural experiences – experiences of blindness, deafness, blackness, and slowness – and the art interpreting and expressing them. Culture plays little role in giving rise to literal blind, deaf, black, or physically slow phenotypes, which is why they have no cultural siblings. And literal blind, deaf, black, or physically slow phenotypes do not play an overwhelmingly exclusive role in causing the cultural experiences to which they give rise. That is why metaphorical phenotypes – cultural spouses – can cause the same kinds of experience or art.

In fact, of all the eight conditions, only plain facial features has no cultural siblings *and* no cultural spouses. It is at once a cultural only child and a cultural single. Because cultural experiences play a minimal role in causing the phenotype of plain facial features – by contrast with the way in which cultural experiences cause, say, anorexia or obesity – it has no cultural siblings.[101] But because the phenotype of plain facial features plays such an exclusive role in causing the cultural experiences to which it gives rise – by comparison with, say, the phenotypes of blindness and deafness – it has no spouse. No other phenotype could come close to causing the same experiences and the same art.

Let me press this a bit further. One might say that the culture of objectification, of emphasizing the value of a woman's looks, shapes the experiences of the woman with a perfect nose and skin every bit as much as those of the woman with a plain nose and skin. Indeed, by selecting certain noses and skins as beautiful and others as plain, doesn't the culture of objectification cause, as a parent does, these phenotypes to come into existence? And if a common cultural experience – in this case, the experience of objectification – underlies or plays through both plain and beautiful phenotypes, then aren't the two siblings? Even if the plain-featured are cured, won't at least part of their cultural tradition – the cultural experiences of objectification and the art dealing with it – survive in the beautifully featured?

No. For again, with facial features, we run into a tension. True, there is a sense in which the woman with beautiful facial features is objectified every bit as much as is the woman with plain facial features. But then objectification is really no more a part of the cultural experience of having plain features than it is of the cultural experience of having beautiful or any other kind of facial features. Those who identify a culture of objectification believe that it constructs every individual, or at least every woman, into a variety of different phenotypes: young, old, maternal, sex object, plain, pretty, beautiful, light-haired, dark-haired. Since the culture of objectification is part of every phenotype, it represents nothing of plainness in particular.

Of course, at one level, all those phenotypes are different. But at that level, the experiences of the underlying culture of objectification are each unique. A plain-featured woman's experiences of objectification differ deeply from those of a beautifully featured woman's and wouldn't survive a cure for plain facial features. At this level, someone who is no longer plain-featured cannot maintain the same experiences of the underlying culture of objectification that she had when she was plain-featured. In this way, she differs from someone who is no longer obese – the Thin Fat Person – who can still embody the same cultural experiences that underlie obesity.

Whatever cultural experiences shape or "construct" plainness, then, they are either universal – in which case they will survive a cure but have nothing especially to do with plainness – or unique, in which case they can bespeak plainness but won't survive. By contrast, the cultural experiences that rise to the level of causing obesity, such as certain kinds of conflicts between maternal and professional roles, are neither unique to obese women nor manifested in all phenotypes universally, only in a set centered on rage or confusion. Roseanne Barr is a cultural sibling to Sandra Bernhard. But Pamela Anderson and Andrea Dworkin – as much as both may be victims, indeed creatures, of a culture of objectification – are not cultural siblings.

Perhaps it is the inkling of this possibility that causes writers, whether or not they think of themselves as plain-featured – and in a way unique among the eight conditions – to lament the loss of cultural diversity that a cure for plain facial features would bring.[102] "Think, in all its immense variety, of the nose," Joseph Epstein writes in his picturesque critique of cosmetic surgery: "from Gogol's long sharp proboscis to Tolstoy's potato nose to W. C. Fields's empurpled lighthouse nose to Jimmy Durante's two-pound cucumber nose to Igor Stravinsky's isosceles-triangle nose to Bob Hope's ski-jump nose to Barbra Streisand's grand depressed-tip, sloping-septum nose."[103] As cosmetic surgeons gain ever greater acuity, the critic Leslie Fiedler mourned, we will "become even more homogeneously, monotonously beautiful. . . ."[104] For some time, Elizabeth Haiken says, "cultural critics have lamented the homogenization of appearance that has resulted from the acceptance of plastic surgery."[105]

One might reply that Fiedler and the others are looking at a disaggregated level. Yes, if we wipe out plain facial features, then all noses will look much the same (falling as they will into a golden-mean ideal range), all eyes will, and so forth. But that doesn't necessarily mean that, at a more aggregate level, all faces will look the same, even though all would be beautiful. Even now, there are innumerable people with different, but beautiful, faces. Still, none of those individuals would be described as plain – in the way in which, in a world of 100 percent seeing people, some of those sighted people could still be (as they are now) described as blind. And in a world of 100 percent thin bodies, some people could still be fat. And in a world of 100 percent nonblack people, many would continue to be black.

Possibly, in a world in which all faces were beautiful, some would eventually be deemed more beautiful than others. But that would simply return us to the situation that I discussed in Part 1, where more and more people attain a new social ideal. Eventually, they render abnormal other people who were formerly normal, thereby giving the latter license to regard their condition – formerly beautiful – as the "new plain" and demand a cure. Once again, after *that* cure, everyone would be beautiful, albeit on a new definition.[106] And none of those phenotypically beautiful people would be metaphorically plain; none would be Beautiful Plain People in the sense of Bruch's Thin Fat People. Indeed, when we think of a beautiful plain person, we tend to think of someone along the lines of George Eliot in Henry James's famous description, who, though phenotypically plain (or, as with James's Eliot herself, ugly), is imbued by and emanates a culture of beauty.[107] We do not, by "Beautiful Plain Person," mean someone physically beautiful who somehow maintains vestiges of a culture of plainness.

Cosmetic surgery often gets criticized by those who believe that plain facial features are not a legitimate medical condition and that curing them is a form of enhancement. In Part 1, I argued against that claim. It is legitimate for people with plain features to regard their condition as socially abnormal and/or to believe that many others have reached a social ideal; and that is what makes for a medical condition. I think, however, that cosmetic surgery (and certainly my imagined perfect and permanent version of cosmetic surgery) can be criticized because it represents a form of cultural genocide. I am not saying that the culture surrounding plain facial features – plain Jane stories, beauty-is-only-skin-deep tropes, and the like – is necessarily richer than the cultures of the deaf, the obese, or American blacks. The question of cultural genocide hangs not on determining what a culture is and who has one, but on what genocide would be.

Genocide is an inflammatory term. Groups who traditionally and justly lay a claim to it do so because it invokes the involuntary eradication of their people, not mass voluntary exit following a cure. As persuasive as that observation is, it's beside the point here, which is that with seven of the eight phenotypes, even if they disappeared there would be an alteration but not an eradication of their cultural traditions. These conditions have cultural spouses and/or cultural siblings. But in one case, the loss would be much closer to complete. With the disappearance of plain facial features – of my big nose and her wrinkled skin and his protruding ears – there is neither spouse nor sibling to survive. The physical phenotype of plain facial features is too preponderantly the exclusive cause of the cultural experiences to which it gives rise, meaning that it has no cultural spouse. But cultural experiences only marginally, if at all, cause the physical phenotype of plain facial features, which means that it can have no cultural sibling. And I suspect that deep down, we are more disturbed by the kind of cultural barrenness portended by a world in which everyone has socially ideal features than we are by the notion that plain features are a legitimate medical condition. We need think only of the suffering that they evidently cause; but more to the point of what I'm arguing, those harboring them can legitimately view their condition as abnormal while believing that others around them have achieved the ideal.[108] Although we have rescued a cure for plain facial features from the charge of enhancement, then, it remains guilty, as much as any cure can, of the charge of cultural genocide.

But more needs to be said. We might well accept that cure bodes a kind of cultural genocide in the case of plain features. And yet, as I have just recalled from Part 1, those with plain features can legitimately view theirs as a medical condition. So why should our avoiding the obliteration of the associated cultural richness necessarily trump our offering the plain-featured a cure? True, we are not objecting to cure by merely pointing to the existence of a cultural tradition to be accommodated, but to actual possibilities for its genocide or disappearance. Nor are we simply pointing to the genocide, or disappearance, of the group, but also to that of the associated cultural motifs themselves in society as a whole and in the individuals who formerly harbored the condition. Still, why would we necessarily reach the limits of medicine here?

I think that there is a difference to be split. In Part 1, I quoted from two kinds of cosmetic surgery patients: those who regard their noses, eyes, lips, or skin as abnormal and seek normality and those who view them as normal and seek to make them ideal.[109] Here, I would point out that those who see the feature in question as abnormal – and who seek simply to place it somewhere within what they can legitimately regard as the norm – are closer to viewing themselves as having a medical condition that should trump cultural concerns. Indeed, even if all the abnormally nosed had normal noses, the world would still have diversity, because we would by no means have all crawled into the realm of the ideal. By contrast, those who acknowledge that their feature already is normal, and who now seek to make it conform to an ideal, pose a greater threat to the cultural richness provided by diversity of features. And they are also missing one of the two possible criteria for deeming their condition a medical one: It may fall outside a populated social ideal, but it does not fall outside the social norm.

True, I argued in Part 1 that a person can legitimately view her facial feature as a medical condition even if she sees it as normal, as long as she wishes to bring it to a social ideal that some others have attained. A person who wants to make her normal feature ideal, then, is asking for something that lies within the limits of medicine if the issue is simply cure versus enhancement. But here the issue is cure versus cultural genocide. And here, by comparison with those who see their features as abnormal and seek only to make them normal, those who see their features as normal and want to make them ideal are further removed from viewing their condition as a medical one necessitating cure. They are also closer to bringing about the monotony of homogeneous looks that, in this case, is tantamount to a kind of cultural genocide. The cure–genocide border, if not the cure–enhancement border, can come between those with what they see as an abnormal feature seeking to make it normal and those who possess what they believe is a normal feature seeking to make it ideal.

Medicine, then, should offer cosmetic surgery to those who view their feature as abnormal and seek to make it normal, but not to those who view it as normal and seek to make it ideal. The possibilities for cultural genocide are stronger, the claim to be a medical condition weaker. Sorting these two groups is not impractical. As I noted in Part 1, cosmetic-surgery seekers so sort themselves. And cosmetic surgeons routinely interview prospective patients to ascertain their motives.[110]

One loose end. In Part 1, I argued that black racial features are not a medical condition. The very notion of "racial" features imports genotypic notions into what could and should otherwise be a more purely phenotypically conceived set of features: skin color, hair texture, lip size, and the like. And so, I said, if we ever get to a point where black racial features get wholly detached from any stereotyped notion of racial "blackness" – where they are no longer viewed as genotypically bundled racial features, but simply as phenotypic facial features – we would have entered the realm of cosmetic surgery. Those features would simply locate themselves on bell curves distributed over society as a whole. And bell curves themselves offer no landmarks as to where normality and abnormality begin and end. Phenotypic dark skin or broad noses, shorn of all racial associations, could legitimately be deemed medical conditions every bit as much as could phenotypic wrinkled skin or pointed noses. Although, of course, they equally legitimately need not be.

But here, in Part 3, I have argued that while phenotypic wrinkled skin and pointed noses may be medical conditions, curing them – since they have neither cultural spouses nor cultural siblings – would come closest of all the eight conditions to cultural genocide. And the same would apply to phenotypic dark skin and broad noses once they are liberated from all racial associations. Seeking to lighten one's dark skin to a socially ideal shade, or narrow one's broad nose to socially ideal proportions, would now amount to cultural genocide in the same way that cosmetic surgery can. A certain kind of diversity would be utterly lost to our culture, not simply altered. Phenotypic dark skin or tightly curled hair, stripped of all racial associations, do not have cultural siblings, since they are not caused by cultural experiences. And, shorn of all racial associations, they would have no cultural spouses, since whatever cultural experiences they did elicit – which, by assumption, would no longer have anything to do with race or blackness – would have to do so exclusively with the phenotype that they would disappear with it.

No matter how you make the cut, a Michael Jackson pill for black racial features would be illegitimate. As racial features, they are not a medical condition, although they are part of a larger culture of blackness that would live on after their disappearance. If they ever came to be seen only as facial features, they could then legitimately fall into the class of medical conditions, but their disappearance would leave no surviving cultural spouse or sibling. Either black racial features are not a medical condition or, if they are seen simply as facial features, then a Michael Jackson pill would come as close as other forms of cosmetic surgery do to being legitimately stamped a form of cultural genocide.[111]

Conclusion

I began by asking us to imagine that we live in a medical utopia of unlimited resources and boundless technology. In this state, we don't have to set priorities or use triage. We are able to cure any and all conditions, any and all phenotypes, that can legitimately be deemed medical ones. In this world, there would be two principal objections to a cure: that it is mere enhancement or that it is cultural genocide. As utopian as it may seem, though, this world is one that our own will always resemble imperfectly. After all, the question as to what limits there are on medical resources and technology itself remains enormously contestable. And so even now, in our current far from utopian state, we engage in lively debates over the final limits to medicine, debates that engross medical ethicists, doctors, activists, patients, and would-be patients.

In the current debate over the final limits to medicine, many cure/enhancement writers and activists tend to make the cut at the societywide level. They deem a treatment to be a cure if it enables people harboring a particular condition to pursue a societywide range of life plans and in that way takes them to a state of social normality. The only alternative that's regularly entertained would direct us to the individual level, stamping a treatment as cure and not enhancement if, given the particular life plan of the person in question, it will make that individual whole. Participants in the cure/genocide debate, by contrast, tend to make their cuts at the group level. They weigh each group of people with a particular condition on an implied scale of cultural richness. If the group's life experiences, or history, or language, or literature rise to a certain level of cultural achievement, then cure would be cultural genocide. But if not, then not.

Both the cure/enhancement and the cure/genocide debates, however, have now hit the roadblocks that I describe in the Introduction. It is
not clear how much further they can move along their current tracks. So
my question in this inquiry has been: What if they were to switch tracks?
What if, in making the cure/enhancement cut, we were to do so at the
group level, defining a treatment as a cure if members of the group harboring the relevant condition could legitimately so deem it? A group
perspective on what is or is not socially normal would offer more nuance
than a societywide approach, one that required a cure to enable a societywide range of life plans, would allow. At the same time, a group-level
perspective on what it takes to make individuals whole would, I argued,
prevent our being held hostage to individual idiosyncracies, on which
anything could be a cure as long as it enabled the particular individual concerned to pursue his particular life plan. And what if, in making
the cure/genocide cut, we were to abandon the group level, jettisoning
group-on-group comparisons of cultural richness? We could then explore
the ways in which cure, though it may wipe out the group itself – the group
known as the phenotypically blind, for example, would no longer exist –
might nevertheless allow the group's culture to live on. Not, of course, in
the no-longer existing group itself, but in the individuals who formerly
composed it and in society as a whole.

My project was to see if there are principles that would help us make
the cuts in these ways. And, I argued, there are. To assist us in making
the cure/enhancement cut, we need to construct concepts of norms, ideals, genuineness, and artificiality that take account of the fact that social
normality or individual wholeness is always changing or growing. And to
help us make the cure/genocide cut, we must develop notions of cultural siblinghood and spousehood that take account of the fact that a
group can disappear while its culture remains alive: changed, certainly,
but living cultures are always changing and growing. In reflective equilibrium fashion, I applied these principles to actual debate and practice surrounding eight phenotypes that provoke contemporary controversy over
the limits to medicine: mild depression, physical slowness, plain facial
features, black racial features, blindness, deafness, obesity, and anorexia.
And then, in light of practice, I sometimes modified those principles and
sometimes, on the basis of the principles, claimed particular arguments
to be wrong.

In Part 1, where I examined the position of each group with respect to
the social norm and the social ideal, I argued that members of seven of
them could legitimately regard their phenotype as a medical condition,

such that cure wouldn't be mere enhancement. The lone exception was blacks seeking to change their racial features. In Part 2, I looked at how each group's condition configures the possibilities for a cure to instill traits that are genuine or, alternatively, artificial. I argued that all groups could view whatever they accomplish with a cure as genuine achievement, not artificial enhancement, except (under certain circumstances) for slow runners. And in Part 3, I argued that of all the eight conditions, it is the plain-featured whose cultural experiences – and the art interpreting and expressing them – would, post-cure, vanish from society as a whole and from the individuals who formerly harbored the condition. Phenotypic plain features are bereft of both cultural spouse and cultural sibling. Ridding the world of all but beautiful facial features could be deemed a form of cultural genocide.

These conclusions accord with what I think many people believe. We should hesitate about offering medical treatments for black racial features, physical slowness, and plain facial features. But the *reasons* I offer might differ from what we would have anticipated. Prior to analysis, we might have expected that the problem with curing plain facial features is that it is an enhancement, not that it spells cultural genocide. And we might have thought that the problem with a Michael Jackson pill for black racial features is that it threatens cultural genocide, apart from any question as to whether or not it could be deemed a legitimate medical procedure, a cure.

As for mild depression, I argue that a cure would be neither enhancement nor cultural genocide. Speaking of mild depressives as a group, curing their condition would bring people who legitimately view themselves as socially (ab)normal to a social ideal that others have attained; and it would do so in a way that allows for genuine, not artificial, individual change on the dominant Kantian approach. Hence it's not enhancement. And since, of all the eight conditions, mild depression is the only one with both surviving cultural spouse and cultural sibling (even if sibling sometimes doubles as spouse), cure would not be genocide. This result might not accord with the views of some ethicists, although I suspect that it does comport with the beliefs of a growing number of doctors and certainly of (would-be) patients. But here, reflective equilibrium suggests, to me, that it's the opposition to cures for mild depression that needs rethinking, at least before we further reconsider the principles that support such cures.

When it comes to the other four conditions – blindness, deafness, anorexia, and obesity – I claim that members of each group can legitimately regard their cure *as* a cure, not an enhancement. Members of these groups can legitimately view their conditions as socially abnormal while deeming others to have reached the social ideal. And they can legitimately claim that a cure would be consonant with genuine, subject-preserving individual change, not artificial, subject-eroding enhancement. I also claim that curing these conditions would not constitute cultural genocide. That's because subsequent to a cure, even if everyone took it and the groups themselves disappeared, the cultural traditions associated with each of these four conditions would continue to live on: altered, but still alive, in society as a whole and in the individuals, now cured, who formerly were blind, deaf, anorexic, or obese. Blindness and deafness have cultural spouses; obesity and anorexia, cultural siblings.

Other contemporary hot topics – human growth hormone for short people, IQ boosters ("purported 'intelligence enhancing agents' "),[1] and Ritalin for ADD – lend themselves to the analysis I have offered. Let me sketch, and I emphasize the word "sketch," how this might work in each case.

Consider human growth hormone. Social norms of height would have to be marked off on the bell-curve distribution of heights in society. The social ideal of height would occupy a golden mean on the same spectrum; that mean might fall on the tall side, but it certainly wouldn't occupy a pole around the shortest short or the tallest tall. On the analysis I offered in Part 1, those anywhere on the short side of the bell curve – whether or not they suffer from human growth hormone deficiency – could legitimately view their shortness as falling outside the range of social normality, since bell curves are silent on the matter. And they could legitimately believe others to have achieved the social ideal, understood as a range around the golden mean.[2] On that score, offering them human growth hormone wouldn't be enhancement. Of course, it would be equally legitimate for any short person, consulting the bell curve, to regard her height as perfectly normal.

On the criterion I offered in Part 2, if individual struggle cannot substitute even one whit for cure, then cure couldn't be enhancement. And, indeed, there is no mode of struggle by which a short person can actually erode her phenotypic condition; for short people, struggle against their phenotype can at most involve them in attempts to pass through the adroit use of footwear and clothing. Such struggle cannot substitute for cure. Hence, if a cure were in turn to substitute for such struggle, rendering it unnecessary, that cure would simply be precluding a kind of struggle that is no more genuine, no more part of the individual subject, than the cure itself would be. Cure, then, couldn't be deemed artificial enhancement by comparison. Height born of a cure would not eat into, or supplant, any height gained by the genuine self's struggle. Instead, it would take its place as a trait outside the subject, no more nefarious than congenital ideal height would be. In this way, a cure for shortness would resemble a cure for plain facial features.

But while a cure for shortness would escape the charge of enhancement, it might fall afoul of the cultural genocide criterion that I discuss in Part 3. Phenotypic shortness, not having been caused by cultural experiences, has no cultural siblings. There are no cultural experiences that give rise to phenotypic shortness in the first place and, therefore, none that at the same time engender and imbue sibling phenotypes that would survive its disappearance. Nor does phenotypic shortness give rise to cultural experiences of a sort provoked by other phenotypes, by phenotypic spouses, apart, of course, from the experience of discrimination and oppression, which I am assuming is never worth the cultural candle. Whatever may remain in terms of the cultural experiences shortness causes, they pretty much redound to the physical phenotype of shortness exclusively. It's hard to imagine a tall or medium-height person undergoing the same kinds of cultural experiences that shortness would elicit in the same way that we can imagine a seeing person undergoing the same kinds of cultural experiences that blindness would elicit. Phenotypic shortness, in other words, has no cultural spouse.

Commenting on David B. Allen and Norman C. Fost's imagined case of Johnny, an eleven-year-old boy with growth hormone deficiency, and Billy, who is just as short but has no deficiency, Erik Parens writes that "while Johnny and Billy are a hard case for those who in general are committed to responding to suffering, treating Johnny and Billy as the same would produce a still larger problem. Treating them the same would entail undermining our fundamental commitment to preserving differences."[3] What worries Parens, it would seem, is not that a cure for nonhormonally based shortness would be mere enhancement because shortness isn't a medical condition; certainly, he acknowledges Billy's suffering. Rather, Parens's concern is a cultural one. Cure would wipe out a form of "difference" from the culture. With a cure for phenotypic obesity, we could still have Thin Fat People. But with a cure for shortness, we would not have

Tall Short People, at least not in the same sense. We might thus consider reining in any cure for shortness in the way I suggested, in Part 3, that we might do with a cure for plain facial features. We might allow it for those who view their height as abnormal and seek to make it normal, but not for those who view their height as normal and seek to make it ideal.

Let us assume for the moment that IQ, as Richard Herrnstein and Charles Murray argued to considerable notoriety, meaningfully measures something called "intelligence" (I will vary this assumption shortly). So understood, socially normal IQ would be determined on a bell curve,[4] with the social ideal occupying a range at the high-end pole. A populated version of that ideal would embrace (say) the top 5 percent, whose IQs range from 135 to 298, or the top 2 percent, or even simply the highest single IQ, 298, that anyone has reached. On the criteria set forth in Part 1, those falling on the low side of the bell curve could therefore deem a pill – one that lifted them from what they legitimately regarded as their abnormal IQ and brought them to what they could legitimately regard as a populated ideal – as a cure, not an enhancement.[5] So, of course, could those who view their IQ as normal – on whatever side of the bell curve they happen to fall – and who seek simply to join a populated ideal range, although, of course, not an unpopulated one of 400 or 500.[6]

Now, what of the Kantian concern about individual (that is, subjective) wholeness? It's possible for a person to struggle, via mental exercise, conceptualization, and analysis, to improve his IQ, just as it's possible for someone to struggle via physical exercise, diet, and training to improve her running speed. Whatever it is that IQ measures, in other words, it is not immutable.[7] Struggle can substitute for cure at least to some extent, although, as with physical slowness, it needn't do so to any great degree. But even where it doesn't, such struggle is admirable on Kantian grounds, not a form of passing. Reversing the arrow, a cure for low IQ could, but needn't, substitute for that struggle. One can readily imagine someone, his IQ now brought to the populated social ideal of mental gifts, continuing to exercise his mind, doing so every bit as much as before, to take himself beyond that ideal. If he did, cure would not encroach upon the genuine self or its accomplishments. It would simply take its place outside the subject, where other people's congenitally socially ideal IQ resides.

But what if someone, now cured of his low IQ and possessed of the socially ideal level of intelligence that others had attained without cure, announces that he has reached his goals in the realm of intelligence, and will now rechannel his struggles from further reading and thinking to his golf game? There can be some disagreement on this point. But I would argue that being brought to the socially ideal level of intelligence is much more a prerequisite for further struggle in the area of intelligence – continued thinking, contemplating, reasoning – than prerequisite to struggles that do not involve intelligence. Certainly that's so if intelligence is understood in Herrnstein and Murray's global sense as embracing all intellectual capacities. In the same way, I argued in Part 2, a cure for physical slowness, one that gives a runner socially ideal gifts, is much more prerequisite to further struggles in the same vein – struggles to diet, exercise, and train to go beyond even the social ideal – than it is prerequisite to other sorts of struggles in life. And so, I claimed, a Kantian doctor could legitimately condition a cure for a runner's physical slowness on the runner's promising to continue to struggle with diet, exercise, and training. Since physical speed isn't obviously a prerequisite for new struggle elsewhere, a letup in diet, exercise, or training in the wake of cure would mean, speaking at a group-general level, that the runner's subject had shrunk. It would mean that some measure of accomplishment that was previously creditable to the runner's genuine subject no longer would be, thus rendering that cure an artificial enhancement.

In the same way, a Kantian doctor could premise a cure for low IQ on the patient's continuing to learn, think, reason, and contemplate. A cure for low (i.e., below-the populated socially ideal) IQ is prerequisite to continued struggle in the realm of learning, thinking, reasoning, and contemplating. Cessation or even a reduction in whatever such struggles the individual had been waging would suggest, rather strongly, that the cure had become merely a form of enhancement – a way of enabling her to do easily what before came with effort. This is doubly so since a socially ideal IQ isn't clearly prerequisite to any other kinds of struggle outside the domain of intelligence, especially when we are conceiving intelligence broadly as learning, thinking, reasoning, and contemplating. "[M]any factors other than intelligence," N. J. Block and Gerald Dworkin write, "contribute to success in other spheres."[8] As a group-general statement, we could not assume that individuals who eased up in their intellectual struggle in the wake of having been brought to the socially ideal IQ would be made more able, or more likely, to embark on new struggle in some other domain – thereby keeping the genuine subject whole.

Recall that my response here embodies a large assumption: that IQ measures global intelligence. Suppose, as many critics say, it instead measures a more confined set of skills that form part, but by no means the bulk, of what we consider to be intelligence: a defined clatch of memory, computational, speed-thinking, problem-solving or test-taking skills, possibly combined with a very particular base of factual knowledge.[9] It would seem to me that if that's what IQ is, then a socially ideal level would indeed be less prerequisite to further struggle in the domain of memory, computational, and problem-solving skills than it would be to struggle of many other sorts. In which case, low IQ would be more like obesity than physical slowness. A person harboring the condition could plausibly say: Cure me of this so that I can cease struggling to improve my memory or computational skills and devote myself to other struggles. On this understanding of low IQ, cure – as a general statement about those who would seek it – wouldn't be enhancement.

What we mean by IQ is enormously debatable. But it's a debate precisely about IQ, not one that touches the approach that I am advancing. Whatever IQ means – or, more exactly, whatever it is in the domain of intelligence for which we might consider developing a cure – the approach that I am suggesting offers an intuitively plausible way of viewing it. Suppose that we are talking about a defined, nonglobal set of intellectual skills. Bringing those with a low level of such skills to the populated social ideal, even if they then cease struggling to develop them further, wouldn't, speaking of the group as a whole, be enhancement. Computational or problem-solving skills generally enable one to embark on struggles in domains that involve other kinds of skills, including broader intellectual skills, far more than they do the further rote development of computational or problem-solving skills. A cure for low IQ, then, would simply take its place outside the undiminished genuine subject, as if it were any other innately based set of skills.

But suppose instead that we are talking about intelligence in some all-inclusive sense. Cure would be enhancement for those who, in its wake, eased up in their previous level of struggle to think, reason, and imagine. A gift for thinking, reasoning, and imagining – especially at a socially ideal level – enables continued struggle to think, imagine, and reason far more than it enables struggle in domains that involve other (i.e., wholly nonintelligence-based) skills. To ease up on one's struggles to think, imagine, and reason in light of a cure for low IQ, even to some degree, would be to allow cure to eat into the subject, at least to some degree, relegating the capacities that the cure instills to the realm of artificial enhancement.

As for the question of whether a cure for low IQ would amount to cultural genocide, again the best analogue is physical slowness. Being challenged intellectually gives rise to a broader type of cultural experience and literature having to do with obstacles and hurdles, frustration and grit, discontents and triumphs: experiences that many other phenotypes, including being challenged physically, can cause.[10] That cultural experience, and the story and song it inspires, would survive a cure for low IQ, and so low IQ has cultural spouses. Indeed, even if all got the gift of a socially ideal intelligence, the experiences of intellectual challenge, defeat, and triumph would persist as each person continued struggling to imagine, inquire, and contemplate in order to reach beyond what her gift alone could achieve. A cure for low IQ may be many things, but it is hard to see how it could amount to cultural genocide.

What of a cure for ADD? In order to avoid the tangled issue of paternalism provoked by debates over childhood ADD, "where those who are treated are not the ones making the choice to seek treatment," let us assume that we are speaking of adult ADD.[11] The capacity to pay attention distributes itself on a bell curve for determining social normality, with the social ideal occupying the high-end pole. It is thus "impossible . . . to draw a sharp boundary between those who are considered 'normal' and those [considered] to be ill," as Richard DeGrandpre writes in *Ritalin Nation*.[12] People located anywhere on that half of the bell curve below the mean could, consequently, legitimately see their attention deficits as falling outside the norm. At the same time, they (along with many on the other half of the curve) could legitimately believe that others – those whose attention spans are the highest known – have attained the polar ideal range on the far side of the spectrum. On the criteria I advanced in Part 1, a cure for ADD would not be enhancement.

When it comes to the criteria I set out in Part 2, having to do with whether a cure for ADD would allow for individual achievements that aren't real or genuine, the best analogue is a cure for anorexia or obesity. An ideal weight is not prerequisite to continued struggle in the realm of weight, but plausibly is prerequisite to new struggle in any number of other realms. Similarly, the capacity to give sustained attention is not prerequisite to continued struggle in the realm of attention but, more plausibly, is prerequisite to new struggle in any number of other realms. Assume that we are speaking of those with ADD as a group and therefore apart from idiosyncratic cases. We can then say that there is no need for a cure to erode – although it certainly will shift – the terrain of a person's traits that fall under his genuine self, understood as that part of the person that struggles to achieve. If a cure eliminated some struggle – the struggle to be attentive – it would, as a general statement about the group, enable even more: the struggle to do mathematics, science, philosophy, any number of trades, and beyond. "[M]edication works like a pair of eyeglasses," Edward M. Hallowell and John J. Ratey write, "helping the individual to focus."[13]

Eric Juengst questions whether the "student whose Ritalin-induced concentration yields a high exam grade from one night's cramming . . . earned the grade; that is, whether the grade is serving its usual function of signaling the disciplined study and active learning that the practice of being a student is supposed to involve . . . . If the grade is not serving that function then, for that student, it is a hollow accomplishment."[14] But why wouldn't this statement apply equally to a student who didn't need Ritalin to cram? It's in fact the cramming, not the Ritalin, that substitutes for any more extensive struggle in the realm of disciplined study and active learning. Cramming aside, there is no reason why a cure for ADD wouldn't, as a group-general statement, enable much more struggle – disciplined study, active learning – than any that it might supplant.[15]

As for the cultural consequences of a cure for ADD, they would seem not so serious. Here the best analogue is mild depression; for, like mild depression, ADD has both cultural siblings and cultural spouses. ADD is not the only phenotypic effect of its underlying cultural causes of image bombardment, sensory overstimulation, increased social and domestic demands, and the other cultural experiences that give rise to ADD.[16] Other effects – phenotypic siblings – include stress and edginess, but also the ability to multitask and absorb information imagistically as well as verbally. Nor is phenotypic ADD the only cause of the kinds of cultural experiences, especially experiences of misfittedness, misunderstanding, and getting the book thrown at you, that are its effects. Other causes – phenotypic spouses – include certain kinds of creativity, boredom, exuberance, mischieviousness, "high energy, inutitiveness and enthusiasm"; being a " 'daydreamer,' [or] 'a spaceshot.' "[17] Whatever value one may place on them, the cultural experiences – and the associated art – surrounding ADD will almost certainly survive a cure. Changed, and cultures are always changing anyway, but very much alive.

I want to acknowledge that much of what I have said is predicated on certain garden-variety liberal assumptions. At different points, I have claimed that pluralism within various groups – disagreement among the mildly depressed or deaf or plain-featured as to whether cure would be enhancement and/or genocide – is inveterate. Liberals tend to assume that people can and should be credited with having come to their different views on the merits, and that concerns about false consciousness and bad faith carry the burden of proof. Those have been my assumptions here, and I have offered some arguments for them. I have also assumed that a certain Kantian-style notion of the genuine self, one that is generally associated with a central strand in modern liberalism, is valid for the purposes of Part 2. Possibly, as I suggest at various points, a different conception of the self – Aristotelian, for example – would lead to different conclusions. In Part 3, I again adopted a liberal view in the tradition of Trudeau and Kymlicka, on which what matters is whether a culture can survive at the social and individual levels, even if the group that fostered it disappears.

The principles for which I have argued also focus attention on whatever the here and now happens to be. If, at this particular moment, a condition falls outside the norm while others have achieved the ideal, then cure is warranted. But if circumstances change, if that ideal, once available to everyone, becomes the new norm, then – I argue in Part 1 – no further medical action may be warranted, unless or until some people set off again for a new ideal. There is, in other words, no recourse to a timeless biological or static social notion of normality. The Kantian doctor in Part 2 takes his patients as he finds them, using whatever measure of struggle they have been waging as the benchmark – the "area" of the subject – to be preserved, not some absolute or peak-level baseline notion of individual wholeness. Cultures, I assumed in Part 3, change over time in the sense asserted by Brian Barry. And so – in gauging whether any given culture would survive a cure – we have to look at cultures at the moment, not set a bar on which every aspect of a culture must be preserved in amber for all time. We have to look at the cultural spouses and cultural siblings that a phenotype has at the present time period, not the imponderable as to whether those spouses and siblings will themselves live on, or retain their current character, forever. But we cannot, I believe, do more than this.

In the Introduction I quoted Jonathan Glover, who said that among readers of his book *What Sort of People Should There Be?*, he hoped for an "understanding of the book's values," if not "general agreement" with everything it says. Along similar lines, I doubt that it would be possible for anyone, certainly at this stage in medical history, to offer conclusive arguments that would end even particular strands in the debate over medicine's limits. My goal has simply been to suggest an alternative way of approaching the serious questions that cure/enhancement and cure/genocide thinkers have raised. I explored what would happen if we took a group approach where cure/enhancement writers have considered only the social and individual levels. And I looked at the social and individual levels where cure/genocide writers have focused on the group. My claim is that reversing lenses like this offers greater hope of conducting a productive debate, one in which controversy is sharpened, not eliminated, and in which ambiguities remain fruitful, not barren.

My position resembles that of the forester who stopped to put on his running shoes when a bear charged, knowing that he would have to run faster only than his camp mate, not the bear. I claim only that the approach for which I have argued may get us further than the current ones, not that it will take us to a destination where we can cease debating.

Notes

Introduction: Reversing Our Lenses

1. Jerome McCristal Culp, Jr., "The Michael Jackson Pill: Equality, Race and Culture," *Michigan Law Review* 92 (1994), p. 2615.
2. See, e.g., Sheila M. Rothman and David J. Rothman's informative *The Pursuit of Perfection: The Promise and Perils of Medical Enhancement* (New York: Pantheon, 2003), p. xii.
3. Arthur L. Caplan, "The 'Unnaturalness' of Aging – A Sickness unto Death?" in Arthur L. Caplan, H. Tristram Engelhardt, Jr., and James J. McCartney, *Concepts of Health and Disease* (Reading, Mass.: Addison-Wesley, 1981), p. 735.
4. It's true that we can deem a condition to be a legitimately medical one without deeming it necessary to pay publicly for the development or the delivery of its treatments, even if we could afford to do so. The further possibility that some people might then be able to access a legitimate medical treatment while others might not raises issues of equity that – like most writers who focus on the question of medicine's legitimate terrain – I want to set aside. Hence, I assume that if a condition is legitimately a medical one, public funding for the treatment will be available. In any event, debates about what medicine could legitimately do, assuming affordability, will continue to be live ones, if for no other reason than that the question as to what limits there are on society's medical budget will also always be contestable.
5. President's Council on Bioethics, *Beyond Therapy: Biotechnology and the Pursuit of Happiness* (Washington, D.C., 2003), p. 13.
6. Eric T. Juengst, "What Does Enhancement Mean?" in Erik Parens, ed., *Enhancing Human Traits: Ethical and Social Implications* (Washington, D.C.: Georgetown University Press, 1998), p. 39.
7. President's Council on Bioethics, Staff Working Paper 7, *Distinguishing Therapy and Enhancement* (Washington, D.C., 2002), p. 2.
8. Norman Daniels, "Health-Care Needs and Distributive Justice," *Philosophy & Public Affairs* 10 (1981), p. 170.

9. Georges Canguilhem, *The Normal and the Pathological*, with an Introduction by Michel Foucault (New York: Zone, 1989), pp. 196–7; see also Mary J. Tiles, "The Normal and the Pathological: The Concept of a Scientific Medicine," *British Journal of the Philosophy of Science* 44 (1993), pp. 738, 739: We must determine "the content of the norms . . . without prejudicing the possibility or impossibility of eventually correcting those norms . . .".

10. Dorothy Dinnerstein, *The Mermaid and the Minotaur: Sexual Arrangements and Human Malaise* (New York: Harper and Row, 1977), pp. 21, 22. See also Robert Wachtbroit, "Normality as a Biological Concept," *Philosophy of Science* 61 (1994), p. 581, arguing against the idea that "claims about biological normality are definable [or] explicable in terms of claims about biological functions . . . . [A]ccounts of biological functions cannot explain the concept of biological normality because they presuppose it"; Andrew Elgar et al., *The Ethical QALY* (Surrey: Euromed, 1998), p. 70 ("the issue of normal human functioning cannot be resolved purely by appeal to natural science, precisely because humans are cultural creatures capable of redefining their 'nature' . . . the medical needs of human beings go beyond the physiological. A healthy human being is a creature that can carry out complex social and cultural functions"); Joseph Margolis, "The Concept of a Disease," *Journal of Medicine and Philosophy* 1 (1976), p. 245; and Arthur Kleinman, *The Illness Narratives: Suffering, Healing and the Human Condition* (New York: Basic, 1988), p. 17.

11. "Normally desirable standards for what level of performance? [it must be asked]. Whether a painless 'blotchy discoloration of the skin' is harmful to the agent, and hence an illness, can be determined only if we know which standard of adequate and desirable performance we are supposed to apply." See Robert Brown, "Physical Illness and Mental Health," *Philosophy & Public Affairs* 7 (1977), pp. 24, 26.

12. Christopher Boorse, "On the Distinction between Disease and Illness," *Philosophy & Public Affairs* 5 (1975), pp. 49–68; see also Boorse, "What a Theory of Mental Health Should Be," *Journal for the Theory of Social Behaviour* 6 (1976), p. 73.

13. *The Nature of Disease* (London: Routledge, 1987), p. 76.

14. President's Council on Bioethics, Third Meeting, April 26, 2002, Session 5: Enhancement 1: Therapy vs. Enhancement, pp. 21, 23. Kass and Fukuyama have championed the idea that medicine's goals, whatever they may be, cannot include altering "human nature." Their descriptions of human nature essentially combine various aspects of biological and current social normality, though, and so fall victim to much the same kind of critique.

15. Erik Parens, "Is Better Always Good? The Enhancement Project," in Parens, ed., *Enhancing Human Traits*, p. 12.

16. Willard Gaylin, "Introduction," in Thomas H. Murray, Willard Gaylin, and Ruth Macklin, *Feeling Good and Doing Better: Ethics and Nontherapeutic Drug Use* (Clifton: Humana, 1984), pp. 5, 4.

17. President's Council on Bioethics, Third Meeting, p. 27.

18. Or see the discussion of obese visual art in R. M. Vaughan, "Soft Flesh Feels Very, Very Good," *Globe and Mail*, February 13, 2004, p. R10.

19. See, e.g., Leslie Heywood, *Dedication to Hunger: The Anorexic Aesthetic in Modern Culture* (Berkeley: University of California Press, 1996).

20. Sondra Solovay, *Tipping the Scales of Justice: Fighting Weight-Based Discrimination* (Amherst, New York: Prometheus Books, 2000), p. 130.

21. Hillel Schwartz, *Never Satisfied: A Cultural History of Diets, Fantasies and Fat* (New York: Free Press, 1986), p. 324.

22. Richard Klein, *EAT FAT* (New York: Pantheon, 1996), p. 182.

23. Quoted in Edward Dolnick, "Deafness as Culture," *The Atlantic*, September, 1993, pp. 37–8.

24. Dolnick, "Deafness as Culture," p. 37; see also Mary Ellen Maatman, "Listening to Deaf Culture," *Hostra Labor Law Journal* 13 (1996), p. 330: "What makes the American deaf community more like Hispanic-Americans than disabled Americans is, of course, its culture, including its language."

25. David Ingram, *Group Rights: Reconciling Equality and Difference* (Lawrence: University Press of Kansas), p. 75.

26. Harlan Lane, *The Mask of Benevolence: Disabling the Deaf Community* (New York: Knopf, 1992), p. 16.

27. James N. Myers, "It's Destructive to Carry Self-Acceptance Too Far," *Dayton Daily News*, July 3, 2001, p. 7A.

28. Irving Faber Lukoff and Martin Whiteman, *The Social Sources of Adjustment to Blindness* (New York: American Foundation for the Blind, 1970), p. 6.

29. Lukoff and Whiteman, *Social Sources*, p. 11; see also Jenny Corbett, *Bad-mouthing: The Language of Special Needs* (London: Falmer, 1996), pp. 53–5.

30. Nils Holtug, "Are We Stuck with Our Appearance? Ethics and Cosmetic Surgery," in Inez de Beaufort, Medard Hilhorst, and Soren Holm, eds., *In the Eye of the Beholder: Ethics and Medical Change of Appearance* (Oslo: Scandinavian University Press, 1996), p. 116.

31. Maatman, "Listening to Deaf Culture," p. 330 (quoting Andrew Solomon, "Deaf Is Beautiful," *New York Times Magazine*, August 28, 1994, p. 65); see also Lane, *Mask of Benevolence*, p. 20 ("Black people don't want to be white; deaf people don't want to hear").

32. Carl Elliott, *Better Than Well: American Medicine Meets the American Dream* (New York: Norton, 2003), p. 195.

33. Terry Poulton, *No Fat Chicks* (Secaucus: Carol, 1997), p. 113. See also Joan Dickenson, "Some Thoughts on Fat," in Lisa Schoenfielder and Barb Wieser, eds., *Shadow on a Tightrope: Writings by Women on Fat Oppression* (Iowa City: Aunt Lute, 1983), p. 42: "No feminist suggests that blacks bleach their skin . . . so why should we insist that fat women aim for thinness?" Or consider this item, reported by Richard Perez-Pena and Grant Glickson in "As Obesity Rises, Health Care Indignities Multiply," *New York Times*, November 29, 2003, p. A1: "Dr. [Butch] Rosser, who performs bariatric surgery at Beth Israel Medical Center in Manhattan, underwent one form of it himself and lost more than 170 pounds. Dr. Rosser, an African-American, said being closer to a healthy weight was like a black person 'passing' for white, in that, for the first time, he would hear other doctors' unguarded comments about morbidly obese people."

34. Elliott, *Better Than Well*, p. 198.

35. See, e.g., Dan Brock, *Life and Death* (New York: Cambridge University Press, 1993), p. 106: "Whether the norm be that of the particular individual, or that typical in the particular society or species, the aim of raising people's function to above the norm is not commonly accepted as an aim of medicine of equal importance to restoring function up to the norm"; and F. Kraupl Taylor, *The Concepts of Illness, Disease and Morbus* (New York: Cambridge University Press, 1979), p. 63: "we can expect that most of the attributes of a healthy person are normal by both population standards and his individual standards. In a person who has fallen ill recently some attributes will be abnormal by both population and his individual standards."

36. Robert M. Veatch, "The Medical Model: Its Nature and Problems," in Caplan, Engelhardt, and McCartney, eds., *Concepts of Health and Disease*, p. 526, and Lester S. King, "What Is Disease?" in *Concepts of Health and Disease*, p. 112.

37. See Daniels, "Health-Care Needs and Distributive Justice," p. 159: "normal ranges are society relative . . . normal opportunity-range abstracts from . . . individual differences . . . ."

38. Dan W. Brock, "Enhancements of Human Function: Some Distinctions for Policymakers," in Parens, ed., *Enhancing Human Traits*, pp. 56–7.

39. Allen Buchanan, Dan W. Brock, Norman Daniels, and Daniel Wikler, *From Chance to Choice: Genetics and Justice* (New York: Cambridge University Press, 2000), p. 168.

40. Brock, "Enhancements," p. 56; see also Parens, "Is Better Always Good?," p. 23.

41. Quoted in Margarette Driscoll, "Why We Chose Deafness for Our Children," *Sunday Times,* April 14, 2002, p. 7.

42. See some of the discussion in Anita Silvers, "A Fatal Attraction to Normalizing: Treating Disabilities as Deviations from 'Species-Typical' Functioning," in Parens, ed., *Enhancing Human Traits*, p. 112.

43. Edmond A. Murphy, "The Pursuit of the Minor Premise: A Comment on Normality," *Metamedicine* 2 (1981), p. 297.

44. Margaret Olivia Little, "Cosmetic Surgery, Suspect Norms, and the Ethics of Complicity," in Parens, ed., *Enhancing Human Traits*, p. 172; see also Daniel Callahan, "Transforming Mortality: Technology and the Allocation of Resources," *Southern California Law Review* 205 (1991–2), p. 208.

45. Onyekachi Wambu, "Adventures in the Skin Trade," *The Independent*, London, July 14, 1998, p. 5; Ralph Ellison, "What Would America Be Like without Blacks?," reprinted in David Roediger, ed., *Black on White: Black Writers on What It Means to Be White* (New York: Schocken, 1998), p. 163.

46. Quoted in Brian Grant, ed., *The Quiet Ear: Deafness in Literature* (Boston: Faber and Faber, 1988), p. 79.

47. See, e.g., Pierre Elliott Trudeau, "The Values of a Just Society," in Thomas S. Axworthy and Pierre Elliott Trudeau, eds., *Towards a Just Society: The Trudeau Years* (Markham, Ontario: Viking, 1990), pp. 363–4.

48. Will Kymlicka, *Liberalism, Community and Culture* (Oxford: Clarendon, 1989), pp. 165, 170, 175.

49. Francis Fukuyama, *Our Posthuman Future* (New York: Farrar, Straus and Giroux, 2002), p. 136.

50. Buchanan, Brock, Daniels and Wikler, *From Chance to Choice*, p. 161.

51. John Harris speaks of classifying medical conditions phenotypically, in the sense that I am using that term, according to "what people look like and what they can do" (see John Harris, *Wonderwoman and Superman: The Ethics of Human Biotechnology* [New York: Oxford University Press, 1992], p. 173). Arthur Kleinman says that the "illness experience includes categorizing and explaining, in common-sense ways accessible to all persons in the social group, the forms of distress caused by those pathophysiological processes." See Kleinman, *The Illness Narratives*, p. 4. For an extended defense of the view that "the soul of sickness is closer to the self than the cell," see Robert A. Hahn, *Sickness and Healing: An Anthropological Perspective* (New Haven: Yale University Press, 1995) (quote from p. 39).

    A focus on the phenotypic level avoids some of the difficulties inherent – and noted by many – in the long-standing attempt to define medical conditions by determining which subphenotypic traits are functional in what supraphenotypic environments. To cite an oft-used example, the phenotype of rickets can arise when the subphenotype of a high melanin content combines with the supraphenotype of a northern climate, since the two together inhibit vitamin D absorption from the sun. If we were trying to describe the medical condition here by speaking at levels other than the phenotypic, we might say one of two things: First, a high melanin content is dysfunctional – and also abnormal – in northern environments but not in southern ones. Or, second and conversely, a northern environment is dysfunctional – and also abnormal – for those with higher amounts of melanin but not for those with lower ones. Either way, by focusing on the subphenotypic and supraphenotypic levels, we don't have a definitive answer to the question of whether the condition is functional or dysfunctional, normal or abnormal. But we do have such an answer if we focus on the phenotype: on rickets. Rickets is dysfunctional in both a hot and a cold climate and for those with both high and low melanin contents. And rickets is abnormal in both kinds of climates and for both levels of melanin as well. Hence it's a medical condition.

52. This is not to deny that "a man with a cancer growing silently in his lung . . . would be regarded by both doctors and laymen as urgently in need of treatment" (see R. E. Kendell, "The Concept of Disease and Its Implications for Psychiatry," in *British Journal of Psychiatry* 127 [1975], p. 307), even if it has not manifested phenotypically in the observable way for which I argue here. The fact that it will manifest phenotypically is what makes it a medical condition; the tumor is a medical condition ultimately because of its phenotypic effects as I understand them: its "physical appearances and features" such as pain, debilitation, and death. If, however, there is reason to believe that such a subphenotypic condition will never manifest itself phenotypically, then there is cause not to view it as a medical condition. "[V]irtually all men may get cancer of the prostate if they live long enough," Phillip V. Davis and John G. Bradley ("The Meaning of Normal," *Perspectives in Biology and Medicine* 40 [1996], pp. 71, 75) observe, "and the overwhelming preponderance of them

suffer no clinically significant ill effects from the disease . . . . In our haste to identify subclinical presentations of disease states, we have developed the ability to measure disease states (or the precursors of disease states) without any assurance that the actual illness event will happen . . . if one can look at thin enough slices of the thyroid gland, the prevalence of histologically verifiable papillary carcinoma could equal 100 percent." In older men, subphenotypic prostate cancer might well not be a medical condition – as long as the normal life span remains as it is – since it will never manifest phenotypically. And in all of us, histologically verifiable papillary carcinoma may not be a medical condition, depending on the likelihood of its ever manifesting phenotypically. All of which implies, for my purposes, that the concept of cure can include prevention, since curing a phenotypic medical condition might require attacking it or warding it off as a subphenotypic phenomenon. For similar inclusions of prevention under the ambit of cure, see Nils Holtug, "Does Justice Require Genetic Enhancements?" *Journal of Medical Ethics* 25 (1999), p. 137; Mark J. Cherry, "Polymorphic Medical Ontologies: Fashioning Concepts of Disease," *Journal of Medicine and Philosophy* 25 (2000), pp. 519–38; and Margolis, "The Concept of a Disease," p. 241. As Martha Nussbaum reminds us, the "whole point of medical research is cure." See *The Therapy of Desire* (Princeton: Princeton University Press, 1994), pp. 33–4.

53. Malcolm Gladwell, "Black Like Them," *New Yorker*, April 29, 1996, p. 80.

54. Rainer Spencer, *Spurious Issues: Race and Multiracial Identity Politics in the United States* (Boulder: Westview, 1999), p. 190; see also Orlando Patterson, *The Ordeal of Integration* (Washington: Counterpoint, 1997), p. xi.

55. Katherine M. Franke, "What Does a White Woman Look Like? Race and Erasing in Law," in Richard Delgado and Jean Stefancic, eds., *Critical White Studies* (Philadelphia: Temple University Press, 1997), p. 467.

56. See the discussion in Kathy Russell, *The Color Complex: The Politics of Skin Color among African Americans* (New York: Harcourt Brace Jovanovich, 1992), p. 79.

57. Michael Shermer, "Blood, Sweat and Fears: Why Some Black Athletes Dominate Some Sports and What It Really Means," *Skeptic* (Summer 2000) (quoting Perolof Astrand), p. 44.

58. See Kathy Davis, *Reshaping the Female Body* (New York: Routledge, 1995), p. 76. Few people evidently like to think that they need radical cosmetic surgery. "Drastic changes in appearance are the rare exception, despite the potential influence of television shows that feature extensive surgery like 'Extreme Makover' and 'The Swan' . . . . Facelifts live, but they have become very specific. It's not the face, but the brow or midface that is done" (see James Gorman, "Plastic Surgery Gets a New Look," *New York Times*, April 27, 2004, p. F1).

59. Peter D. Kramer, *Listening to Prozac* (New York: Viking, 1993), p. 289.

60. Connie Strong and Terence Ketter, "Stanford Researchers Establish Link between Creative Genius and Mental Illness," *Business Wire*, May 21, 2002, p. 1; see also Wayne Katon and Peter P. Roy-Byrne, "Mixed Anxiety and Depression," *Journal of Abnormal Psychology* 100 (1991), p. 337.

61. See Peter D. Kramer, "The Valorization of Sadness," in Carl Elliott, ed., *Prozac as a Way of Life* (Chapel Hill and London: University of North Carolina Press, 2004), p. 49.
62. Kramer, *Listening to Prozac*, p. 253.
63. Andrew Solomon, *The Noonday Demon: An Atlas of Depression* (New York: Scribner, 2001), p. 16.
64. See also Nicci Gerrard, review of Andrew Solomon's "Noonday Demon," *Observer*, May 6, 2001, p 16.
65. Jonathan Glover, *What Sort of People Should There Be?* (Harmondsworth: Penguin, 1984), p. 73.
66. See, e.g., the discussion in Reznek, *The Nature of Disease*, ch. 4.
67. See, e.g., W. French Anderson, "Human Gene Therapy: Why Draw a Line?," *Journal of Medicine and Philosophy* 14 (1969), p. 687.
68. See, for similar assumptions in discussions of these topics, President's Council on Bioethics, Third Meeting, pp. 20–1.
69. Rachel Cottam, "Obesity and Culture," *The Lancet* 364 (2004), p. 1202.
70. "Obesity and Culture," p. 1202.
71. Y. Michael Barilan and Moshe Weintraub, "The Naturalness of the Artificial and Our Concepts of Health, Disease and Medicine," *Medicine, Health Care and Philosophy* 4 (2001), p. 319.
72. Tod Chambers, "Prozac for the Sick Soul" in Elliott, ed., *Prozac as a Way of Life*, p. 203.
73. Parens, "Kramer's Anxiety," in Elliott, ed., *Prozac as a Way of Life*, p. 26.
74. *Prozac Nation* (New York: Riverhead Books, 1995), p. 315.
75. Jeungst, "What Does *Enhancement* Mean?", p. 30 ("enhancements are by definition and description improvements: changes for the good").
76. Quoted in Memuna Forna, "Beyond the Pale," *Guardian*, November 2, 1992.
77. See Jack D. Pressman, *Last Resort: Psychosurgery and the Limits of Medicine* (New York: Cambridge University Press, 1998).
78. Holtug, "Are We Stuck with Our Appearance?", p. 115.
79. Gregory Stock, *Redesigning Humans: Our Inevitable Genetic Future* (Boston: Houghton Mifflin, 2002), p. 190. See, as well, Maxwell J. Mehlman, *Wondergenes: Genetic Enhancement and the Future of Society* (Bloomington: Indiana University Press, 2003), p. 97.
80. Marcia Millman, *Such a Pretty Face: Being Fat in America* (New York: Norton, 1980), p. xi; see also Michael Fumento, *The Fat of the Land* (New York: Viking, 1997), p. 262.
81. Shelley Bovey, *The Forbidden Body: Why Being Fat Is Not a Sin* (London: Pandora, 1994), p. 3.
82. See, e.g., Susan Bordo, "*Braveheart, Babe* and the Contemporary Body," in Parens, ed., *Enhancing Human Traits*, p. 199 and Daniels, "Health-Care Needs and Distributive Justice," p. 174.
83. G. A. Cohen, "On the Currency of Egalitarian Justice," *Ethics* 99 (1989), p. 934.
84. Elizabeth Anderson, "What Is the Point of Equality?," *Ethics* 109 (1999), pp. 287–337.

85. See, e.g., Peter Conrad and Joseph W. Schneider, *Deviance and Medicalization* (Philadelphia: Temple University Press, 1992), pp. 26–7, 32; Thomas Szasz, *Ceremonial Chemistry* (New York: Doubleday, 1974), p. 149; and H. Tristram Engelhardt, Jr., *The Foundations of Bioethics*, 2nd edition (New York: Oxford University Press, 1996), p. 224. Christopher Boorse ("What a Theory of Mental Health Should Be," *Journal for the Theory of Social Behaviour* 6 [1976] p. 63) says that a "disease becomes an illness only if it is (i) undesirable for its bearer; (ii) a title to special treatment; and (iii) a valid excuse for normally criticizable behavior." We can now see that not only is (i) hostage to individual idiosyncrasy, relying too heavily on an individual's own view of whether he is ill; and not only is (ii) circular – something is entitled to special treatment because it's an illness, not an illness because it's entitled to special treatment – but any claim based on (iii) will rest on views of autonomy that are too irresolvable to do the criterial work Boorse expects of them.

86. See, e.g., Jurgen Habermas, *The Future of Human Nature* (Cambridge: Polity, 2003), pp. 82, 87.

87. Thomas H. Murray, "Drugs, Sports and Ethics," in Murray et al., eds., *Feeling Good*, p. 120.

88. Glover, *What Sort of People Should There Be?*, p. 18.

89. So I am not addressing, for example, questions of medical futility, which have to do with medicine's technological limits, or matters of rationing, which have to do with medicine's financial limits. I assume, in what follows, that neither of these limits is an issue.

1. Between the Normal and the Ideal

1. Bill McKibben, *Enough: Staying Human in an Engineered Age* (New York: Times Books, 2003), p. 24; see also Lauren Slater, "Dr. Daedalus: A Radical Plastic Surgeon Wants to Give You Wings," *Harper's*, July 2001, p. 58.

2. I stress that my concern lies with group views of what's *socially* normal and *socially* ideal, not with group views of what's normal or ideal for the group itself. Some deaf advocates, for example, believe in the ideal of "the deafer, the better." But it is an ideal they hold out for the deaf alone, not for society as a whole, and so society has no obligation to help realize it. I'll look at this issue later in Part 1.

3. Joseph Margolis, "The Concept of Disease," in Arthur L. Caplan, H. Tristram Engelhardt, Jr., and James J. McCartney, eds., *Concepts of Health and Disease* (Reading, Mass.: Addison-Wesley, 1981), p. 569; and Robert M. Veatch, "The Medical Model," in Caplan, Engelhardt, and McCartney, eds., *Concepts of Health and Disease*," p. 541.

4. Lester S. King, "What Is Disease?,"in Caplan, Engelhardt, and McCartney, eds., *Concepts of Health and Disease*, pp. 110–11; see also Georges Canguilhem, *The Normal and the Pathological* (New York: Zone, 1989), p. 8.

5. Canguilhem, *The Normal and the Pathological*, pp. 196–7; see also Michel Foucault, *The Birth of the Clinic: An Archaeology of Medical Perception* (New York: Vintage, 1975), p. 34.

6. Amid I. Ismail, Hana Hasson, and Woosung Sohn, "Dental Caries in the Second Millennium," paper presented at the NIH Consensus Development Conference on Dental Caries Diagnosis and Management, March 26–8, 2001, p. 4; Arthur Ward Lufkin, *A History of Dentistry* (Philadelphia: Lea and Febiger, 1948), pp. 241, 246; Maurice Smith, *A Short History of Dentistry* (London: Wingate, 1958), pp. 46, 48–9; Thomas M. Marthaler, "Dentistry between Pathology and Cosmetics," *Community Dentistry and Oral Epidemiology* 30 (2002), p. 3. "What one society considers a disease, another may not. [Even now, m]any societies . . . where teeth are normally lost with aging . . . would reject the claim that most of their population was suffering from . . . periodontal disease"; see Harlan Lane, *The Mask of Benevolence: Disabling the Deaf Community* (New York: Knopf, 1992), p. 210.

7. See, generally, Henry W. Noble, "Decline of Decay in the Twentieth Century," *History of Dentistry Research Group Newsletter* 9 (2001), p. 240. Cavity-prevention awareness and the toothpaste tube are both phenomena of the 1890s.

8. L. Jackson Brown, Thomas P. Wall, and Vickie Lazar, "Trends in Caries among Adults 18–45 Years Old," *Journal of the American Dental Association* 133 (2002), pp. 827–34; Fred B. Skrepcinski et al., "Oral Health of Adults and Elders," *The IHS Primary Care Provider* 27 (2002), p. 3.

9. As I will argue shortly, the fact that others had reached the nondecay ideal would justify dentistry's providing a cure – cavity filling, fluoride treatments, sealants – to bring the rest of the population there *only if* those others would have reached that ideal by means (e.g., personal hygiene, better diet) other than the cure. This is likely to have been the case, since access to professional dental care was far from widespread during the period discussed. More generally, if an ideal must have begun to be populated in order for us to justify our delivering a cure to bring the rest of us there, then the cure itself cannot be what started to populate the ideal in the first place. Such a stipulation prohibits the mere invention of a technology for curing a condition from itself justifying us in deeming the condition a medical one. What medicine ought to do should be as independent of what medical technology can do at any given time as of what it can't do.

10. Perhaps " '[i]n one hundred years, everyone will have perfectly-shaped, perfectly white teeth,' predicts Prof. [Elizabeth] Kay" of Dental Health Research Services at the University of Manchester. See Elizabeth Heathcote, "Is This the Body of the Future?", *The Independent*, November 3, 2002, p. 1.2; see also Seth Stevenson, "The Great Whitening Way," *Slate*, April 1, 2002 [online].

11. Roberta Pollack Seid, *Never Too Thin: Why Women Are at War with Their Bodies* (New York: Prentice Hall, 1989), p. 308.

12. See Gerald N. Grob, *The Deadly Truth: A History of Disease in America* (Cambridge, Mass.: Harvard University Press, 2002), pp. 55, 57, 127, 137.

13. Elena Conis, "Capsules, Supplements Like Vitamin C, Only Better – Its Makers Say," *Los Angeles Times*, November 17, 2003, p. F2.

14. See Joseph Margolis, "The Concept of Disease," in Caplan, Engelhardt, and McCartney, eds., *Concepts of Health and Disease*, p. 569.

15. Edmond A. Murphy, "The Pursuit of the Minor Premise: A Comment on Normality," *Metamedicine* 2 (1981), p. 296.

16. President's Council on Bioethics, *Beyond Therapy: Biotechnology and the Pursuit of Happiness* (Washington, D.C., 2003), p. 80.
17. President's Council on Bioethics, Third Meeting, p. 22.
18. See the critical discussion in Mary Eberstadt, "Why Ritalin Rules," *Policy Review* 94 (1999), pp. 24–40.
19. Len Barton, *Disability and Society: Emerging Issues and Insights* (London: Longman, 1996), p. 180.
20. Abraham Rudnick, "The Ends of Medical Intervention and the Demarcation of the Normal from the Pathological," *Journal of Medicine and Philosophy* 25 (2000), p. 578.
21. Theresa Glennon, "Race, Education and the Construction of a Disabled Class," *Wisconsin Law Review* (1995), p. 1305.
22. See, e.g., Anita Srikameswaran, "Tall Enough," *Pittsburgh Post-Gazette*, November 4, 2003, p. D1.
23. See Sheila M. Rothman and David J. Rothman, *The Pursuit of Perfection: The Promise and Perils of Medical Enhancement* (New York: Pantheon, 2003), p. xii. For disagreements with or qualifications of WHO's definition of osteoporosis as a loss of bone density of greater than 2.5 standard deviations below the mean, see Gina Kolata, "Bone Diagnosis Gives New Data But No Answers," *New York Times*, September 28, 2003, p. 1.1; and Sandra G. Boodman, "Hard Evidence," *Washington Post*, September 26, 2000, p. Z12. Daniel Offer and Melvin Sabshin, in *Normality* (New York: Basic, 1974), pp. 52, 54, describe normal IQ as falling within one standard deviation of the mean, while Phillip V. Davis and John G. Bradley ("The Meaning of Normal," *Perspectives in Biology and Medicine* 40 [1996], p. 90) claim that "[n]ormal intelligence . . . falls within two standard deviations of the mean. . . ." And R. E. Kendell ("The Concept of Disease and Its Implications for Psychiatry," *British Journal of Psychiatry* 127 [1975], pp. 308–9) declares that "the boundary between mental subnormality and normal intelligence" is simply "an arbitrary one." In *The Concepts of Illness, Disease and Morbus* (New York: Cambridge University Press, 1979), p. 61, F. Kraupl Taylor says that it "becomes less and less obvious where normal variation ends and abnormality begins. Is, for instance, hypertension a disease, and if so what is the level beyond which blood pressure is abnormal. . . .?" For similar comments on myxoedema, a thyroid condition, see Lawrie Reznek, *The Nature of Disease* (London: Routledge, 1987) p. 127.
24. Christopher Boorse, "On the Distinction between Disease and Illness," *Philosophy & Public Affairs* 5 (1975), p. 50.
25. As Robert Wachtbroit says, "[w]hen normality is understood as a statistical concept, it may be defined as the mean, median or mode – or in terms of some portion of a distribution of items" around them. See "Normality as a Biological Concept," *Philosophy of Science* 61 (1994), p. 580.
26. It's true that there can be disagreement as to where exactly the tail of a skewed curve begins, although unlike with the bell curve, a couple of possibilities suggest themselves. Perhaps, for example, the tail begins where the range around the mean ends, i.e., at the point where there are just as many people on that side of the "mean range" closer to the tail as there are on the side of the mean range closer to the median range.

27. Pregnancy is unusual in that it is a dichotomous condition. True, one could change the dichotomous curve "pregnant/not pregnant" distributed over (adult) society to a more continuous "number of weeks pregnant" distributed over (adult) society. But there would still be a mode of zero weeks and a mean of some number of weeks. More to the point, such a curve would ill reflect what it means to be pregnant, since it would suggest that being eight or nine months pregnant was abnormal, while being a few weeks pregnant was not (such that later abortions would be more medically justified than earlier ones). Pregnancy, because it is viewed as a dichotomous condition, should be arrayed on a dichotomous 'curve.'

    It's also true that many other conditions can be described both dichoto-mously and continuously. For example, a dichotomous curve on which there were only two possibilities, neurotic or nonneurotic, would presumably skew heavily toward the neurotic side. On it, *non*neurotics would be socially abnor-mal and liable for medical cure. But we could also formulate a continuous curve from "no neurosis" to "a great deal of neurosis." We would then (as further discussion in the text will suggest) face a normal curve. My assump-tion in what follows is that when a dichotomous curve suggests one approach and a continuous curve another, we should (unless there are special reasons to the contrary, as with pregnancy) go with the latter.

28. Certainly, a woman can view pregnancy as a normal condition – not a med-ical condition – and yet legitimately seek prenatal care to prevent what are abnormal conditions (diabetes, fetal hemorrhaging), conditions that she legitimately deems medical ones, from besetting herself or her fetus. She could also regard pregnancy as abnormal, as a medical condition, and yet deem traditional delivery instead of abortion to be the cure. The fact that pregnancy can legitimately be regarded as an abnormal condition, in other words, is a necessary but not sufficient prerequisite for the legitimacy of abor-tion, given the other issues it raises, to be classed as an appropriate cure.

    I want to acknowledge the following implication of what I'm saying here: As noted, a woman can regard her pregnancy as socially abnormal, assum-ing that she locates the normal range around the *mode* on the dichotomous curve of pregnant/not pregnant distributed across the adult population. But equally, a man could view his inability to get pregnant as abnormal, and hence a medical condition, if he located the normal range around the *mean*. If the only issues were philosophical, not material or technological, it would – on this curve and on the argument I am advancing – fall within the purview of medicine to furnish him a cure.

29. Perhaps the analogy between cystic fibrosis and homosexuality, on these criteria, would be closer if we discovered that there exists a "gay gene," or at least some genetic basis for sexual orientation. At the genotypic level, a gay gene would be abnormal, just as a cystic fibrosis gene is. But we would, I think, still have a conflict of curve: one between a curve at the genotypic level skewed toward not having the gay gene and a bimodal one at the phenotypic level distributing sexual orientation across society as a whole. My approach says that – in cases of conflict – we should rely, for the purposes of defining legitimate medical conditions, on the less genotypically, more phenotypically constructed curve. The fact that a gay man has a gay gene but – on the

appropriate phenotypic curve of sexual orientation – can legitimately view himself as perfectly normal in being attracted to men means that he doesn't have a medical condition.

30. By contrast, suppose that with cystic fibrosis we created a curve, distributed over society, in which one pole bundled the two traits "carrier of the cystic fibrosis gene" and "phenotypically manifests cystic fibrosis" and the other pole bundled the two traits "noncarrier of the cystic fibrosis gene" and "doesn't phenotypically manifest cystic fibrosis." This curve would skew heavily toward the latter pole. But – unlike with homosexuality – if we then constructed two separate curves over society, one from carrier to noncarrier, and the other from phenotypically manifests cystic fibrosis to doesn't phenotypically manifest cystic fibrosis, we'd also have two curves skewed in exactly the same way. Cystic fibrosis gives rise to no conflict in curve.

31. I'll take this opportunity to note that bimodal distributions of phenotypic characteristics (unlike genotypic, cellular, or biochemical characteristics) are rare apart from gender-related distributions (sexual characteristics, sexual orientation), so I will say no more about them here. I note that since a bimodal curve over society as a whole is simply two normal curves in a series, gay men could not only legitimately regard their sexual orientation as normal (something they could not do on the curve skewed toward "sexual orientation to women" distributed over men only), they could also legitimately regard their sexual orientation as abnormal, hence a medical condition to be cured. But so could straight men legitimately regard their sexual orientation as abnormal, hence a medical condition to be cured. (For an analysis of organized psychiatry's discussions of these issues, see Herb Kutchins and Stuart A. Kirk, *Making Us Crazy: DSM: The Psychiatric Bible and the Creation of Mental Disorders* [New York: Free Press, 1997], ch. 3.)

32. As a society's natality increases – as it comes to contain more young people – the bell curve distributing muscle strength over society as a whole might begin skewing toward the high muscle-strength pole. Conversely, as mortality decreases, the curve could begin skewing toward the low muscle-strength pole. In either case, though, a seventy-year-old woman could still view her weak muscles as socially abnormal.

33. Norman Daniels, "Health-Care Needs and Distributive Justice," *Philosophy & Public Affairs* 10 (1981), p. 170.

34. Marc Steinbach, "The Normal in Cardiovascular Diseases," *Lancet* 7369 (1964), p. 1117. See also Cathryn Jakobson Ramin, "In Search of Lost Time," *New York Times Magazine*, December 5, 2004, p. 81: "Years ago, [the clinical psychologist Thomas Crook III] noted the insensitivity implicit in telling older patients who complained about their memories that what they were experiencing was inconvenient but typical. If they were in complaining that they could no longer read, he wrote in 1993, 'it would scarcely occur to the clinician to inform them that their problems are no worse than those of other persons of the same age and, therefore, that they do not merit treatment.' "

35. W. Miller Brown points out that once we begin dividing society into biologically based groupings, there's no obvious stopping point and subdivisions can grow ever finer. See "On Defining 'Disease,'" *Journal of Medicine and Philosophy* 10 (1985), p. 315.

36. Andrew Pollack, "Forget Botox. Anti-Aging Pills May Be Next," *New York Times*, September 21, 2003, p. 3.1; and Margolis, "The Concept of Disease": "There are diseases that are lethal but *there are no diseases that are classified as such merely because they result in death*" (p. 570).

37. See David Gems, "Is More Life Always Better? The New Biology of Aging and the Meaning of Life," *Hastings Center Report*, 33 (July/August 2003), pp. 31–9.

38. It may well be that to cure phenotypic manifestations of aging we have to attack aging at the genotypic or cellular level, and that if we do so, we will postpone or even eliminate death. Nevertheless, it's not necessarily the case that cures for phenotypic aging need rely on stopping cellular aging, or that even if they do, that means that cellular aging itself – let alone death – is a medical condition.

39. Arthur L. Caplan, "The 'Unnaturalness' of Aging – A Sickness Unto Death?" in Caplan, Engelhardt, and McCartney, *Concepts of Health and Disease*, p. 728.

40. See some related discussion in Christopher Boorse, "A Rebuttal on Health," in James M. Humber and Robert F. Almeder, eds., *What Is Disease?* (Totowa: Humana, 1997), p. 91.

41. Peter D. Kramer, "The Valorization of Sadness," in Carl Elliott, ed., *Prozac as a Way of Life* (Chapel Hill and London: University of North Carolina Press, 2004), p. 50.

42. F. Kraupl Taylor, "The Medical Model of the Disease Concept," in Caplan, Englehardt, and McCartney, eds., *Concepts of Health and Disease*, p. 580.

43. Julie Poppen, "Private IQ Tests Raise Concerns," *Rocky Mountain News*, April 13, 2002, p. 3B. Those who fall on the high half of the IQ bell curve must view their condition as normal but, with respect to the populated polar ideal of IQ, could still be a "group harboring the condition" in that they could legitimately demand a cure to take them to that ideal.

44. Ronald Kotulak, "Redefining Humanity: Brain Research Forces an Agonizing Reappraisal," *Chicago Tribune*, May 15, 1988, p. 1.

45. *The Pursuit of Perfection*, pp. xv–xvi.

46. *The Pursuit of Perfection*, p. xv.

47. In a related vein, Rothman and Rothman worry that if we begin a process of making human growth hormone available to (say) the lowest 10 percent on the height distribution, then those "who had been one step above the lowest percentiles in height would now drop to the bottom; they would then seek treatment, and the reshuffling process would begin all over again" (*The Pursuit of Perfection*, p. 183). Yes, but – on the approach that I am advancing – even if this process were taken to the nth degree, it would come to a stop where everyone is just as tall as the socially ideal group is now, and I presume that that ideal would be a golden mean located somewhere between the shortest and the tallest. Beyond that, there would be no medical call for human growth hormone.

48. Lester S. King, "What Is Disease?" in Caplan, Engelhardt, and McCartney, *Concepts of Health and Disease*, pp. 110–11.

49. *The Pursuit of Perfection*, p. xiii.

50. Cass R. Sunstein, "Keeping Up with the Cloneses," *New Republic*, May 6, 2002, p. 32.

51. King, "What Is Disease?", p. 111.

52. See Jerome C. Wakefield, "The Concept of Mental Disorder," *American Psychologist* 47 (1992), p. 376.

53. See Debra Viadero, "Researchers: Nature × Nurture = Startling Jump in IQs," *Education Week* 21 (January 23, 2002), p. 8: "Better nutrition, the increasing complexity of daily life, 'smarter' genes, video games and computers – even, goes one theory, the prevalence of mazes and word games on fast-food placemats and cereal boxes – all may have played a role in boosting IQ power across time." And medicine could match only whatever IQ level these slow-moving broader forces had already populated at any time.

54. I am assuming that, as Ezekiel J. Emanuel says (see *The Ends of Human Life: Medical Ethics in a Liberal Polity* [Cambridge, Mass.: Harvard University Press, 1991], p. 22), "the ends of medicine are not self-defining but are in need of specification"; and further, as Emanuel says, that such specification requires a "political" account and debate. For our purposes here, I don't need to take the radical position that the internal practices of medicine themselves disclose no information that could help determine the boundaries of medicine as a social institution, just that they cannot supply a complete description. "The right to define a problem and to locate it within one social domain rather than another – to construe it as a problem of medicine, education, rehabilitation, religion . . . is won by struggle and enterprise," in particular, political argument and debate. See Harlan Lane, "Cochlear Implants: Their Cultural and Historical Meaning," in John Vickrey Van Cleve, ed., *Deaf History Unveiled* (Washington, D.C.: Gallaudet, 1993), p. 278; see also Project Report, "The Goals of Medicine," in Mark J. Hanson and Daniel Callahan, eds., *The Goals of Medicine* (Washington, D.C.: Georgetown University Press, 1999), pp. 6, 13, 17.

55. Peter J. Whitehouse, Eric Juengst, and Maxwell Mehlman ("Enhancing Cognition in the Intellectually Intact," *Hastings Center Report* 27 [1997], p. 14), in discussing cognitive functioning, acknowledge the twin possibilities of using social norm and social ideal to determine whether a particular condition is a medical one but then dismiss them. Two "alternatives," they write, "would be to fall back on the statistical average cognitive capacity of the population to indicate the ceiling of legitimate requests for enchancement, or to set the ceiling by the best available example of excellent cognitive functioning and to bring people up to that level on request." But "[t]hese alternatives," Whitehouse et al. go on to say, "raise [a] problem [having to do with] fairness. . . .[Specifically,] it becomes difficult to resist an 'equalizing' policy that would discriminate against the naturally fortunate. If a statistical norm is used as a goal for services, then all those born above the norm will be denied access [to medical services]. Even if the ceiling were set at the level of the species' cognitive champion, the less fortunate would have a disproportionate claim on enhancement resources." It's not clear to me how the notion that the less fortunate would have a greater claim on medical resources than the more fortunate counts as an argument against a scheme for defining

medicine's role. And if it doesn't, then this objection to using norms and ideals to define medical conditions is problematic.

56. "Although one might argue that the notion of the 'ugly' is parasitic on that of 'beauty,' " Kathryn Pauly Morgan writes, "this is not entirely true since the ugly is also contrasted with the plain." See "Women and the Knife: Cosmetic Surgery and the Colonization of Women's Bodies," *Hypatia* 6 (1991), p. 45.

57. Kathy Davis, *Reshaping the Female Body* (New York: Routledge), p. 161.

58. Medard Hilhorst, "At Face Value and on Second Thoughts," in Inez de Beaufort, Medard Hilhorst, and Soren Holm, eds., *In the Eye of the Beholder: Ethics and Medical Change of Appearance* (Oslo: Scandinavian University Press, 1996), p. 78.

59. Ben Pappas and Eric Anderson, "I Got an Extreme Makeover," *Us Weekly*, April 14, 2003, pp. 60–1.

60. Holtug, "Are We Stuck with Our Appearance?," p. 111.

61. Sander L. Gilman, *Creating Beauty to Cure the Soul: Race and Psychology in the Shaping of Aesthetic Surgery* (Durham: Duke University Press, 1998), p. 4.

62. Davis, *Reshaping the Female Body*, p. 100.

63. Richard Simpson, "Hollywood's Best Parts (for Plastic Surgeons)," *Evening Standard* (London), March 15, 2001, p. 3. See also Anna Kirkland and Rosemarie Tong, "Working within Contradiction: The Possibility of Feminist Cosmetic Surgery," *Journal of Clinical Ethics* 7 (1996), p. 151 and Thomas D. Rees, "The Surgery of Aesthetics: A Modern Dilemma," *Aesthetic Plastic Surgery* 15 (1991), p. 101: "Surgeon[s] thus are asked to expand their practices to include improving the appearance of people who want to look better than 'normal' or 'average' – that is, who want to more closely approximate cultural ideals. . . ."

64. Of Maria Shriver, the journalist Heather Mallick writes that "[s]he's too taut, her jaws look like Wusthof knives" (see "I'll Take Paul and Dalton Any Day," *Globe and Mail*, October 4, 2003, p. F2). Alessandra Stanley describes the producer Robert Evans's "face [as] unnaturally taut" (see "The Kid Stays in the Cartoon," *New York Times*, October 22, 2003, p. E1).

65. See J. H. Langlois and L. A. Roggman, "Attractive Faces Are Only Average," *Psychological Science* 1 (1990), pp. 115–21.

66. David Brown, "Attractive Facial Features Aren't Just Average Matter; Slight Distortion of Certain Dimensions Found to Create a More Pleasing Appearance," *Washington Post*, March 21, 1994, p. A03.

67. Wendy Chapkis, *Beauty Secrets: Women and the Politics of Appearance* (Boston: South End Press, 1986), p. 174.

68. Naomi Wolf, *The Beauty Myth* (New York: Anchor, 1992), p. 143; see also Kuni J. Simis, "What Is Beautiful Is Good, But . . . ," in de Beaufort, Hilhorst, and Holm, eds., *In the Eye of the Beholder*, pp. 176, 178.

69. Consider the spectrum from wrinkled to smooth skin. Doesn't the ideal here, too, fall at the polar end of smoothness, not at a golden mean between it and wrinkledness? Yes, but "smooth" skin, though occupying a polar ideal on the wrinkled–smooth spectrum, is actually an aggregate of a couple of golden-mean ideals from two other spectrums: the spectrum from loose to taut skin, where ideal skin is a golden mean with some healthy hypodermic

fat, and the spectrum from oily to dry, where it occupies a golden mean of dewiness. See, e.g., Anahad O'Connor, "In Case of the Falling Face, Gravity Is Acquitted," *New York Times*, October 26, 2004, p. F6.

70. Carl Elliott, *Better Than Well: American Medicine Meets the American Dream* (New York: Norton, 2003), p. 234.

71. In stating that penis size is distributed on a bell curve, am I not confining the distribution to men? No. If we distributed penis size over society as a whole, we would get a mode, or hump, at zero inches and then a bell curve distributed over a range between a very small and a much larger number of inches. Such a distribution over society as a whole would in effect be neither a bell nor a skewed nor even a bimodal curve, but a hybrid of all three. Nevertheless, anyone who fell anywhere on the bell curve portion – almost all of whom would be men – could ask to be brought to any other point on it, since the bell curve itself is silent on cutoffs.

 Here, though, is what I think is a better way of putting it: If we are going to distribute any characteristic over society as a whole, then it has to be described in a gender-neutral way, such as "size of the sexual organs," not "size of the penis." In which case, again, we'd get a bell curve, on which anyone could regard his or her condition as normal – or abnormal.

72. See President's Council on Bioethics, *Beyond Therapy*, p. 237: "When we analytically separate out any one dimension for description – say, for example, the range from cheerful to gloomy – we notice that people distribute themselves along a full and continuous spectrum of 'normal' mood states and dispositions, and this seems true across the board."

73. Taylor, "The Medical Model," p. 580. See also Daniel Offer and Melvin Sabshin, *Normality* (New York: Basic, 1974), pp. 50, 54: "the Bell-shaped curve . . . determin[es] statistically normal distributions of behavior . . . with both extremes connoting pathology. One either has too much anxiety or too little." Hence the "wide variation in observed behavior engaged in by 'normal' people" (p. 62).

74. Kramer, *Listening to Prozac* (New York: Viking, 1993), p. 265.

75. William Skidelsky, "Jagged Little Pills," *Guardian*, February 14, 2002, p. 2.14; see also Lauren Slater, *Prozac Diary* (New York: Random House, 1988), p. 22.

76. Peter C. Whybrow, *A Mood Apart: Depression, Mania, and Other Afflictions of the Self* (New York: Basic Books, 1997), p. 255.

77. Abraham Maslow and Bela Mittelmann, "The Meaning of 'Healthy' ('Normal') and of 'Sick' ('Abnormal')," in Caplan, Engelhardt, and McCartney, eds., *Concepts of Health and Disease*, p. 48. See also Philip Rieff, *Freud: The Mind of a Moralist* (New York: Anchor, 1961), p. 389.

78. Kramer, *Listening to Prozac*, p. 12.

79. Kramer, *Listening to Prozac*, p. 269.

80. Those who, in discussing such issues, claim that no one has reached an ideal mental state tend to speak about someone who is totally free of all neuroses, not free of this or that neurosis. See, e.g., Offer and Sabshin, *Normality*, p. 46: "According to the dominant psychoanalytic motif, . . . perfection is an ideal that living man can never reach, albeit a few select individuals have, at times, come close to the ideal"; see also p. 103.

Freud viewed normality as an ideal, an understanding that comports with the notion of a golden-mean ideal range overlaying the peak in the bell curve distributing any given neurotic quality. True, Freud believed that no single person is likely ever to achieve the normal-ideal mental state on each and every spectrum: anxious to tranquil, solemn to vivacious, gloomy to cheerful. But he did believe it possible for people, from time to time, to reach a normal-ideal range along one or another particular dimension in isolation. In aggregate or in total, in other words, "a normal ego . . . is, like normality in general, an ideal fiction." In a disaggregated sense, however, "[e]very normal person, in fact, is only normal on the average . . . the degree of [his ego's] remoteness from one end of the series [distributing a particular mental trait] and of its proximity to the other will furnish us with a provisional measure of what we have . . . termed an 'alteration of the ego.' " See "Analysis Terminable and Interminable" (1937) in Joseph Sandler, ed., *On Freud's "Analysis Terminable and Interminable"* (New Haven: Yale University Press, 1991), p. 22; and also Robert Brown, "Physical Illness and Mental Health," *Philosophy & Public Affairs* 7 (1977), p. 22.

81. The BMI is controversial, but principally because it's not clear to what extent overweight carries increased mortality or health risks of other sorts, e.g, diabetes, heart disease. Here, though, the question is whether overweight/obesity per se can be seen as a medical condition.
82. Libby Brooks, "Size Matters," *Guardian*, March 16, 2002, p. 16.
83. Sharlene Hesse-Biber, *Am I Thin Enough Yet?* (New York: Oxford University Press, 1996), p. 63.
84. Deborah A. Sullivan, *Cosmetic Surgery: The Cutting Edge of Commercial Medicine in America* (New Brunswick: Rutgers University Press, 2001), p. 22.
85. Susan Bordo, "Reading the Slender Body," in Mary Jacobus, Evelyn Fox Keller, and Sally Shuttleworth, eds., *Body/Politics* (New York: Routledge, 1990), pp. 97, 100, 102.
86. Beth MacInnis, "Fat Oppression," in Catrina Brown and Karin Jasper, eds., *Consuming Passions: Feminist Approaches to Weight Preoccupation and Eating Disorders* (Toronto: Second Story, 1993), p. 73.
87. Alessandra Stanley, "Prime Time Gets Real with a Plump Heroine," *New York Times*, October 8, 2002, p. E1.
88. Richard Klein, *EAT FAT* (New York: Pantheon, 1996), p. 13; Seid, *Never Too Thin*, pp. 315, 216.
89. See, e.g., Leanne Joanisse and Anthony Synnott, "Fighting Back," in Jeffrey Sobal and Donna Maurer, eds., *Interpreting Weight: The Social Management of Fatness and Thinness* (New York: Aldine de Gruyter, 1999), p. 65.
90. Holtug, "Are We Stuck with Our Appearance?," p. 112.
91. Joanne Finkelstein, *The Fashioned Self* (Cambridge: Polity Press, 1991), p. 88.
92. Eva A. Szekely and Patricia DeFazio, "Gaps between Feminist Understandings of Eating Disorders and Personal Experience," in Brown and Jasper, eds., *Consuming Passions*, p. 369.
93. Barbara McFarland and Tyeis Baker-Baumann, *Shame and Body Image: Culture and the Compulsive Eater* (Deerfield Beach: Health Communications, 1990), pp. 67, 93.

94. Szkely and DeFazio, "Gaps," p. 367. See also Steve Clarke, "Oh the Joys . . . Oh the Pleasures," *Daily Telegraph,* April 14, 1994, p. 15; "Fat People Rally in Defence of Obesity," *Ottawa Citizen,* May 14, 2000, p. A7; Grant Pick, "What's Wrong with This Picture?," *Chicago Tribune Magazine,* July 9, 2000, p. 17; and, of course, Klein, *EAT FAT.*

95. In Part 3, I give an explanation of the difference between lifestyle and culture.

96. See Lane, *The Mask of Benevolence,* p. 228.

97. Being pleasingly plump, *zaftig,* or curvaceous, if ideal, all fall within legitimate conceptions of the golden-mean social ideal; these are not group ideals for the fat. I note that the idea of a "thin fat" person does come up in Part 3, but the context and meaning are totally different.

98. Brooks, "Size Matters," p. 16.

99. Hilde Bruch, *Eating Disorders: Obesity, Anorexia Nervosa and the Person Within* (New York: Basic, 1980), p. 89.

100. Thomas F. Cash and Edwin A. Deagle III, "The Nature and Extent of Body-Image Disturbances in Anorexia Nervosa and Bulimia Nervosa: A Meta-Analysis," *International Journal of Eating Disorders* 22 (1997), pp. 109, 114.

101. Rita Freedman, *Beauty Bound* (Lexington, Mass.: Lexington Books, 1986), p. 151.

102. See, e.g., Brooke Adams, "Culture of Thinness Drives Eating Disorders," *Salt Lake Tribune,* July 5, 2004, p. C1; and also, more generally, A. J. Gruber et al., "Why Do Young Women Diet? The Roles of Body Fat, Body Perception, and Body Ideal," *Journal of Clinical Psychiatry* 62 (2001), pp. 609–11.

103. *www.livejournal.com/community/ed_recovery*

104. *www.livejournal.com/community/anagothica*

105. *www.livejournal.com/community/ana_bella*

106. Cynthia Billhartz, "'Ana' and 'Mia' . . . On the Web and Out of Control," *St. Louis Post-Dispatch,* March 5, 2002, p. E1.

107. Quoted in Cash and Deagle, "The Nature and Extent of Body-Image Distortions," p. 119.

108. Seid, *Never Too Thin,* p. 310.

109. Billhartz, " 'Ana' and 'Mia', " p. E1; see also Lucy Atkins, "It's Better To Be Thin and Dead Than Fat and Living," *Guardian,* July 23, 2002, p. 10.

110. *www.livejournal.com/community/fat_ana*

111. *Jaoii.lunarpages.com/articles/art.html*

112. *www.livejournal.com/community/ana_bella*

113. Mary Ann Sighart, "Mary Ann Sighart Rebels Against the Model Body," *The Times* (London), April 9, 1994 [online].

114. Marya Hornbacher, *Wasted: A Memoir of Anorexia and Bulimia* (New York: HarperFlamingo, 1998), pp. 107, 253.

115. Seid, *Never Too Thin,* p. 304.

116. In fact, only conditions that distribute themselves on bell curves for determining social normality, and that use a polar range for determining social ideal – as running does – will routinely have such a subgroup: I'm referring to those who, falling as they do on the high half of the bell curve but below

the high-end pole, cannot legitimately consider themselves socially abnormal, but can deem themselves to fall short of a populated social ideal and so seek a cure.

117. See, e.g., Elmer Sterken, "From the Cradle to the Grave: How Fast Can We Run?" *Journal of Sports Sciences* 21 (2003), pp. 479–91.

118. See, e.g., Hal Higdon, "Getting Started – Beginning Runner's Guide: – Breathing," "Juggling Your Workouts," and "Injuries," www.runnersworld. com/home/0,1300.5–60–63–245,00.html; 5–60–68–256,00.html; 1300,2–51–54–1032,00.html

119. Quoted in Tom Derderian, *Boston Marathon* (Champaign, Ill.: Human Kinetics, 1996), p. 587.

120. President's Council on Bioethics, *Beyond Therapy*, p. 102; Ron Rapoport, *See How She Runs: Marion Jones and the Making of a Champion* (Chapel Hill: Algonquin, 2000), p. 133.

121. Mary J. Tiles, "The Normal and the Pathological: The Concept of a Scientific Medicine," *British Journal of the Philosophy of Science* 44 (1993), p. 738.

122. Sterken, "From the Cradle to the Grave," p. 489.

123. See, e.g., Catherine Edman, "Footfest Soccer Tournament Puts Focus on Fun," *Daily Herald* (Arlington, Va.), March 2, 2000, p. 1; Kim Skinner, "Win or Lose, Everyone Gets a Ribbon," *Dayton Daily News*, March 2, 1995, p. Z.2.8; and Carl Honore, *In Praise of Slow* (Toronto: Knopf, 2004), p. 38. I discuss the notion of accommodation further in Part 3.

124. "If everyone were similarly enhanced . . . new expectations for higher records would arise, thus preserving opportunities to reveal character through effort." See Michael H. Shapiro, "The Technology of Perfection: Performance Enhancement and the Control of Attributes," *Southern California Law Review* 65 (1991–2), p. 79.

125. Sigmund Loland, *Fair Play in Sport* (London: Routledge, 2002), p. 59: "A 60-year-old cross-country skier may compete with and indeed beat a 20-year-old opponent. A 75-year-old runner may perform better than her 50-year-old competitor."

126. President's Council on Bioethics, *Beyond Therapy*, p. 297.

127. See *Vision Problems in the U.S.* (Chicago: Prevent Blindness America, 2002), p. 4. According to the Center for Disease Control's *Summary Health Statistics for U.S. Adults: National Health Interview Survey 1999*, 84.3% of Americans over eighteen say that they have good hearing and 91.4% say that they have no vision trouble. See also Carol Padden and Tom Humphries, *Deaf in America: Voices from a Culture* (Cambridge, Mass.: Harvard University Press, 1988), p. 4; and www.hearink.com/hlfacts.htm: "78% of people over 55 have normal hearing."

128. Floyd Matson, *Walking Alone and Marching Together: A History of the Organized Blind Movement in the United States 1940–1990* (Baltimore: National Federation of the Blind, 1990), p. 1020.

129. See Robert A. Scott, *The Making of Blind Men: A Study of Adult Socialization* (New York: Russell Sage, 1969), p. 24 and Robert Amendola, "Perceptual Rehabilitation: The Replication of Visual Perception through Nonocular Sensory Perceptions," in John F. Muldoon, ed., *Essays on Blindness*

Rehabilitation (New York: American Foundation for the Blind, 1990), p. 56.

130. Naomi Schor, "Blindness as Metaphor," *Differences: A Journal of Feminist Cultural Studies* 11 (1999), p. 99.

131. Amendola, "Perceptual Rehabilitation," p. 56. See also Andrew Potok, *Ordinary Daylight: Portrait of an Artist Going Blind* (New York: Holt, Rinehart and Winston, 1980), p. 240.

132. Margarette Driscoll, "Why We Chose Deafness for Our Children," *Sunday Times*, April 14, 2002, p. 7.

133. Beryl Lieff Benderly, *Dancing without Music: Deafness in America* (Garden City: Doubleday, 1980), pp. 226, 248. See also Oliver Sacks, *Seeing Voices: A Journey Into the World of the Deaf* (Berkeley: University of California Press, 1989), p. 2; and Lennard J. Davis, *My Sense of Silence: Memoirs of a Childhood with Deafness* (Urbana: University of Illinois Press, 2000), pp. 146–7.

134. Rod Michalko, *The Mystery of the Eye and the Shadow of Blindness* (Toronto: University of Toronto Press, 1998), p. 93. Of course, those who occupy the hump of the curves skewed toward seeing or hearing – whether or not they view their vision or hearing as normal – can also ask to be brought to that populated polar-range ideal.

135. Michael E. Monbeck, *The Meaning of Blindness: Attitudes Toward Blindness and Blind People* (Bloomington: Indiana University Press, 1973), pp. 146–7.

136. And it is a curve: Racial features vary "gradually rather than by the sharp, clearly demarcated disjunctions fundamental to the myth that races can be readily differentiated. The physical features that code as race do not change abruptly between those who are White and those who are Black or Yellow. Instead, these features permute gradually, permitting no easy divisions." See Ian F. Haney Lopez, *White by Law: The Legal Construction of Race* (New York: New York University Press, 1996), p. 82.

137. "Race, Education and the Construction of a Disabled Class," p. 1294.

138. See Ronald E. Chennault, "Giving Whiteness a Black Eye: An Interview with Michael Eric Dyson," in Joe L. Kincheloe et al., eds., *White Reign: Deploying Whiteness in America* (New York: St. Martin's, 1991), p. 302.

139. Maurice Berger, *White Lies* (New York: Farrar, Straus and Giroux, 1999), pp. 210, 212.

140. See Haney Lopez, *White by Law*, p. 184: "Whiteness exists as a pole around which evolve imaginary racial meanings."

141. Vivian Owusu, "Fade to White: Lightening Creams: Skin-Bleaching Products a Hot Seller – and a Controversial Issue," *National Post*, January 21, 1999, p. B9.

142. Ann Cook, "Black Pride? Some Contradictions," in Toni Cade Bambara, ed., *The Black Woman: An Anthology* (New York: New American Library, 1970), p. 152.

143. Kim Shayo Buchanan, "Creating Beauty in Blackness," in Brown and Jasper, eds., *Consuming Passions*, p. 40.

144. Quoted in Joy Bennett Kinnon, "Is Skin Color Still an Issue in Black America?" *Ebony* 55, April 2000, pp. 52–6.

145. Elliott, *Better Than Well*, p. 166.

146. Berger, *White Lies*, p. 23 (emphases mine).

147. Ruth Frankenberg, "The Mirage of Unmarked Whiteness," in Birgit Brander Rasmussen et al., eds., *The Making and Unmaking of Whiteness* (Durham: Duke University Press, 2001), p. 80.

148. Birgit Brander Rasmussen et al., "Introduction," in Rasmussen et al., eds., *The Making and Unmaking of Whiteness*, p. 10; Ruth Frankenberg, *White Women, Race Matters* (Minneapolis: University of Minnesota Press, 1993), p. 193.

149. Tiles, "The Normal and the Pathological," p. 734.

150. Lionel K. McPherson and Tommie Shelby, "Blackness and Blood: Interpreting African American Identity," *Philosophy & Public Affairs* 32 (2004), p. 181. Of course, while there are genetic bases for hair color and skin color and nose shape – in other words, for each of the individual characteristics that make up putative black and white racial phenotypes – there is (at present) no known genetic basis for sexual orientation, only for gender: the two components that make up putative straight and gay phenotypes.

151. Joseph L. Graves, Jr., "Symposium: Is There a Biological Basis for Race and Racial Differences?" *Insight on the News*, May 28, 2001, p. 40: "Sri Lankans, Nigerians and Australoids share a dark skin tone but differ in hair type."

152. Jon Entine, "The Straw Man of 'Race'," *The World & I* 16 (2001), pp. 294–317.

153. See the discussion in S. O. Y. Keita, et al., "Conceptualizing Human Variation," *Nature Genetics Supplement* 36 (2004), p. S17.

154. Jon Entine, *Taboo: Why Black Athletes Dominate Sports* (New York: Public Affairs, 2000), p. 112; Armand Marie Leroi, "A Family Tree in Every Gene," *New York Times*, March 14, 2005, p. A21.

155. Luigi Luca Cavalli-Sforza, *Genes, People and Languages* (San Francisco: North Point Press, 2000), p. 11.

156. See Haney Lopez, *White by Law*, pp. 100–1 ("races have no biological basis") and Andrew Hacker, "Saved?" *New York Review of Books*, August 14, 2003, p. 23 ("the notion of 'race' [has] no basis in genetics or biology").

157. Cavalli-Sforza, *Genes, People and Languages*, p. 11. As Robin Marantz Henig ("The Genome in Black and White [and Gray]"), *New York Times Magazine* October 10, 2004, p. 50) writes: "In Northern Europe, for instance, people carrying mutations of lighter skin color thrived, probably because the scarcity of sunlight made dark-skinned people especially susceptible to Vitamin D deficiency and rickets." But, of course, "most of the variations occurred in the non-functional regions of the genome."

158. Virginia L. Blum, *Flesh Wounds: The Culture of Cosmetic Surgery* (Berkeley: University of California Press, 2003), p. 264.

159. Indeed, even now, blacks who seek to lighten their skin via cosmetics often claim to be doing so to reach a beauty norm, not a race norm. Yet as long as the notion of racial norms intervenes on them, those beauty norms will themselves remain "racialized" (see Susan Bordo, "*Braveheart, Babe*," p. 193). Consider Carl Elliott's statement, which I quoted earlier: Black Americans, Elliott writes, "run the danger of constantly seeking an ideal of beauty that they will never quite reach." The reference is to an ideal of beauty, not of race. But the ideal of beauty to which Elliott refers is a polar racialized ideal

at the white end of the spectrum. If and when the notion of race is totally expunged from the social construction of facial features, then cosmetic surgery could be a legitimate cure. But at that point, we would be talking about cosmetic surgery not for racial features, but for facial features, and confronting not polar but golden-mean ideals.

160. Unlike blindness, autism confronts a conflict of curve, a situation that in effect causes some autistic spokespeople to explicitly identify with black Americans (see Frank Klein, "Don't Cure Autism Now!", *home.att.net/~ascaris1/dontcure.html*, p. 1). Autism consists of a number of phenotypic traits – "communications difficulties . . . sensory issues, . . . overexcitability [and] self-destructive behavior" but also "far-reaching memory skills, . . . extraordinary 3D simulating skills [and] mathematical abilities" – each of which any given autistic person might display to a greater or lesser extent (see "Don't Cure Autism Now!", p. 1, and Letter from Edan, "Re-branding Asperger's," *www.aspergia.com*). If these traits are seen as all of a piece – as intertwined characteristics of a single phenotype called "autism" – then such a phenotype clearly falls on the tail of the skewed curve distributing that phenotype over society as a whole. Placed on such a curve, where the hump is occupied by the nonautistic majority, autism and even mild autism/Asperger's syndrome would uncontroversially be deemed abnormal, hence medical conditions.

On another view, however, each of autism's particular traits can be unbundled from the others and placed on its own bell curve. One such bell curve would distribute society as a whole over the spectrum from "unable to read people" to "uncannily sensitive to people"; another, from "overly calm" to "overly excitable"; still another, from "overly susceptible to sensory stimulation" to "underresponsive to sensory stimulation"; and so on. Bell curves, unlike skewed curves, are themselves silent on the matter of where to draw cutoffs between normality and abnormality. As Morton Ann Gernsbacher ("Autistics Need Acceptance, Not Cure," *www.autistics.org/library/acceptance.html*) writes, "autistic traits," looked at one by one, "are distributed into the non-autistic population." Accordingly, autistic writers who wish to deny that autism is a medical condition refuse to view it as a unitary "collection . . . of traits," an interconnected "bundle of problems," or a "bundle of abnormalities" (see "DSM," *www.autcom.org/dsm.html*; Michelle Dawson, "We Are Not Your Community," *www.sentex.net/~nexus23/naa_asol.html*, p. 3; and Amanda Baggs, "The World I Want to Live In," *www.autistics.org/library/want.html*, p. 2). Instead, they regard autism as a series of disparate phenotypes that would essentially fall along a series of different bell curves: "[a]utistic people vary widely across multiple dimensions," so "[w]here do you draw the line and who draws it?" (Dawson, "We Are Not Your Community," p. 8). On any such curve, as the buttons sported by attendees at a recent advocacy conference put it, an autistic person can deem his phenotype "Mildly Normal," "Profoundly Normal," or "Moderately Normal" (see *www.autcom.org/reflections.html*). Of course, any given autistic person could alternatively view his position on any of these bell curves as abnormal and seek a cure.

2. A Visit to the Kantian Doctor

1. See, e.g., Erik Parens, "Is Better Always Good?," in Erik Parens, ed., *Enhancing Human Traits: Ethical and Social Implications* (Washington, D.C.: Georgetown University Press, 1998), p. 13 and Bill McKibben, *Enough* (New York: Henry Holt, 2003), pp. 6, 49.

2. Staff Working Paper, *Distinguishing Therapy and Enhancement* (April 26, 2002), p. 4.

3. Robert L. Simon. "Good Competition and Drug-Enhanced Performance," in William J. Morgan and Klaus V. Meier, eds., *Philosophic Inquiry in Sport* (Champaign, Ill.: Human Kinetics, 1995), p. 210; see also Norman Fost, "Banning Drugs in Sports: A Skeptical View," *Hastings Center Report*, August 1, 1986, pp. 5–10.

4. Roger Gardner, "On Performance-Enhancing Substances and the Unfair Advantage Argument," in Morgan and Meier, eds., *Philosophic Inquiry in Sport*, p. 228.

5. "Unlike . . . drugs that change the agent directly, the equipment that boosts our performance does so indirectly. . . . We can see how the springier running shoes, the lighter tennis racket, and the bigger baseball glove enable their users to go faster, hit harder, and reach the formerly unreachable – yet without apparently changing them in their persons or native powers"; see President's Council on Bioethics, *Beyond Therapy: Biotechnology and the Pursuit of Happiness* (Washington, D.C., 2003), p. 124. "Yet," the President's Council then goes on to say, "appearances are deceiving. That . . . they remain but visible tools in our hands does not mean that we remain in fact unaltered" (p. 125).

6. See, e.g., Michael Lavin, "Sports and Drugs: Are the Current Bans Justified?," in Morgan and Meier, eds., *Philosophic Inquiry in Sport*, pp. 232–8.

7. McKibben, *Enough*, pp. 6–7.

8. President's Council on Bioethics, *Beyond Therapy*, p. 128.

9. *Beyond Therapy*, p. 129.

10. Lavin, "Sports and Drugs," p. 233.

11. See some of the discussion in David DeGrazia, "Prozac, Enhancement, and Self-Creation," *Hastings Center Report*, March–April 2000, pp. 34–40.

12. See generally the essays from *Journal of the Philosophy of Sport* collected in Morgan amd Meier, eds., *Philosophic Inquiry in Sport*; and, more specifically and explicitly, Gardner, "On Performance-Enhancing Substances," p. 227.

13. Comments of Council member William B. Hurlbut, President's Council on Bioethics, Fifth Meeting, July 11, 2002, Session 4: Enhancement 2: Potential for Genetic Enhancement in Sports, p. 32; see also Anjan Chatterjee, "Cosmetic Neurology," *Neurology* 63 (2004), p. 971.

14. Dan W. Brock, "Enhancements of Human Function: Some Distinctions for Policymakers," in Parens, ed., *Enhancing Human Traits*, p. 58.

15. Track shoes or running blocks might not seem like cures in the way a pill does, but of course, prosthetic shoes and leg braces are considered curative (in the sense of being medical devices). And so the question would be whether

there's any reason for the former not to be deemed legitimately medical if the latter are.

16. Michael Walzer, *Thick and Thin: Moral Argument at Home and Abroad* (Notre Dame: University of Notre Dame Press, 1994), pp. 23–4.

17. See, e.g., Doug Robinson, "Bonds' Hitting Feats Clouded by Steroids," *Deseret News*, December 20, 2004, p. D1: "Bonds recently admitted to a grand jury that he took steroids but didn't know what it was. Not that it matters. The result is the same: He gained an illegal advantage."

18. The premise here is not that struggle, and the traits born of it, are always valuable, always a source of good things. That would constitute a utilitarian justification for struggle. Rather, the premise, a Kantian one, is that struggle, and any traits born of it, are genuine ones however much or little anyone might value them. Not everyone, after all, values the trait of being a champion shot putter, even if it was attained through years of struggle. But most will agree that the person concerned will have acquired his abilities genuinely, not artificially.

19. David Osterman, "Trying to Keep Track," *Orange Country Register,* April 20, 1998, p. D1.

20. Linford Christie, *To Be Honest with You* (London: Michael Joseph, 1995), p. 23.

21. Sigmund Loland, *Fair Play in Sport* (London: Routledge, 2002), p. 57.

22. Mike Stroud, *Survival of the Fittest: Understanding Health and Peak Physical Performance* (London: Jonathan Cape, 1998), p. 36.

23. Carl Elliott, *Better Than Well: American Medicine Meets the American Dream* (New York: Norton, 2003), p. 39.

24. See *Muscle: Confessions of an Unlikely Bodybuilder* (New York: Poseidon, 1991), p. 123.

25. Michael J. Sandel, "The Case against Perfection," *The Atlantic*, April, 2004, p. 56.

26. See Michael J. Sandel, "What's Wrong with Enhancement?," paper prepared for the December 2002 meeting of the President's Council on Bioethics.

27. G. A. Cohen, "On the Currency of Egalitarian Justice," *Ethics* 99 (1989), p. 934.

28. See, e.g., "Harry Frankfurt, "Identification and Wholeheartedness," in Ferdinand Schoeman, ed., *Responsibility, Character and the Emotions* (New York: Cambridge University Press, 1987), pp. 27–45.

29. "The Case against Perfection," p. 62.

30. "The Case against Perfection," p. 54.

31. Chris Schombs, "What Makes Special Olympics Special," *St. Petersburg Times*, March 29, 1990, p. 2.

32. Johnny Watterson, "IOC Must Watch Out for Flying Amputees," *Irish Times*, Sepetmber 24, 2004, p. 23.

33. In effect, the current doping tests assume a Kantian equation of natural gifts with a cure, since a sample "will be deemed to contain a Prohibited Substance [if the sample] so deviates from the range of values normally found in humans that it is unlikely to be consistent with normal endogenous production." In other words, an athlete whose levels deviate sufficiently from

the norm will be penalized regardless of whether such levels are innately or exogenously caused. See World Anti-Doping Agency (WADA), *The World Anti-Doping Code: The 2005 Prohibited List International Standard* (Montreal: WADA, 2005), p. 2. WADA, of course, is not operating in a world in which it's legitimate for medicine to bring the social norm to a populated ideal. But if it were, then the premise of its testing is that medical cures – steroids – that brought a runner to an already populated social ideal would be no less legitimate than a natural gift that did the same.

34. Nicci Gerrard, review of Andrew Solomon's *Noonday Demon, Observer,* May 6, 2001, p. 16.

35. Peter D. Kramer, *Listening to Prozac* (New York: Viking, 1993), p. 277; see also Stephen Braun, *The Science of Happiness* (New York: Wiley), pp. 3–4, 17.

36. "The quest for self-improvement [via Prozac] make[s] the 'self' smaller," the President's Council on Bioethics says; see *Beyond Therapy,* p. 301.

37. Morag MacSween, *Anorexic Bodies: A Feminist and Sociological Perspective on Anorexia* (London: Routledge, 1993), p. 93. "It's a struggle everday to get through this," Catherine Holahan quotes another as saying; see "Yahoo to Withdraw Eating-Disorder Sites," *Dayton Daily News,* August 5, 2001, p. 19A; see also Kim Chernin, *The Obsession: Reflections on the Tyranny of Slenderness* (New York: Harper and Row, 1981), p. 53.

38. *www.livejournal.com/community/ana_bella*

39. *www.livejournal.com/community/peo_reality*

40. *www.livejournal.com/community/ed_recovery.* Of course, anorexics also describe the struggle to *become* anorexic in similar terms. That doesn't mean that anorexia is not a medical condition, only that the trait of being anorexic can be a genuine one in the terms I'm using.

41. We may "be put off by the prospect of treatment as it appears to render one passive," Susie Orbach writes; we "might well ask where one might find a therapeutic context that honours . . . the client and her struggle. . . . Self-help has a role to play in coming to grips with and recovering from anorexia . . . in order to get through the anorexia it will be necessary to struggle. . . ." See *Hunger Strike: The Anorectic's Struggle as a Metaphor for our Age* (New York: Norton, 1986), pp. 119–20, 122.

42. See, generally, Michael Fumento, *The Fat of the Land* (New York: Viking, 1997); Jeanne Schinto, "Think Thin (Fat Chance)," *Nation,* November 3, 1997, pp. 54–7, and Editorial, "No Willpower? Pop This Pill," *Norfolk Virginian-Pilot,* November, 21, 2004, p. J4: "Many of [the weight-reduction pill] Accomplia's salutary effects could be had in time with hard work, but Americans want instant results, preferably with no more effort than washing down a pill with a glass of water."

43. See also, e.g., Gloria Cahill, "The Serious Side of Rosie O'Donnell," *Radiance: The Magazine for Large Women* (Winter 1997)[online], in which Rosie O'Donnell speaks of the nobility involved in her "struggle" against obesity.

44. Irving Faber Lukoff and Martin Whiteman, *The Social Sources of Adjustment to Blindness* (New York: American Foundation for the Blind, 1970), p. 169.

45. Georgina Kleege, *Sight Unseen* (New Haven: Yale University Press, 1999), pp. 17, 19.

46. Kleege, *Sight Unseen*, p. 19; Rod Michalko, *The Mystery of the Eye and the Shadow of Blindness* (Toronto: University of Toronto Press, 1998), p. 115.

47. Mary Ellen Maatman, "Listening to Deaf Culture: A Reconceptualization of Difference Analysis Under Title VII," *Hostra Labor Law Journal* 13 (1996), p. 331; Douglas C. Baynton, *Forbidden Signs: American Culture and the Campaign against Sign Language* (Chicago: University of Chicago Press, 1996), p. 146.

48. Joseph P. Shapiro, *No Pity: People with Disabilities Forging a New Civil Rights Movement* (New York: Times Books, 1993), p. 11.

49. Maatman, "Listening to Deaf Culture," p. 334.

50. *Narrative History of Deaf America* (Silver Spring: National Association of the Deaf, 1981), p. 360.

51. Margarette Driscoll, "Why We Chose Deafness for Our Children," *Sunday Times*, April 14, 2002, p. 7.

52. Beryl Lieff Benderly, *Dancing without Music: Deafness in America* (Garden City: Doubleday, 1980), pp. 224–5.

53. John Hull, *Touching the Rock* (New York: Pantheon, 1990), p. 205. Oliver Sacks speaks of Hull's having come "to accept [his blindness] with remarkable equanimity . . . . " See "The Mind's Eye," *New Yorker*, July 28, 2003, p. 50.

54. Autistic spokespeople compare themselves with the deaf in this way. It's true that, often with the assistance of the controversial Applied Behavior Analysis (ABA) technique, many autistics have partially or even wholly succeeded in eroding or rolling back their tendencies to self-injure, and to "flap, finger-flick, rock, twist, rub, clap, bounce, squeal, hum, scream, hiss, and tic," replacing them with "typical, expected behaviors . . . such as pointing, joint attention, appropriate gaze, and eye contact. . . . " (Michelle Dawson, "The Misbehaviour of the Behaviourists," *www.sentex.net/~nexus23/naa_aba.html*, pp. 4, 13). Yet although "[y]ou can train an autistic person to act superficially normal," his brain nevertheless "is still wired in a way that makes it autistic, and the thoughts in the head are still the thoughts of an autistic" (Frank Klein, "ABA Proponents Attack Autistics: Showing Their True Character," *home.att.net/~ascaris1/attacking-autistics.html*, p. 4). Our question, then, should not be whether struggle can overcome or even eliminate autistic behaviors, but whether it can overcome or eliminate the underlying mental states, just as the question, for deafness, is not whether struggle can eliminate deaf behavior, but deafness itself. And the answer in both cases is no. That's why many autistic activists deride ABA, as deaf activists do oralist lipreading, as forms of passing – struggles against the phenotype of autism or of deafness that merely mask it without altering it (Jane Meyerding "Thoughts on Finding Myself Differently Brained," *anmi.autistics.us/jane.html*, p. 5). ABA, one website says, "does not treat autism; it teaches the autistic to hide that he or she is autistic. That's like claiming you can 'treat' deafness by harassing the person into semi-successfully lipreading" (*Moggy Mania*, April 13, 2004, *www.sonic.net/mustang/moggy/archives/001521.html*, p. 1). What follows from this, however – at least on the approach that I am advancing – is that a cure for autism would not be enhancement, since it would not supplant any

genuine achievements a person had scored over her phenotype, only, at most, those that mask it.

55. Elliott, *Better Than Well*, p. 192.
56. Lawrence Blum, *I'm Not a Racist, But.* . . . (Ithaca and London: Cornell University Press, 2002), pp. 86, 83.
57. I borrow this phrasing from David R. Roediger, *Colored White* (Berkeley: University of California Press, 2002), p. 17.
58. Maurice Berger, *White Lies* (New York: Farrar, Straus and Giroux, 1999), p. 103.
59. See Joseph R. Washington, Jr., *Marriage in Black and White* (Boston: Beacon Press, 1970), pp. 141, 328; Anthony Appiah, "But Would That Still Be Me? Notes on Gender, 'Race,' and Ethnicity as Sources of 'Identity'," *Journal of Philosophy* 87 (1990), p. 498; and Adrian Piper, "Passing for White, Passing for Black," in Elaine K. Ginsberg, ed., *Passing and the Fictions of Identity* (Durham and London: Duke University Press, 1996), p. 268.
60. Anna Kirkland and Rosemarie Tong, "Working within Contradiction: The Possibility of Feminist Cosmetic Surgery," *Journal of Clinical Ethics* 7 (1996), p. 154.
61. Wendy Chapkis, *Beauty Secrets: Women and the Politics of Appearance* (Boston: South End Press, 1986), pp. 175, 171; see also Sara Halprin, *Look at My Ugly Face!* (New York: Viking, 1995), p. 57, equating "struggling to match some [beauty] standard" with the attempt to pass.
62. Rita Freedman, *Beauty Bound* (Lexington, Mass.: Lexington Books, 1986), p. 210.
63. Freedman, *Beauty Bound*, p. 54.
64. "[B]eauty aids," Mary Winter writes ("Implants for Harding?" *Rocky Mountain News*, July 21, 2001, p. 2F), "are just as disingenuous as cosmetic surgery."
65. Robin Tolmach Lakoff and Raquel L. Scherr, *Face Value: The Politics of Beauty* (London: Routledge and Kegan Paul, 1984), pp. 24, 25.
66. Cosmetic-surgery patients no longer seem concerned to hide the fact that they've had surgery (which is, of course, not to say that they no longer wish to conceal plain facial features; quite the contrary). They are, in other words, no longer concerned that people think that their noses or eyes or skin are innate as opposed to being the result of a cure. On a Kantian understanding, however, there is nothing remarkable here. One's innate looks are no more or less genuine (or otherwise creditworthy) than one's surgically corrected or cured features would be. Another way of making the point would be to say that if skin with a certain youthful appearance or breasts of a certain shape are meant to signal a biological reality – fertility – then their resulting from a cure would be something to conceal. The fact that so many don't so conceal underscores the extent to which such phenotypes are valued more for their social than their biological "functionality"; or, put another way, they are testimony to the extent to which sex is understood in recreative, not procreative, terms. In which case, the difference between a breast of a certain size and shape due to an implant and one due to natural tissue is apparently irrelevant. For some related discussion, see

William Ian Miller, *Faking It* (New York: Cambridge University Press, 2002), pp. 208–10.

67. See Hoberman, "The Sportive Agon in Ancient and Modern Times," in Janet Lungstrum and Elizabeth Sauer, eds., *Agonistics: Arenas of Creative Contest* (Albany: SUNY Press, 1997), pp. 300–1. "[A] player is missing the point if she *doesn't* practice and struggle," Michael H. Shapiro says. See "The Technology of Perfection: Performance Enhancement and the Control of Attributes," *Southern California Law Review* 65 (1991–2), p. 60.

68. It's possible that pre-cure, when his gifts were well below the social ideal, a sprinter's diet, exercise, and training had shaved an extra 0.5 second off his time. Now that his gifts are at the socially ideal level, thanks to cure, the same amount of diet, exercise, and training can shave only 0.2 second off simply because he is approaching the outer limits of current human possibility. Still, that means only that the 0.2 second post-cure represents the same achievement as 0.5 second pre-cure, not that his post-cure struggle has necessarily diminished.

69. President's Council on Bioethics, Session 4, Enhancement 2: Potential for Genetic Enhancement in Sports, July 11, 2002, p. 23 (emphasis mine).

70. Elsewhere, Kass has expressed the non-Kantian view that there is a pertinent difference between natural and cure-born gifts; see Kass and Eric Cohen, "The Price of Winning at Any Cost," *Washington Post*, February 1, 2002, p. B5.

71. Thomas H. Murray, "Drugs, Sports, and Ethics," in Thomas H. Murray, Willard Gaylin, and Ruth Macklin, eds., *Feeling Good and Doing Better: Ethics and Nontherapeutic Drug Use* (Clifton: Humana, 1984), pp. 123, 124.

72. "Bonds' Hitting Feats Clouded by Steroids," p. D1.

73. Matt Marrone "Bonds Signature Still Carries Juice," *New York Daily News*, December 12, 2004, p. 73.

74. J. N. Gelberg, "The Rise and Fall of the Polara Asymmetric Golf Ball: No Hook, No Slice, No Dice," *Technology in Society* 18 (1996), p. 97.

75. Gelberg, "The Rise and Fall," p. 99.

76. Gelberg, "The Rise and Fall," p. 99.

77. Roger Angell, "Sammy's Sin," *New Yorker*, June 30, 2003, pp. 33–4.

78. So, for example, a golfer with a greater natural gift for accuracy would have to use less of the "saved" struggle that the distance ball affords him, while one with a smaller natural gift for accuracy would have to use more.

79. Quoted in Simon Hughes, "Leading Scientist Warns That Football Could Fall Victim to Blood-Boosting Drug," *Daily Telegraph*, December 20, 2001, p. 4.

80. Keith R. Williams, "Biomechanical Constraints and Economy of Movement in Endurance Performance," in R. J. Shephard and P.-O. Astrand, eds., *Endurance in Sport: Volume II of the Encyclopaedia of Sports Medicine*, 2nd edition (Oxford: Blackwell Science, 1992), p. 245.

81. Amy Shipley, "Stimulants Are a Major League Hit," *The Washington Post*, March 2, 2003, p. D1.

82. T. J. Quinn, "Greenie War Could Change the Look of MLB," *New York Daily News*, January 16, 2005, p. 71. Of course, if a player takes so much in the way of stimulants that he exceeds the populated social ideal of alertness and energy,

i.e., the highest level attained without any such stimulants, then he's gone too far. As Timothy Noakes says, with the aid of stimulants some "athletes, quite simply, have moved off the natural bell-shaped curve of normal human performance," and if they do, then on criteria set out in Part 1, medicine has exceeded its proper bounds. See Timothy Noakes, "Tainted Glory – Doping and Athletic Performance," *New England Journal of Medicine*, 351 (2004), p. 849.

83. Steve Wilstein, "Misleading Supplements Confuse, Trap NFL Players," *National Post*, November 22, 2002, p. S2.

84. Brittany L. Agro, "Outrunning His Asthma," *Daytona Beach News Journal*, November 15, 2003, p. 4C.

85. Greg Botelho, "Sports Talk in the Valley – Perseverance Needs More Than a Deep Breath," *Providence Journal*, October 1, 1999, p. C3.

86. John Korobanik, "Many Athletes Depend on Controversial Drug," *Edmonton Journal*, July 20, 2001, p. H2.

87. K. F. Dyer and T. Dwyer, *Running Out of Time: An Examination of the Improvement in Running Records* (Kensington, Australia: New South Wales University Press, 1984), p. 131.

88. Dick Patrick, "Sprinter Tells of Descent," *USA Today*, December 3, 2004, p. C12.

89. Quoted in Patrick, "Sprinter Tells of Descent," p. C12.

90. See also Steven Downes, "Searching for Blood on the Tracks," *Sunday Herald*, Glasgow, August 6, 2000, p. 12: "steroids . . . only permit the user [sic] to train harder, or to recover from their exertions more quickly. The steroid cheat still has to work hard. EPO, however, is different: it delivers an immediate 10% improvement in performance." The same issues arise with high-altitude training, which produces more red blood cells. On the one hand, undergoing the training requires struggle: "I went up there to altitude," swimmer Mike Johnson told *Newsday*, "and I died the first few days of training . . . . It really hit me hard." On the other hand, high-altitude training apparently can relieve struggle: "those training at altitude, after swimming their best times at sea level, felt they had something left," according to U.S. Swimming Federation coach John Troup. See John Jeansonne, "The Controversy Surrounding Blood Doping," *Newsday*, April 5, 1988, p. 105. Whether more struggle is relieved than imposed is a matter for individual cases.

91. Steroids allow you to "take the easy way out"; they "substitute for hard work," according to high school coach Ray Fenton; see John Scafetta, "Hard Work or Cutting Corners?," *Las Vegas Review*, January 4, 2005, p. 5E. Even Kelli White, on another occasion, said, " 'It was too easy,' when describing how she won while on performance-enhancing drugs." See Alan Loyd, "Steroid Issue Hits upon Our Values," *South Bend Tribune*, January 6, 2005, p. 1.

92. What about dietary practices such as carbohydrate loading? Are they enhancements? Again, it depends on the ease with which they can be executed. Carbohydrate loading requires a kind of struggle, such as restricting one's diet and fasting at certain times. It also necessitates engaging in "a lot of sprints to deplete the muscle glycogen already there . . . so that the muscle cells supercompensate" using the loaded carbohydrates, thereby rendering

the runner's "stores of muscle glycogen . . . optimal on the day of the race" (Robert Cross, "Marathon," *Chicago Tribune*, October 17, 1985, p. 1). Observations such as these take carbohydrate loading out of the realm of enhancements and place them in the domain of genuine struggle, such that whatever the athlete accomplishes as a result of carbohydrate loading can be seen as redounding to the subject as genuine achievement. It may be easier – require less struggle – for him to endure during the race as a result of having loaded, but he has to struggle so much more to undertake the loading properly. Of course, while the criterion is a Kantian one, it may well be – for any given athlete – that the ease-up in struggle to endure during the race that loading in fact enables is greater than the new quantum of struggle required by the loading process itself. In which case, on the Kantian criterion, carbohydrate loading would reduce the domain of accomplishments attributable to the genuine subject and enhance his performance artificially.

93. Elliott, *Better Than Well*, p. 215.

94. *Listening to Prozac*, p. 278.

95. Elio Frattaroli, *Healing the Soul in the Age of the Brain* (New York: Viking, 2001), p. 385.

96. "Permit a somewhat outrageous thought experiment," The President's Council on Bioethics says (see *Beyond Therapy*, p. 256): "might St. Augustine's physician, were it available, have offered him a mood-brightener? With it, he might still have mourned [his mother's loss], but with less misery. He might have had to struggle less . . . . " Yet the Council also says that "SSRIs [such as Prozac] do not completely sever how one feels from how one lives. On the contrary, in many therapeutic uses, they probably re-link feeling and living, permitting passionate experience its proper role in fostering further growth" (p. 260).

In opposing the use of Prozac for mild depression, critics often try to belittle its effectiveness. "SSRIs [such as Prozac] cannot implant a groundless emotion, and they cannot instantly transform a soul," *Beyond Therapy* says (p. 254). In so claiming, though, *Beyond Therapy* necessarily, and ironically, buttresses claims made by the defenders of Prozac that it indeed does not bring about a great transformation, but rather simply allows the patient to confront reality unclouded by neurosis. Obviously, this doesn't happen in all cases of Prozac use, but it would with our hypothesized super-Prozac. "[W]hile they do not live falsely," *Beyond Therapy* concludes (p. 254), "many of [those on Prozac] do live different lives than they would otherwise have lived." But so do we all, at every moment.

97. See, e.g., Lois Finelli, "Revisiting the Identity Issue in Anorexia," *Journal of Psychosocial Nursing and Mental Health Services* 39 (2001), p. 25 ("insight-oriented psychotherapy may be useful but only after starvation has been treated successfully").

98. There might be some perverse incentives here in that, knowing that physicians are proposing to give them a cure that will take them from their struggle-born achievement to the social ideal, individuals won't struggle much at all. That may be. But I will shortly amend this point in a way that will make the

perverse incentives concern irrelevant when I discuss a response that the patient could make to such a proposal by her physician.

99. See, e.g., "Anti-Obesity Drugs: Still Useful If Used Appropriately, But No Instant Fix," *Royal College of Physicians News*, April 24, 2003 [online] and Lesley White, "A Slim Hope Still Beats a Fat Chance," *Sunday Times*, January 26, 1997.

100. Philip Terzian, "Well-Intentioned Tyrants Are Worse Than Smoking," *Las Vegas Review-Journal*, May 9, 1997, p. 15B.

101. Eve Ensler, *The Good Body* (New York: Villard, 2004), p. xiv.

102. "I am 'recovered'. . . now . . . [and] am completing my honors degree in psychology . . . there is life after anorexia." See Bagsofjoy, "Life After Anorexia," posted November 20, 2002, on *www.pale-reflections.com*

103. Saying that a cure for anorexia or obesity can be requisite for embarking on many other struggles in life isn't the same as saying that such cures are necessary for the pursuit of a "great many life plans." That's an argument that's used, with limited success, as I argued in the Introduction, to try to determine what cures are necessary to bring people to a state of social normality: The socially normal person is someone possessed of those capabilities necessary for many life plans. Here the task is to gauge whether a cure is likely to leave an individual personally genuine, not make her socially normal. And for a cure for anorexia or obesity to leave an individual personally genuine – for the cure not to be enhancement – we must be able to presume plausibly that she actually will embark on another project. In addition, we must be able to assume that any such project will involve as much struggle as she was waging before. By contrast, for a cure to bring a person to social normality on the great many life plans view, she needn't actually engage in any of those life plans; nor need any of them involve struggle. All that matters is that she's now normal.

104. A query: What if we were to accommodate (more on this in Part 3) obesity and anorexia? What if, in other words, we changed social attitudes and reconfigured the environment so that a socially ideal body size was no longer prerequisite, as it can now reasonably be felt to be, for struggle – effort, exertion, and quest – in numerous social domains such as romance, politics, sports, or business? Under these circumstances, we would raise an eyebrow at someone who said, to a Kantian doctor, "Cure me of my obesity so that I can stop the struggle to diet and exercise, enter the realm of politics or business or romance, and wage my subject-expansive struggle there." In this respect, obesity would have become like slow running: A cure would not be prerequisite to struggle in other spheres. In another respect, though, difference would remain. With slow running, a cure that endows the runner with a permanent gift for running at the socially ideal level can, nevertheless, be prerequisite to continued full struggle – continued diet, exercise, and training – in aid of even further success in the sphere of running. But a cure for obesity, one that (permanently, as I am assuming) brought the person to a socially ideal body size, would never be prerequisite to any further struggle – diet, exercise – in the sphere of weight control. And so the Kantian doctor

could not reasonably extract a continued commitment to such struggle as a condition of cure.

105. Robyn Norwood, "The List of Professional Athletes Turning to Laser Surgery to Improve the Way They See Is Growing," *Los Angeles Times*, April 25, 2000, p. 1.

106. John Garrity, "James McLean Battles the Effects of an Old Illness That Hurt His Putting," *Sports Illustrated Golf Online*, May 7, 2003. Of course, Woods might argue that he undertook the laser surgery in order to embark on a new struggle, say learning to fly a plane, that would bring a compensating area of personal achievement within the realm of the subject to make up for his no longer having to struggle to do eye exercises or squint to see the green. But while laser surgery can be prerequisite to struggles in domains other than golf, being able to see the green would still not be a credible prerequisite to struggle in the domain of music.

107. Kramer, *Listening to Prozac*, p. 258.

108. See, generally, Adam Phillips, *On Kissing, Tickling and Being Bored: Psychoanalytic Essays on the Unexamined Life* (Cambridge, Mass.: Harvard University Press, 1993), especially the Introduction and ch. 11.

109. Frank Klein, "Autism, Genius, and Greatness," *http://home.att.net/ ~ascaris1/index.html*, p. 2.

110. Peter D. Kramer, *Against Depression* (New York: Viking, 2005), pp. 83, 264.

111. Randolph M. Nesse, "Is Depression an Adaptation?," *Archives of General Psychiatry* 57 (2000), pp. 14–20.

112. Hence, if we were to cure the mild depressive's diffidence without eradicating the underlying depressive mental state, this would cause him increased pain – increased painful encounters and endeavors – just as would eradicating autistic flapping or withdrawal without eliminating autistic mental states or trying to stamp out ASL, as many oralists had hoped to do, without eradicating deafness. If eradicating diffidence without expunging the underlying depressive mental state is a recipe for increased pain, then what, so psychoanalysis asks, about eradicating the depressive mental state without resolving whatever underlying conflict caused it? It seems, however, much more likely that curing a depressive mental state even without resolving the underlying conflict will reduce total pain, while curing diffident behavior without curing the underlying depressive mental state will increase pain.

113. Kramer, *Against Depression*, pp. 64, 67.

114. See Erica Goode, "Seeing Pessimism's Place in a Smiley-Faced World," *New York Times*, August 5, 2000, p. F7; President's Council on Bioethics, *Beyond Therapy*, p. 258.

115. Elliott, *Better Than Well*, ch. 3.

116. *Listening to Prozac*, pp. 291–5.

117. Anthony Daniels, "Mental Instability or Mindless Activity?" *Sunday Telegraph*, February 24, 2002, p. 13; David Healy, *The Antidepressant Era* (Cambridge, Mass.: Harvard University Press, 1997), p. 29; and Matt Seaton, "Health: When You're Up, You're Up, But When You're Down . . . ," *Guardian*, July 19, 2001, p. 2.14.

118. See, e.g., John P. Hewitt, Michael R. Fraser, and LeslieBeth Berger, "Is It Me or Is It Prozac?: Antidepressants and the Construction of Self," in Dwight Fee, ed., *Pathology and the Postmodern* (London: Sage, 2000), pp. 170, 176; and Kyung M. Song, "Some Experts Say Drug Makers, Doctors Too Quick to Medicate Social Phobias," *Knight Ridder Tribune Business News*, September 22, 2004, p. 1: "John Walker, a clinical psychologist and director of the Anxiety Disorders Program at St. Boniface General Hospital in Winnipeg, Canada . . . said people fall into a natural distribution curve between outgoing and bold and being shy and cautious. It's difficult to pinpoint where on that bell curve social phobia lies. 'Any cutoff point you make will automatically be aribitrary,' said Walker."

119. Ronald Kotulak, "Depression Looks More Like a Physical Thing," *Knight Ridder Tribune News Service*, July 12, 2002, p. 1; see also President's Council on Bioethics, *Beyond Therapy*, p. 234: "Some of us are very hard on ourselves, filled with self criticism and doubt about self-worth at even the smallest falling short; others of us are very self-content or even self indulgent, able to brush aside even large failures with what looks like blithe indifference."

120. Karen Horney refers to this neurotic as the "expansive" type in contrast to the "self effacing" type. Expansive types "tend to overrate their capacities or their special gifts" and are "smug"; also, the expansive type's "need for proving his mastery often . . . gives him the incentive to have a try at tasks which others might be wary of tackling." See *Neurosis and Human Growth: The Struggle Toward Self-Realization* (New York: Norton, 1950), pp. 311, 317, 312.

121. In all of the preceding, the Kantian subject should not be confused with the Cartesian subject. In his "Canguilhem and the Cyborgs" (*Economy and Society* 2 [1998], p. 209), Ian Hacking critiques the idea that we could ever "use a system of machines (computers) and chemicals to modify the body, so that the mind can be left free to explore, to create, to think, to imagine." Hacking's objection is that our "mental stuff" could not possibly remain unaltered if we tinker so radically with the body, as if mind and body were hermetically sealed off from one another; he rejects what he sees as the "Cartesian dualism" behind such a stance. But nothing in my discussion assumes that if a person takes a cure for slow running or a pill for obesity or–obviously–super-Prozac, then his mind, the Cartesian subject, won't be altered. The Kantian subject as I am construing it here is not the mind. It is that part of the self that both struggles and includes the fruits of struggle; it can comprise both mental traits like humility or courage and physical traits like speed or thinness. And this Kantian subject needn't remain unchanged, only undiminished, in the face of a cure. The President's Council also explicitly opts for a Cartesian over a Kantian conception of the self, as I am construing it, when it states: "The importance of human effort in human achievement is here properly acknowledged: the point is less the exertions of good character against hardship, but the manifestations of an alert and self-experiencing agent making his deeds flow intentionally from his willing, knowing and embodied soul." President's Council on Bioethics, *Beyond Therapy*, p. 293.

3. Cultural Spouses, Cultural Siblings

1. Jan Branson and Don Miller, *Damned for Their Difference: The Cultural Construction of Deaf People as Disabled* (Washington, D.C.: Gallaudet University Press, 2002), p. 227.
2. Charles Taylor, *Multiculturalism: Examining the Politics of Recognition* (Princeton: Princeton University Press, 1994), p. 69.
3. Steven Lukes, "Toleration and Recognition," *Ratio Juris* 10 (1997), p. 215.
4. Len Barton, *Disability and Society: Emerging Issues and Insights* (London: Longman, 1996), pp. 59, 32.
5. See, generally, Anita Silvers, "A Fatal Attraction to Normalizing: Treating Disabilities as Deviations from 'Species-Typical' Functioning," in Erik Parens, ed., *Enhancing Human Traits: Ethical and Social Implications* (Washington, D.C.: Georgetown, University Press, 1998), pp. 95–123.
6. Carl Elliott, *Better Than Well: American Medicine Meets the American Dream* (New York: Norton, 2003), pp. 196, 197 (emphasis mine).
7. Terry Teachout, "The Bard of Discomfort," *Wall Street Journal*, December 17, 2004, p. W9.
8. See Marcia Millman, *Such a Pretty Face: Being Fat in America* (New York: Norton, 1980), p. 221 and Lawrence M. Thomas, "Split-Level Equality: Mixing Love and Equality," in Susan E. Babbitt and Sue Campbell, eds., *Racism and Philosophy* (Ithaca: Cornell University Press, 1999), pp. 195–201.
9. Douglas Fuchs and Lynn S. Fuchs, "Competing Visions for Education Students with Disabilities: Inclusion versus Full Inclusion," *Childhood Education* 74 (1998), p. 313.
10. See, e.g., Jeffrey O. Cooper, "Overcoming Barriers to Employment: The Meaning of Reasonable Accommodation and Undue Hardship in the Americans with Disabilities Act," *University of Pennsylvania Law Review* 139 (1991), p. 1456.
11. Anne Locke Davidson, *Making and Molding Identity in Schools: Student Narratives on Race, Gender and Academic Engagement* (Albany: SUNY Press, 1996), p. 29.
12. Anna Day Wilde, "Mainstreaming Kwanzaa," *The Public Interest* 119 (1995), p. 78.
13. Sara Rimer, "Colleges Find Diversity Is Not Just Numbers," *New York Times*, November 12, 2002, p. A1.
14. Dirk Johnson, "Segregation or Salvation? Milwaukee Creates Schools for Black Males," *New York Times*, September 30, 1990, p. 11; Joyce Mercer, "Marching to Save Black Colleges," *Chronicle of Higher Education*, May 11, 1994, p. A28.
15. Randall Kennedy, *Interracial Intimacies* (New York: Pantheon, 2003), p. 333.
16. Joseph P. Shapiro, *No Pity: People with Disabilities Forging a New Civil Rights Movement* (New York: Times Books, 1993), p. 229. See also Avishai Margalit and Moshe Halbertal, "Liberalism and the Right to Culture," *Social Research* 61 (1994), p. 491 and Ayelet Shachar, *Multicultural Jurisdictions: Cultural Differences and Women's Rights* (Cambridge: Cambridge University Press, 2001).

17. In fact, one could argue that the greater the number of conditions that can legitimately be viewed as medical ones – and certainly, by some lights, the approach I am advancing expands that number – the less any given condition's being so viewed will be stigmatizing. Antony Black, for example, believes that to brand a condition a medical one can be stigmatizing, and yet he notes that one consequence of the contemporary expansion of medical conditions is that "the stigma of taking a . . . pharmaceutical [has been] largely lifted." See "Medicating Normality," *Biopsychiatry Illuminated* 10 (November 2003), issue 67, p. 2, and 17 (November 2003), issue 68, p. 6. (*www.adhd.report.com/biopsychiatry/bio-38.html*).

18. Allen Buchanan, Dan W. Brock, Norman Daniels, and Daniel Wikler, *From Chance to Choice: Genetics and Justice* (New York: Cambridge University Press, 2000), p. 265; see also Erik Parens, "Is Better Always Good?," in Parens, ed., *Enhancing Human Traits*, p. 26.

19. Buchanan, Brock, Daniels, and Wikler, *From Chance to Choice*, p. 279.

20. Quoted in Jacob Sullum, "Fat Chances," *Reason* 29 (1998), pp. 52–5.

21. David Ingram, *Group Rights: Reconciling Equality and Difference* (Lawrence: University Press of Kansas), p. 76; see also Virginia L. Blum, *Flesh Wounds: The Culture of Cosmetic Surgery* (Berkeley: University of California Press, 2003), p. 51.

22. On the latter, see Jim Souhan, "Down on the Farm: Tradition Has a New Home: Generations Have Come to Love Minor League Baseball in Cedar Rapids," *Minneapolis Star Tribune*, July 15, 2002, p. 1C.

23. Kathy Davis, *Reshaping the Female Body: The Dilemma of Cosmetic Surgery* (New York: Routledge, 1995), pp. 4–5; see also Margaret Olivia Little, "Cosmetic Surgery, Suspect Norms, and the Ethics of Complicity," in Parens, ed., *Enhancing Human Traits*, p. 176; Jo Spence, *Cultural Sniping: The Art of Transgression* (London: Routledge, 1995), p. 211; Joanna Frueh, "Monster/Beauty: Midlife Bodybuilding as Aesthetic Discipline," in Kathleen Woodward, ed., *Figuring Age: Women, Bodies, Generations* (Bloomington: Indiana University Press, 1999), p. 214. See also Arthur W. Frank, "Emily's Scars: Surgical Shapings, Technoluxe, and Bioethics," *Hastings Center Report*, 34 (March–April 2004), p. 24: "participation in disability rights – claiming one's disability as a cultural difference, even as a positive value – is one available body project. Another project is to minimize disability through surgery. Many people – probably an increasing number – will mix both projects, since the projects are mutually exclusive in theory more than in practice."

24. In the case of black racial features, of course, the Michael Jackson pill would not be a legitimate cure, but we can still ask whether there is an additional objection to it on cultural genocide grounds.

25. The phrase is Leon Wynter's, quoted in Joel Kotkin and Thomas Tseng, "Happy to Mix It All Up," *Washington Post*, June 8, 2003, p. B01; see also Leon Wynter, *American Skin: Pop Culture, Big Business and the End of White America* (New York: Crown, 2002), pp. 8, 268.

26. Bhikhu Parekh, *Rethinking Multiculturalism: Cultural Diversity and Political Theory* (Cambridge, Mass.: Harvard University Press, 2000), pp. 191, 101.

27. Avishai Margalit and Moshe Halbertal argue that Kymlicka's theory merely justifies an individual's right to *a* culture on the grounds that it is only culture that provides individuals with the context necessary to make choices in life. It fails, however, to justify an individual's right to *his own* culture, which the individual requires to structure his identity. Since I am staying away from issues of choice, I adopt what I would call Margalit and Halbertal's adaptation of Kymlicka's view. See "Liberalism and the Right to Culture," *Social Research* 61 (1994), pp. 505–6.

28. Lawrence Blum, "Recognition, Value and Equality," in Cynthia Willett, ed., *Theorizing Multiculturalism* (Malden, Mass.: Blackwell, 1998), p. 77.

29. Brian Barry, *Culture and Equality: An Egalitarian Critique of Multiculturalism* (Cambridge, Mass.: Harvard University Press, 2001), p. 257; see also Hans-Rudolf Wicker, "From Complex Culture to Cultural Complexity," in Pnina Werbner and Tariq Modood, eds., *Debating Cultural Hybridity* (London: Zed Books, 1997), p. 38 and Amy Gutmann, *Identity in Democracy* (Princeton: Princeton University Press, 2003), p. 74 ("Cultures are continually changing by virtue of the creative interpretations and actions of people who identify with them and their interactions with other people and cultures").

30. Blum, "Recognition, Value and Equality," p. 81.

31. Obviously, there are other grounds for preferring to eradicate racial oppression by wiping out prejudice instead of the oppressed's racial phenotype. But here I am concerned simply with the cultural consequences of (say) a widely taken Michael Jackson pill for black racial features and the extent to which those consequences would (and would not) resemble the cultural consequences of an end to racial prejudice.

32. *Stigma: Notes on the Management of Spoiled Identity* (Englewood Cliffs: Prentice Hall, 1963), p. 11.

33. Quoted in Brian Grant, ed., *The Quiet Ear: Deafness in Literature* (Boston: Faber and Faber, 1988), p. 79.

34. See, e.g., Mervyn Rothstein, "Making Theater Accessible to People with Trouble Hearing," *New York Times*, July 18, 2002, p. E5.

35. Naomi Schor, "Blindness as Metaphor," *Differences: A Journal of Feminist Cultural Studies* 11 (1999), pp. 76, 83. See also "Metaphorical Blindness" in Moshe Barasch, *Blindness: The History of a Mental Image in Western Thought* (New York: Routledge, 2001), pp. 121–30.

36. Kleege, *Sight Unseen*, p. 107.

37. "The Mind's Eye," *The New Yorker*, July 28, 2003, p. 55.

38. Schor, "Blindness as Metaphor," pp. 88, 92.

39. *What's That Pig Outdoors?: A Memoir of Deafness* (New York: Farrar, Straus and Giroux, 1990), p. viii. For similar expressions concerning deafness, see Nicole Markotic, "Oral Methods: Pathologizing the Deaf 'Speaker,' " *Mosaic* 34 (2001), p. 127; and Lennard Davis, *Enforcing Normalcy: Disability, Deafness and the Body* (London: Verso, 1995), p. 104.

40. Trent Batson and Eugene Bergman, *Angels and Outcasts: An Anthology of Deaf Characters in Literature*, 3rd edition (Washington, D.C.: Gallaudet University Press, 1985), p. 198.

41. *Deaf in America: Voices from a Culture* (Cambridge, Mass.: Harvard University Press, 1988), p. 1.

42. The only exceptions to this claim arise concerning occasions when ASL is itself the explicit topic of deaf poetry and plays (see ch. 5).

43. Toni Morrison, "Talk of the Town," *The New Yorker*, October 5, 1998, p. 32; see also Lionel K. McPherson and Tommie Shelby, "Blackness and Blood: Interpreting African American Identity," *Philosophy & Public Affairs* 32 (2004), p. 177.

44. Maurice Berger, *White Lies* (New York: Farrar, Straus and Giroux, 1999), p. 60; see also Debra J. Dickerson, *The End of Blackness* (New York: Pantheon, 2004), pp. 11–2.

45. James M. Jones, "Racism: A Cultural Analysis of the Problem," in John F. Dovidio and Samuel L. Gaertner, eds., *Prejudice, Discrimination, and Racism* (New York: Harcourt Brace Jovanovich, 1986), p. 295.

46. Jones, "Racism," p. 295.

47. Stephan Talty, *Mulatto America: At the Crossroads of Black and White Culture: A Social History* (New York: HarperCollins, 2003), p. 224.

48. Onyekachi Wambu, "Adventures in the Skin Trade," *The Independent*, London, July 14, 1998, p. 5.

49. Lawrence Blum, *I'm Not a Racist, But. . . .* (Ithaca and London: Cornell University Press, 2002), p. 172.

50. Talty, *Mulatto America*, p. 223.

51. David R. Roediger, *Colored White* (Berkeley: University of California Press, 2002), p. 225, 230.

52. Vron Ware and Les Back, *Out of Whiteness: Color, Politics and Culture* (Chicago: University of Chicago Press, 2002), pp. 252, 261 262 (emphasis mine).

53. See *Was Huck Black? Mark Twain and African-American Voices* (New York: Oxford University Press, 1993).

54. "What Would America Be Like without Blacks?," reprinted in David Roediger, ed., *Black on White: Black Writers on What It Means to Be White* (New York: Schocken, 1998), pp. 163, 164, 165.

55. See some of the related discussion in Richard Thompson Ford, *Racial Culture: A Critique* (Princeton: Princeton University Press, 2005), p. 157.

56. See also some of the discussion in Margaret Homans, "'Racial Composition' Metaphor and the Body in the Writing of Race," in Elizabeth Abel, Barbara Christian, and Helen Moglen, eds., *Female Subjects in Black and White: Race, Psychoanalysis, Feminism* (Berkeley: University of California Press, 1997), p. 77.

57. Kennedy, *Interracial Intimacies*, p. 333.

58. See., e.g., Virginia Ironside, "Health: Keep Taking the Tablets," *The Independent*, December 14, 2004, p. 6.7.

59. Quoted in Mary Elizabeth Cronin, "Tea Party–Author Sheds Some Light on Those Dark Moods," *Seattle Times*, April 2, 1997, p. E1.

60. "[T]he psychic pains of [neurosis] are akin or sufficiently similar to the psychic pains of ordinary life"; see President's Council on Bioethics, *Beyond Therapy: Biotechnology and the Pursuit of Happiness* (Washington, D.C., 2003), p. 61.

61. When discussing blackness, I had used the terms "literal" blackness and "metaphorical" blackness to describe the two phenotypes (and the same with blindness and deafness). Here, I am using the terms "neurotic" and

"nonneurotic" depression. The point is that whatever modifier might be used to distinguish the phenotypes, the noun indicates the common cultural experience.

62. In *Against Depression* (New York: Viking, 2005), pp. 230, 265, 287, Peter D. Kramer wants to reassure us about the cultural consequences of depression's eradication – and I note that he is speaking of major, not mild, depression – but he adopts a tack that reverses the one I am taking. Kramer denies any "metaphorical" link between depression and existential alienation – the "distance between" the two, he says, "is great" – and he notes that even if depression disappears, we would still have "different artists, different subjects, different stories." His purpose is to argue against the notion that all serious art rests on depression and that curing depression would therefore wreak cultural devastation. But in the process, by urging that even the art and experience of existential alienation bears no resemblance to that of depression, Kramer is (at least in my terms) actually making the case that eradicating depression would be a form of cultural genocide. It would eliminate experiences and art that are different from anything else out there. Whatever may be the case about the distinctions between major depression and ordinary existential alienation/unhappiness, I claim, for reasons stated in the text, that mild depression and ordinary alienation/unhappiness are cultural spouses.

63. Lance Armstrong with Sally Jenkins, *It's Not about the Bike* (New York: Putnam, 2000), pp. 70–1. I am assuming, following much writing in sports medicine that questions whether we are anywhere close to an ultimate limit to human speed and, as per Part 1, that though a cure might bring every runner to the populated social ideal, sooner or later, one or another runner will light out for a new ideal. Gradually, that new ideal will become sufficiently populated by nonmedical means that a new cure could be demanded by those who haven't reached it. But during that interim period, the experience of physical slowness will itself recur.

64. Carl Honore, *In Praise of Slow* (Toronto: Knopf, 2004), pp. 276–7.

65. Will Kymlicka, *Liberalism, Community and Culture* (Oxford: Clarendon Press, 1991), p. 175.

66. One might say that physical obesity and wealth give rise to common cultural experiences of gluttony and accumulation. But apart from recent research that effectively questions whether fat people as a whole are gluttonous as opposed to tricked by their bodies into a constant feeling of starvation even when sated, the cultural responses to fat (disapproving) and to wealth (approving) are vastly different.

67. See Anton Leist, "What Makes Bodies Beautiful," *Journal of Medicine and Philosophy* 28 (2003), p. 203. On the distinction between "ugliness" and "plainness," see Sara Halprin, *Look at My Ugly Face!* (New York: Viking, 1995), p. 209.

68. See also "Can a Person Be Too Good Looking?," *San Francisco Chronicle*, March 28, 1989, p. A22. Earlier, I quoted Walker Percy describing deafness, metaphorically, as a universal experience. By that he meant (in my terms) that any person can experience metaphorical deafness, not that any

phenotype can give rise to it, which is the sense in which I am using "universal" here. None of this is to deny that the conditions of being phenotypically plain-featured and phenotypically beautiful may both be "socially constructed" by the same culture of "objectification." I will say more about this later.

69. John Tottenham, "Tutti Frutti, Call Him Rudy," *The Oregonian*, April 21, 1996, p. B1.

70. Eminem has lived out a "drama of black brotherhood, [being] a white Negro [growing up] poor . . . single mother, absent father, living in a trailer besieged by debts and meager opportunities . . . [black rappers] realized [that theirs] was his language too, and his life as much as theirs." See Andrew O'Hagan, "Imitation of Life," *New York Review of Books*, November 6, 2003, pp. 27–8.

71. It's possible that obesity, anorexia, and plain features can be deemed cultural spouses to one another, although some have argued that the cultural experiences of the obese and the plain-featured in fact allow them to "feel little kinship." See Note, "Facial Discrimination: Extending Handicap Law to Employment Discrimination on the Basis of Physical Appearance," *Harvard Law Review* 100 (1987), p. 2037. In any case, I set aside these possibilities here, since we are talking about curing all of them.

72. See, e.g., Susie Orbach, *Hunger Strike: The Anorectic's Struggle as a Metaphor for Our Age* (New York: Norton, 1986), pp. 167–9; Frances Cooke Macgregor, *Transformation and Identity: The Face and Plastic Surgery* (New York: Quadrangle, 1974), p. 176; and Macgregor, *After Plastic Surgery: Adaptation and Adjustment* (New York: Praeger, 1979). ABC's show "Extreme Makeover" has a "psychologist available to talk about all the emotional and physical changes that typically go hand-in-hand with plastic surgery"; see Donna Petrozello, "Nips, Tucks and Cutting Remarks," *New York Daily News*, November. 13, 2003, p. 54.

73. Michael J. Morgan, *Molyneux's Question: Vision, Touch and the Philosophy of Perception* (Cambridge: Cambridge University Press, 1977), p. 183; and Alberto Valvo, *Sight Restoration after Long-Term Blindness: The Problems and Behavior Patterns of Visual Rehabilitation* (New York: American Foundation for the Blind, 1971), pp. 14, 38. For similar observations regarding the deaf, see Harlan Lane, *The Mask of Benevolence*, (New York: Knopf, 1992), p. 229; and Batson and Bergman, *Angels and Outcasts*, p. 315.

74. See, e.g., Werner Sollors, *Neither Black Nor White Yet Both* (New York: Oxford University Press, 1997), pp. 252–3.

75. If people sought cures for metaphorical blindness, metaphorical deafness, or ordinary unhappiness, say, then these cultural traditions too would expire. But on criteria set out in Part 1, and in a society such as our own in which all of us are metaphorically blind, metaphorically deaf, or ordinarily unhappy – and where no one has reached an ideal of not having these conditions – they could not be deemed medical ones and cured.

76. Mary Briody Mahowald, "To Be or Not Be a Woman: Anorexia Nervosa, Normative Gender Roles, and Feminism," discussing Susan Bordo, in Carol Donley and Sheryl Buckley, eds., *The Tyranny of the Normal: An Anthology* (Kent, Ohio: Kent State University Press, 1996), p. 132.

77. Becky W. Thompson, *A Hunger So Deep and Wide: American Women Speak Out on Eating Problems* (Minneapolis: University of Minnesota Press, 1994), p. 93.

78. Joan Jacobs Brumberg, *Fasting Girls: The Emergence of Anorexia Nervosa as a Modern Disease* (Cambridge, Mass.: Harvard University Press, 1988), p. 3.

79. Elliott, *Better Than Well*, p. 175.

80. Morag MacSween, *Anorexic Bodies: A Feminist and Sociological Perspective on Anorexia* (London: Routledge, 1993), p. 252. Susan Bordo, in *Unbearable Weight: Feminism, Western Culture, and the Body* (Berkeley: University of California Press, 1993), p. 154, remarks that "[n]inety percent of all anorectics are women. We do not, of course, need to know that particular statistic to realize that the contemporary 'tyranny of slenderness' is far from gender-neutral." So for those reasons, and since in any event male anorexia could be cured without coming close to expunging anorexia itself or its culture, I will confine my discussion to female anorexia.

81. Mara Selvini Palazzoli, *Self Starvation* (Northvale: Jason Aronson, 1996), pp. 19, 35.

82. Even so, as Paul E. Garfinkel and David M. Garner say, the family is a "culture bearer . . . a significant force in adapting the growing child to his culture." See *Anorexia Nervosa: A Multidimensional Perspective* (New York: Brunner/Mazel, 1982), p. 175.

83. Bryan S. Turner, *The Body and Society: Explorations in Social Theory*, 2nd edition (London: Sage), pp. 125, 181.

84. MacSween, "Anorexic Bodies," p. 83; Catherine J. Garrett, "Recovery from Anorexia Nervosa: A Sociological Perspective," *International Journal of Eating Disorders* 21 (1997), p. 264.

85. Leslie Heywood, *Dedication to Hunger: The Anorexic Aesthetic in Modern Culture* (Berkeley: University of California Press, 1996), p. 33. If I can extrapolate from Elaine Showalter's interpretation of phenotypic hysteria in the nineteenth century, it may be that – when it comes to what I am calling cultural siblings – it is the physical phenotype that can be deemed the metaphor and the nonphysical one that's better understood as literal. "Nineteenth-century hysterical women suffered from the lack of a public voice to articulate their economic and sexual oppression," Showalter writes, "and their symptoms – mutism, paralysis, self-starvation, spasmodic seizures – seemed like bodily metaphors for the silence, immobility, denial of appetite, and hyperfemininity imposed on them by their societies." See Showalter, *Hystories: Hysterical Epidemics and Modern Culture* (New York: Columbia University Press, 1997), pp. 54–5; and Orbach, *Hunger Strike*, p. 24: "although the anorectic response to our cultural conditions may strike one as extreme . . . [that] very extremeness . . . illuminates the experience of women today. Anorexia nervosa – self – starvation – is both a serious mental illness affecting thousands upon thousands of women, and a metaphor for our age . . . a dramatic expression of the internal compromise wrought by Western women . . . in their attempt to negotiate their passions and desires in a time of extraordinary confusion" and "contradictory requirements of their role. . . ."

86. Richard A. Gordon, *Eating Disorders: Anatomy of a Social Epidemic*, 2nd edition (Oxford: Blackwell, 2000), pp. 96–7; and, again, Orbach, *Hunger Strike*,

pp. 128–9: "the ways in which an individual psyche absorbs and interprets cultural values [and] the pressures that all women experience are the same ones the anorectic takes into herself in a particularly debilitating way."

87. Rita Freedman, *Beauty Bound* (Lexington, Mass.: Lexington Books, 1986), p. 100.

88. J. Seth Riley, "Cultural and Ideological Crisis in Television's *Ally McBeal,*" *www.llp.armstrong.edu/courses/4700/sriley/ally.htm*; see also Leslie Heywood, "Hitting a Cultural Nerve: Another Season of 'Ally McBeal,' " *Chronicle of Higher Education*, September 4, 1998, p. B9: "Ally [is] a heroine who, like so many of us, is split down the middle by traditional ideas about gender and love (ideas that cling despite our most rational, sincere critiques of them), and by the progressive feminist ideals that really do give us a fighting chance." Of course, it is the actor Calista Flockhart who harbors "putative anorexia" (Karen Durbin, *New York Times*, December 28, 1998, p. 2.39), but that condition gets read into her character. While observers insist that Flockhart is or was anorexic, she herself denies this. But she has attributed what she acknowledges as her below-normal weight to the stress involved in reconciling her own working life with her desire for a personal life. See, e.g., Sharon Churcher, "Ally McBeal – Skinny But Not Dipping," *Daily Mail*, January 31, 1999, p. 17.

89. Of course, it's possible that obesity and anorexia themselves are cultural siblings.

90. *Fat Is a Feminist Issue + Fat Is a Feminist Issue II* (London: Arrow, 1998), p. 81. Of her stomach, Eve Ensler writes that like "a toxic dump, it is where the explosive trajectories collide . . . the patriarchal mandate that women be quiet, be less; the consumer-state imperative to be better" (see *The Good Body* [New York: Villard, 2004], pp. x–xi).

91. Sander L. Gilman, *Fat Boys* (Lincoln: University of Nebraska Press, 2004), p. 229. If not all obesity is a feminist issue, then other cultural experiences apart from conflicting societal female roles – the experiences of poverty and dislocation, for example – can and do cause obesity in both men and women (see, e.g., K. Ball, G. D. Mishra, and D. Crawford, "Social Factors and Obesity: An Investigation of the Role of Health Behaviours," *International Journal of Obesity Related Metabolic Disorders* 3 (2003), pp. 394–403). More to the point, the cultural experiences of poverty and dislocation manifest themselves in both obese and nonobese phenotypic siblings. And so what goes for the phenotypic obesity caused by the cultural experiences of female role conflict goes, as well, for the phenotypic obesity caused by the cultural experiences of poverty and dislocation: Both obesities, stemming as they do from broader cultural causes, have siblings that will survive post-cure. (As I noted earlier, poverty and dislocation can also form part of a metaphorical black phenotype, which is simply to say that obesity and metaphorical blackness are often united in the same person.)

92. Bruch, *Eating Disorders*, p. 195. See also Michael Fumento, *The Fat of the Land* (New York: Viking, 1997), p. 259.

93. Catherine Dawson March, "Roseanne Feels the Hot Flashes of TV," *The Globe and Mail*, July 16, 2003, p. R3.

94. Since I've said that phenotypes, not individuals, are cultural siblings, I am here invoking Roseanne Barr as shorthand for a Fat Fat phenotype and Sandra Bernhard as shorthand for a Thin Fat Phenotype.

95. *Listening to Prozac* (New York: Viking, 1993), p. 264.

96. Lionel Trilling, "Art and Neurosis," in *The Liberal Imagination* (Garden City: Doubleday, 1950), p. 178.

97. See, e.g., generally, "Art and Unhappiness," Chapter One, in Robert Pack, *Affirming Limits: Essays on Mortality, Choice and Poetic Form* (Amherst: University of Massachusetts Press, 1985): "the artist [will continue to] confront . . . his most fundamental temptation: an engagement with the theme of unhappiness" (p. 18).

98. Elizabeth Wurtzel, "The Shrug Drug," *Guardian*, January 21, 1999, p. T2.

99. Kay Redfield Jamison, *Touched with Fire: Manic-Depressive Illness and the Artistic Temperament* (New York: Macmillan, 1993). See also Don Morgenson, "A Creative Madness," *Ottawa Citizen*, November 2, 2003, p. A12.

100. Some autistic spokespeople, along similar lines, claim that there is something uniquely autistic about Einstein's or Glenn Gould's brilliance. One could not, therefore, cure autistic social withdrawal or stimulant behavior without destroying revelatory scientific or artistic insights. To view autism in this way, as a whole whose components cannot be prised apart, is, however, to import genotypic or neurological conceptions into the construction of phenotype. It is the autistic "genotype" or autistic "neurology" that, giving rise as it does to what would otherwise seem to be a variety of disparate phenotypes – from scientific-artistic talents to withdrawal/overstimulation propensities – allows commentators to unite them into a single phenotype. Frank Klein, for example, speculates that both Einstein's "intelligence" and his "lack of interest in others" are traceable to his autistic "neural pathways" (Frank Klein, "Autism, Genius, and Greatness," *http://home.att.net/~ascaris1/index.html*, p. 2). "We are people who have a culture," Michelle Dawson writes; "a large published literature, art, music, architecture, design, technology, science, and engineering . . . . The world cannot do without autistic genetics. . . . " (Michelle Dawson, "Is Autism a Plague?" *www.sentex.net/~nexus23/naa_plag.html*, p. 1). To view autism thusly as a single phenotype – and therefore to call attention to how its various traits are nonculturally (neurologically/genotypically) caused – is to deny the possibility of autism's having any cultural siblings. As well, when it is viewed as a single genotypically/neurologically bundled phenotype, autism is readily seen to give rise to its own unique culture of socially withdrawn Einsteins and overstimulated Glenn Goulds, minimizing the possibility of real cultural spouses – of other geniuses who would have quite the same edge. For those who take this holistic, bundled view of autism, a cure naturally appears to be genocide (Frank Klein, "The Evil in Preventing Autism," *home.att.net/~ascaris1/evil.html*, p. 1). Of course, such a view also necessarily renders autism abnormal, since most people do not display this holistic phenotype; see Frank Klein, "How Abnormal am I?," (*home.att.net/~ascaris1/abnormal.html*, pp. 2–3); Geraldine Dawson et al.,

"Defining the Broader Phenotype of Autism: Genetic, Brain, and Behavioral Perspectives," *Development and Psychopathology* 14 (2002), pp. 584, 600.

If, however, one doesn't rely, in describing autism, on pointing to genetic or neurological connections between its various traits, then it is easier to view them in an unbundled way, each distributed over society on its own bell curve. There is the bell curve from "still to fidgety" or from "self-destructive to self-protective" or from "mathematically challenged to mathematically gifted," and anyone, not just autistics, can occupy any point on these curves. According to this view – which, as I showed in note 160 in Part 1, other autistic spokespersons advance – any autistic person can deem her various traits to be normal and hence not a medical condition. But also, on this unbundled view, even if all those diagnosed with autism took a cure, each of the phenotypes that comprise it would continue to exist – and literally, not just metaphorically – in the nonautistic population. Cure, on this unbundled view of autism, could not be cultural genocide.

101. At most, the experience of tension between various cultural demands placed on women might contribute to the development of one type of phenotypic plain facial feature: wrinkled skin. But when it comes to wrinkled skin, biological causes, especially cellular aging, are proportionately far more dominant than are biological causes in the cases of obesity and anorexia, where culture plays a comparatively greater (though by no means exclusive) role. There is, consequently, far less discussion of the culture's role in causing wrinkled skin of the sort that is so dominant in discussions of obesity and anorexia.

102. The only exception here concerns black racial features, about which I say more shortly. I note, though, that there is a liberal argument to be made that society would benefit from the disappearance of phenotypic racial differences between blacks and whites, but there is none comparable that argues that we would otherwise benefit from a disappearance of phenotypic facial differences between the plain-featured and the beautiful.

103. Joseph Epstein, "Prozac, with Knife," *Commentary*, July–August 2000, p. 56.

104. Leslie A. Fiedler, "The Tyranny of the Normal," in Donley and Buckley, eds., *The Tyranny of the Normal*, p. 9.

105. Elizabeth Haiken, *Venus Envy: A History of Cosmetic Surgery* (Baltimore: Johns Hopkins University Press, 1997), p. 220; see also George J. Annas, "The Man on the Moon, Immortality, and Other Millennial Myths: The Prospects and Perils of Human Genetic Engineering," *Emory Law Journal* 49 (2000), p. 772.

106. See some of the discussion in David A. Hyman, "Aesthetics and Ethics: The Implications of Cosmetic Surgery," *Perspectives in Biology and Medicine* 33 (1990), p. 201.

107. "To begin with she is magnificently ugly-deliciously hideous. She has a low forehead, a dull gray eye, a vast pendulous nose, a huge mouth, full of uneven teeth and a chin and jaw-bone *qui n'en finnissent pas*. . . . Now in this vast ugliness resides a most powerful beauty which, in a very few minutes,

steals forth and arms the mind, so that you end as I ended, in falling in love with her. Yes behold me literally in love with this great horse-faced blue-stocking. I don't know in what the charm lies, but it is thoroughly potent." See also Karen Burshtein, "Pretty Ugly," *National Post*, June 5, 2004, pp. SP6–7, on the phenomenon of the *jolie laide*.

108. See, e.g., Fay Weldon, "Sex and the Art of Love in 2099," *Daily Mail*, January 1, 2000, p. 3.

109. Some "people who choose medical interventions to change appearances motivate their choice by appealing to a normal look, or a less abnormal one . . . these women [merely] desire to become ordinary and to be treated as such." See Inez de Beaufort, Ineke Bolt, Medard Hilhorst, and Henri Wijsbek, *Beauty and the Doctor: Moral Issues in Health Care with Regard to Appearance* (Report to the European Commission, Biomedical and Health Research Programme, 2002), p. 64 [online]. Others, though seek, to make "normal features into perfect ones"; see Blum, *Flesh Wounds*, p. 263.

110. See, e.g., de Beaufort et al., *Beauty and the Doctor*, p. 54; and Hyman, "Aesthetics and Ethics," p. 194: "Cosmetic surgeons are advised to probe carefully the patient's hopes and fears and analyze his reasons for selecting an operation." In a sense, the case of plain facial features inverts that of deafness (or blindness). Deafness is both a medical condition and quite arguably, as well, a culture deserving of certain kinds of social accommodation. Even so, a cure would not constitute cultural genocide, since metaphorical deaf phenotypes would live on past the end of literal deafness. Conversely, plain facial features can constitute a medical condition yet are also vulnerable to cultural genocide – they have no metaphorical spouses or siblings – even though they might well not comprise a culture worthy of social accommodation (a question I didn't explore).

111. Although I didn't explore this in detail, the approach I am advancing also creates categories for conditions that are not medical ones but would be both cultures deserving various forms of accommodation and vulnerable to cultural genocide (various ethnic groups), and others that are neither medical conditions nor cultures deserving accommodation nor vulnerable to cultural genocide (these would be 'lifestyles').

Conclusion

1. See, e.g., Maxwell J. Mehlman and Jeffrey R. Botkin, *Access to the Genome: The Challenge to Equality* (Washington, D.C.: Georgetown University Press, 1998), p. 37.

2. Bryan Appleyard, "There's More to Life Than Being Joe Normal," *The Independent*, June 6, 1999, p. 21. Soo, too, could individuals falling on the tall half of the curve view their height as abnormal or as falling outside the golden-mean ideal and seek a cure.

3. Parens, "Is Better Always Good? The Enhancement Project", in Parens, ed., *Enhancing Human Traits: Ethical and Social Implications* (Washington, D.C.: Georgetown University Press, 1998), p. 6; see also David B. Allen and

Norman C. Fost, "Growth Hormone Therapy for Short Stature: Panacea or Pandora's Box?" *Journal of Pediatrics* 117 (1990), p. 18.

4. So we are told by Herrnstein and Murray, although there is reason to question whether their data actually do fall on a bell curve; see Claude S. Fischer et al., *Inequality by Design: Cracking the Bell Curve Myth* (Princeton: Princeton University Press, 1996), pp. 31–4. I am going to assume here that they do; if they instead fall on a skewed curve, as Fischer et al. suggest, then the situation would lend itself to the kind of analysis I suggest when curves are skewed.

5. See NewScientist.com News Service, "Stupidity Should Be Cured, says DNA Discoverer," February 28, 2003.

6. IQ resembles running speed in distributing itself on a bell curve for determining norm and using a polar range for determining ideal. Hence there's a subgroup – consisting of those who fall on the high half of the bell curve but below the high-end pole – who cannot legitimately consider themselves abnormal but who nevertheless fall short of a populated ideal range. In the same fashion as I did with slow runners, I will include those whose IQ is normal but not ideal in the class of "low IQ," since they too can legitimately seek a cure. Someone with low IQ, then, is anyone short of a populated polar ideal.

7. See, e.g., Nathan Glazer, "Is Intelligence Fixed?," in Russell Jacoby and Naomi Glauberman eds., *The Bell Curve Debate* (New York: Times Books, 1995), pp. 338–41; N. J. Block and Gerald Dworkin, "IQ, Heritability and Inequality," in Block and Dworkin, eds., *The IQ Controversy: Critical Readings* (New York: Random House, 1976); and James Flynn, "Massive IQ Gains in 14 Nations," *Psychological Bulletin* 101 (1987), pp. 171–91.

8. Block and Dworkin, "IQ, Heritability, and Inequality," in Block and Dworkin, eds., *The IQ Controversy*, p. 437.

9. Fischer et al., *Inequality by Design*, pp. 68, 158.

10. See, e.g., Mary Jo Bane and Christopher Jencks, "Five Myths about Your IQ," in Block and Dworkin, eds., *The IQ Controversy*, p. 333.

11. President's Council on Bioethics, *Beyond Therapy: Biotechnology and the Pursuit of Happiness* (Washington, D.C., 2003), p. 92. See also Edward M. Hallowell and John J. Ratey, *Driven to Distraction* (New York: Pantheon, 1994), p. 73: "[W]e are only beginning to discover how extensive ADD is – probably over 10 million American adults have it. . . ." Technically, Hallowell and Ratey also note (p. x), "the correct current diagnostic label is attention-deficit hyperactivity disorder, which incorporates the symptom of hyperactivity into the diagnosis. It is an imperfect label for several reasons. The syndrome is not one of attention deficit but of attention inconsistency; most of us with ADD can in fact hyperfocus at times. Hyperactivity may or may not be present; in fact, some children and adults with ADD are quite dreamy and quiet."

12. *Ritalin Nation* (New York: Norton, 1999), p. 133.

13. *Driven to Distraction*, p. 21.

14. Eric T. Juengst, "What Does Enhancement Mean?" in Erik Parens, ed., *Enhancing Human Traits*, p. 39.

15. In its discussion of ADD, which focuses on children, the President's Council wants to argue against Ritalin because life is "not only about school, work, and networking, it is also about leisure, play and friendship. At no time of life are these truths more evident – and more realizable – than in childhood. Life soon enough becomes serious, driven, and hard. The sweetness, freshness, and spontaneity of life are available in their purest form only to the as-yet-unburdened young" (*Beyond Therapy*, p. 94). But if Ritalin makes it easier for a child with ADD to do well in school without sweating it, as the President's Council also fears, then wouldn't it enable children with ADD to more easily turn their concerns to the sweetness and leisure of youth?

16. See, e.g., President's Council on Bioethics, *Beyond Therapy*, p. 81. This is not to deny that ADD also has a biological basis (see Hallowell and Ratey, *Driven to Distraction*, p. 71).

17. *Driven to Distraction*, pp. x, xi; Robert Pear, "Effort on Mood Drugs for Young Is Backed, "*New York Times*, March 21, 2000, p. A18.

Index